About the Author

Stephen Sturgess has been practising yoga and meditation since 1969, when he was first introduced to it by Swami Pragyamurti, a direct disciple of Paramhansa Satyananda Sarasvatī of the Bihar School of Yoga in India.

During the years since, Stephen has studied, practised and experienced the different paths of yoga and meditation – *hāṭha, rāja, kriyā, kuṇḍalinī, tantra, jñanā, karma* and *bhakti* – which have increased his spiritual insights, experience and spiritual knowledge. Stephen was initiated by Swami Satyananda Sarasvatī in 1979 and given the spiritual name of Shankara. It was also in this year that he received the 'British Wheel of Yoga Teaching Diploma' and began teaching yoga.

In 1982 Stephen met Swami Kriyānanda (a direct disciple of Paramhansa Yogananda). The night after this meeting, Paramhansa Yogananda appeared to Stephen in a super-conscious dream, and told him that he was his guru, and that the Kriyā Yoga path is the path he should follow.

In addition to his primary devotion to yoga and meditation, and related subjects, Stephen has a BA (Hons) Ayurveda degree from Thames Valley University (2004). He is also a graphic designer, artist and writer. He lives in London and continues to guide and inspire others on the spiritual path of Kriyā Yoga meditation.

Stephen is the author of *The Yoga Book,* published by Watkins Publishing (1997, 2002) and *Yoga Meditation* (2014).

Stephen's website is www.yogananda-kriyayoga.org.uk; or email: stephensturgess@hotmail.com.

Also by Stephen Sturgess

THE YOGA BOOK

YOGA MEDITATION

The Book of CHAKRAS & SUBTLE BODIES

Stephen Sturgess

WATKINS PUBLISHING
LONDON

This edition first published in the UK and USA 2014 by
Watkins Publishing Limited
PO Box 883
Oxford, OX1 9PL
UK

A member of Osprey Group

For enquiries in the USA and Canada:
Osprey Publishing
PO Box 3985
New York, NY 10185-3985
Tel: (001) 212 753 4402
Email: info@ospreypublishing.com

1 3 5 7 9 10 8 6 4 2

Edited and typeset by Donald Sommerville

Printed and bound by CPI Group (UK) Ltd, Croydon, CR0 4YY

A CIP record for this book is available from the British Library

ISBN: 978-1-78028-682-2

Watkins Publishing is supporting the Woodland Trust, the UK's leading woodland conservation charity, by funding tree-planting initiatives and woodland maintenance.

www.watkinspublishing.co.uk

Publisher's Note

The information in this book is not intended as a substitute for professional medical advice and treatment. If you are pregnant or are suffering from any medical conditions or health problems, it is recommended that you consult a medical professional before following any of the advice or practice suggested in this book. Watkins Publishing Ltd., or any other persons who have been involved in working on this publication, cannot accept responsibility for any injuries or damage incurred as a result of following the information, exercises or therapeutic techniques contained in this book.

Contents

APPENDICES

Dedication

This book is dedicated and offered with love and gratitude to my spiritual masters: Jesus Christ, Babaji, Lahiri Mahasaya, Swami Śrī Yukteswar, and my beloved guru Paramhansa Yogananda, who has shown me the true path to God.

I also dedicate this book to Swami Kriyānanda and Roy Eugene Davis, two direct disciples of Paramhansa Yogananda who have inspired and initiated me into the ancient technique of Kriyā Meditation, that was passed down in succession of gurus from Mahavatar Babaji.

And finally I dedicate this book to Giulia Tripepi, a beautiful soul who has been a constant support and love to me in my life. To the memory of my mother and father. To my dearest sister, Tanis Smith. And also to my special friends: Liladevi and Jayadev at Ananda, and Richard and Christine Fish, who have remained loyal spiritual friends to me on the Kriyā Yoga path for 30 years.

May this book inspire you, the reader, to live in the higher consciousness of your true Self within, that you may find true inner joy and peace.

Stephen Sturgess

The law of life is this: The less one lives in harmony with the truth within, the more one suffers; but the more one lives in harmony with that truth, the more one experiences unending happiness.

Paramhansa Yogananda

Paramhansa Yogananda
(1893–1952)

Introduction

The Kingdom of Light Within

God made man's senses pointing outwards from the time of his birth, so that man always looks outside of himself and never within. Extremely rare is that wise person, who, desiring immortality, directs his senses inward and perceives the truth of his own innermost Self.

Katha Upaniṣad, 2.1.1

The Pharisees asked Jesus: 'When will the kingdom of God come?'

And Jesus replied: 'The kingdom of God does not come with your careful observation, nor will people say, "Here it is," or "There it is," because the kingdom of God is within you.'

Luke 17: 20–21

To find, know, and experience this inner kingdom, and to discover the truth of who we are and what God is, a shift of emphasis must be made from the external to the internal world. You need to discard the old outworn concepts of God being far away sitting on a throne up there and out there, somewhere at the end of the universe, rewarding those who are good and punishing those who are bad. And where is heaven? Heaven is where God is and God is everywhere. God is omnipresent. There is no presence within you that is not God's presence, so you cannot be separate from God. God is present within you as you are within God. 'In God we live and move and have our being' (Acts 17: 28). God is not more present in heaven than He is on earth, for omnipresence means that God is eternally present, undivided, and that He pervades everything. There is nothing outside of the ultimate Reality, God.

The difference between heaven and hell is in the awareness *not* the location. Heaven and hell are not objective places set in time and space. When you are aware that God alone is, when your consciousness is in God, that is heaven. When there is an absence of awareness, that is hell.

Be Still and Know Your Self

Self-knowledge is the awareness that the Self alone is. The Self is the kingdom of God within us. Due to being forgetful of our true nature we continually search outward in the objective world for happiness and joy. The Self is the joy we are searching for. Joy is within you now; it is not something which is attained in the future. You do not have to go to the Himalayas or anywhere else to find that infinite Joy, which is your God-Self, for it is as close to you as your own breath. The Self is the Kingdom of God; there is nothing outside the Self. It is always present within you here and now. All you have to do to realize the kingdom of God is to *be still and know your Self.*

Be still, and know that I am God.

Psalm 46: 10

In stillness there is no ego-sense of 'I', only the pure 'I am'. There is no movement of the mind because you are beyond space and time. You are present in the now-moment. By becoming aware of the oneness of your being, the Self, you will realize God's all-pervading presence within you and in everything.

When your eye is single, your whole body will be filled with light.
Matthew 6: 22

In this verse, Jesus is making a mystical statement that has largely been misunderstood and mistranslated by Christian theologians and followers of Christianity. The deeper meaning of this succinct statement is referring not to the physical body but to the subtle body, the astral body of light, within which the *chakras* are located.

When Jesus said, 'When your eye is single . . .' he was not referring to the gross physical eye, but to the 'Spiritual Eye', the positive pole of the *ājñā chakra* (also known as the third eye, and Christ Consciousness Centre), the fifth centre of consciousness, situated in the astral spine or *suṣumnā.* The Spiritual Eye is the centre of spiritual perception and intuition that yogis meditate on at the midpoint between the eyebrows. The Spiritual Eye's inner vision can be achieved without the physical eyes that see in the waking state, and the mental eye that sees in the dream state. When the mental eye is closed the physical eye has no vision. In comparison, the Spiritual Eye perceives the truth of everything from within, through intuitive awareness in the present, in the 'now' moment. By meditating on the Spiritual Eye, you become aware of the Self, your pure existence, through the light of the Self. Just as you can see your eye only through the reflection in a mirror, the Self can see itself only through the mirror of the mind. When the mirror of the mind is removed, your true Reality, the Self, remains present.

When your thoughts are single and concentrated, then your mind becomes one-pointed, to abide in the silence of the Self. When your Spiritual Eye is single, then your whole astral body is filled with light.

The spinal cord may be likened to a wire. In it are located seven centres of light which are the subcentres for the conduction and distribution of life current throughout the body. The body is nothing but a condensation of this spinal energy. Just as invisible hydrogen and oxygen atoms can be condensed into visible vapour, water, and ice, so light can be transformed into body which is nothing but frozen energy.

Paramhansa Yogananda

The gross physical body is connected to the vital force in the astral and causal bodies by seven main subtle energy centres known as *chakras,* vortices of energy and consciousness. Cosmic energy flows in through the medulla oblongata ('The Mouth of God') and is stored in the brain and distributed through a network of subtle channels (*nāḍīs*) into the spine and into its seven centres (*chakras*), and into the body.

The soul must leave the physical, astral and spiritual bodies through the seven astral doors [*chakras*] in order to reach, and merge into, the Spirit. After it lifts its consciousness from the physical body, it must unlock, and pass through, the seven astral doors in the spine.

Paramhansa Yogananda.

Divinity's Descent

Hāṭha Yoga comes in with a brilliant system. It suggests that the polarized consciousness descends in a spiralling movement of energy, and as it descends, as it ramifies, as it stretches out, it becomes matter. Consciousness moving becomes energy, and when the movement is slowed down it becomes matter. This is pure physics. As consciousness condenses into matter it forms the various elements, and the difference between one element and another is a difference in the frequency and wavelength of their vibrations.

As consciousness descends there is space (ether) – everything is in space. And when something starts moving in that space, it becomes air. When air moves there is friction and therefore fire, and when the gases collide and fire is generated, water is also generated, and then water condenses into solid substances. One is not totally different from the other – the difference is merely one of vibratory frequency.

We have this whole system of elemental stages of creation and the *chakras* from *Sāṁkhya* philosophy and Hāṭha Yoga. These subtle elements (earth, water, fire, air, ether) represent the various stages of manifestation outward from Spirit to matter, the descent of the soul-consciousness into matter; and when reversed the ascent from matter to Spirit.

The theory starts at the base of the spine, at the *mūlādhāra chakra*, where the final point of descent has been reached. Energy apparently moving away from the centre has become solid, earth. The earth is considered the *mūlādhāra chakra*. How do you contemplate this? How do you visualize this? How can you focus your attention on this? For that purpose the yogi sages suggest a physical or physiological counterpart as a focal point of attention. The earth centre is that part of your anatomy which comes into contact with the earth, it is as simple as that! A little way above there is the water element, the next subtle element, located where water collects in the body. This centre (*svādhiṣṭhāna chakra*) represents both water in its simple form, and also the nectar of immortality. Just a little higher from there is the *maṇipūra chakra*, the fire element region – we even call it the gastric fire. It is quite simple. Higher still is the heart region (*anāhata chakra*) which represents air, which is obvious – the lungs and oxygenation. The throat region (*viśuddha chakra*) is a little space (ether) in the throat. Then we go on to the mind – the *ājñā chakra* in the forehead.

Divine Consciousness via the soul has descended from the causal sphere to the gross sphere through seven levels of consciousness, from subtle to gross. As the soul descends stage by stage through the seven levels of consciousness into the physical body, it becomes more and more identified with the body and mind, until it seems to have forgotten its original nature. On its descent down through the *chakras*, the soul first feels itself distinct or separate from God at the *ājñā chakra*, located at the junction between the eyebrows. It is interesting that the lotus symbol of this *chakra* has only two petals, and in that state there is already a sense of duality. At the *ājñā chakra* the soul is still ever aware of God; it has not forgotten God. Although there is a distinction, there is no bondage at this stage.

But as the soul descends farther down through the other *chakras*, it begins to lose its conscious fellowship with God. His presence is not very clear, it is partly obscured. When the soul reaches the heart centre, the awareness of God is still there, but the longing for God is beginning to diminish. As the soul continues to descend to the lowest three *chakras*, below the heart level, it becomes more and more entangled in bondage. The soul forgets the existence of God or Spirit, and its direction goes toward matter. The soul in this state is fully enclosed in the consciousness of its own gross physical form. In this form the soul is identified with the body and mind, and is primarily concerned with the three lowest *chakras* – *mūlādhāra* (coccyx centre at the base of the spine), *svādhiṣṭhāna* (second *chakra* or sacral centre), and *maṇipūra* (third *chakra* or lumbar centre, opposite the navel). *Vṛttis*, subtle vortices of energy created by *saṁskāras* (the conditioned patterns of response that drive our behaviour), karmic actions, and waves of like and dislike that create our mental tendencies, desires and habits, enter the subconscious mind and spine, and then get submerged in these lower *chakras*.

Gateways to Higher Consciousness

We perceive reality through the *chakra* in which our awareness is most dominant. If it is the first *chakra* (*mūlādhāra*), then our awareness and experience will revolve around insecurities about our basic needs and instincts, such as our need for food, shelter, and procreation. If it is the second *chakra* (*svādhiṣṭhāna*) then sexual energy and pleasure can dominate our awareness. At the third *chakra* (*maṇipūra*) the ego can assert itself. A need for dominance or power can manifest as anger, aggression, control and intolerance.

Each *chakra* represents a higher level of human evolution of awareness. The aim of *chakra* awareness and meditation is initially to bring the lower *chakras* into balance with the upper or higher *chakras*, so that our lives are not conditioned and governed in a mundane existence by lower *chakra* consciousness. Most people in the world have lost awareness of their divine nature as a result of involvement in the world of illusions and limitations. Their consciousness is imprisoned in the lower *chakras*. The higher consciousness in the so-called normal person is practically asleep. Some might even say it is non-existent. Only a rare few souls take the initiative to develop beyond conditioned living in ego-consciousness, and seek to regain their freedom by awakening and raising their consciousness to a higher level.

It is only when the spiritual nature of a person becomes sufficiently unfolded that the divine power hidden within the person's heart begins to awaken. Then we transcend the illusions and limitations that have imprisoned us, and regain full awareness of our real Self.

Yoga and meditation techniques assist us in raising our consciousness by influencing life-force (*prāṇa*) and energy in the spine. When energy is liberated from a *chakra*, it can then be channelled and integrated into our whole being. Stimulating and activating each *chakra* gradually awakens consciousness at that level. In the upward return journey through the seven levels of consciousness the soul becomes more and more disidentified with the mental–physical form, and becomes more and more aware of God. As a result the soul rises from the gross to the subtle state of consciousness. In this higher state of consciousness we regain the memory of our true identity: that our true essential nature is the Self, separate from body and mind, and not separate from one another as we had thought.

As we transcend further, we go beyond even the subtle state and come to the causal state, where we feel we are Godlike in nature; we feel one with God – there is no separation. But even this is not the highest. The highest is still beyond this causal state.

Unless you become transformed from your present limited state to a state where you can directly perceive God, how will you perceive Him? The fact is that higher Consciousness is here and now, but because we are unaware and not paying attention to it, we are not cognizant of it; it is hidden from us. It has to be brought forward so that we can become aware of it. And since our state of consciousness is also our state of being, we not only have to become aware of it, we have to become identified with it, and function with it. That is the purpose of all spiritual effort. My guru, Paramhansa Yogananda, emphasized a number of times that we **need** to make a '**strong, persistent effort**' or '**intense effort**' on the spiritual path to Self-realization. In his *Yoga Sutras*, Patañjali, the codifier of Yoga science, gives us two of the most important foundation principles of Yoga – *abhyāsa* and *vairāgya*. *Abhyāsa* means 'repeated practice' and involves cultivating a strong conviction, a persistent effort consistently to choose practices with actions, speech and thoughts that lead in the direction of a stable tranquility. *Vairāgya* means non-attachment, dispassion. It involves learning actively to let go of the many attachments, fears, aversions and false identities that obscure the true Self. *Abhyāsa* and *vairāgya* are like the two wheels of a car – they work together. Practice leads you in the right direction, while non-attachment allows you to continue the inner journey without any diversions into pleasures and pain along the way. As *abhyāsa* becomes well grounded, *vairāgya* also happens. Neither *vairāgya* nor *abhyāsa* can be practised independently. What is needed here is zeal, urgency. Very few of us have that urgency. It is something that cannot be taught; it has to develop from within oneself. In the *Bhagavad Gītā*, Arjuna raised the problem of the difficulty of controlling the mind. He said: 'I find it as difficult to hold the mind as to hold the air with one's fist.' Śrī Krishna answered: 'Yes, O mighty-armed one, without doubt, the mind is unsteady and difficult to control, but through *abhyāsa* and *vairāgya* the mind can be brought under control.' In other words Śrī Krishna propounded the two methods: *abhyāsa* and *vairāgya*.

This higher state of consciousness has to be realized here; and everyone sooner or later is destined to realize it. The object of that consciousness is the infinite, eternal Being, Pure Consciousness, Absolute God. Higher Consciousness is perfect consciousness, and therefore that of which this consciousness is aware is also perfect.

Turning Inward

Meditation is simply reminding yourself again and again that you are not the limited physical body, but the Infinite Spirit. Meditation is arousing the memory of your real Self and forgetting what you imagine you are.

Paramhansa Yogananda

The concept of the *chakras* is a system of understanding our consciousness, of understanding who and what we really are. Meditation on the *chakras* is a means for dissolving the deep-seated and latent *saṁskāras* and obstacles blocking our spiritual awareness to the ultimate goal of Self – God-realization.

Yoga meditation is a journey from the restless and emotional distracted state of mind to a state of inner calm and stillness. As the mind becomes quiet and calm you develop an awareness of yourself as a silent witness – a calm and steady centre of consciousness from which you can quietly observe other mental activities without distraction and involvement. In this meditative state you become aware of your own awareness, and in doing so you become aware of the reality deep within.

Meditation replaces the continuous mind-stream of thoughts and feelings with the quiet, effortless, one-pointed focus of inner awareness and attention that leads you to inner joy. The phenomenal worldly joys are momentary and transient, but the joy of yoga meditation is immense and everlasting.

Don't wait until tomorrow, make meditation a top priority in your life now and practise it regularly. Connect your life with conscious awareness in the stillness of God. Persist in your practice of meditation, do not give up, then you will begin to experience the joy of being fully present, here and now. Meditation will give you the inner strength to deal with all of life's problems. Make meditation a fundamental part of your life, and live in the divine consciousness of your Self, then all forms of creativity, and success will find expression in your life. Realizing the divine image of God Self within you is the ultimate success. Meditation will introduce you to your real Self, and will reveal your purpose here on earth. Ultimately, meditation will liberate you from all suffering, and separation, and take you into the love, peace, and eternal bliss of oneness with the Divine, the source of lasting happiness and security.

Jesus said: 'Seek ye first the kingdom of God and all these things shall be added unto you.'

Matthew 6: 33

Part 1

THE SUBTLE BODIES AND THE CHAKRAS

Chapter 1

The Subtle Bodies

Although our physical bodies appear to be dense and solid, at the most fundamental level they are composed of trillions of molecules and atoms, or energy in constant transformation. In addition to the physical body, the soul (the indwelling pure spirit – the essential reality of who we really are) has several interdependent nonmaterial, subtle bodies or energy fields, surrounding and interpenetrating the physical form, each of which is a luminous field of energy vibrating at a particular frequency. These human energy fields are the manifestation of Universal Energy.

We are spiritual beings, immortal spirit-souls temporarily embodied in both material and nonmaterial fields of energy. These nonmaterial fields of energy or subtle bodies interpenetrate and surround each other in successive layers. Each succeeding subtle body is composed of finer substances and higher vibrations than the preceding body that it surrounds and interpenetrates. The abode of the conscious *ātman* or *puruṣa* (soul), in this body composed of material elements, is likened to a castle. There are three parts of this castle – the physical, astral, and causal bodies. Each of these bodies conditions the soul-consciousness to a varying degree. The individual soul-consciousness expresses itself through five sheaths (*kośas*), which are divided between the three bodies.

The physical, astral and causal bodies serve respectively as mediums for our daily experience in the three states of mind – the waking, the dreaming and the dreamless deep-sleep states. The soul is beyond these three states, being a witness to them.

The five *kośas* and three bodies are inert modifications of matter; they have no permanent reality. They appear to have consciousness because they reflect the consciousness of the Self (*ātman*). The entire *antaḥkāraṇa* (internal instrument of cognition, consisting of consciousness, intellect, ego and mind) is the centre of energy for the soul (*jīvātman* or *puruṣa*). Although inert, the *citta* (field of consciousness) receives consciousness from its contact with the soul. Thereby it becomes active and goes on generating life every moment in the form of subtle *prāṇa;* with the help of the ego it infuses life in the causal, astral and gross bodies. Essentially, this *citta* generates the energy of knowledge and action, rather like positive and negative electrical energy. So much energy is generated that it is difficult to measure it, and because it is so subtle it is very difficult to visualize it with the general light of meditation. Rising from the field of consciousness, and coming out of the orb of ego, this process appears in the form of subtle *prāṇa*.

Out of these currents, the positive current of knowledge nourishes *citta* and *buddhi* (intelligence: the first hierarchical derivative of *Prakṛti* [Nature] and an integral component of the *antaḥkāraṇa* [inner instruments of cognition]). The negative current of activity continues offering the energy of action to the ego (*ahaṁkāra*) and mind (*manas*). The essence of the life-principle is *sūkshma prāṇa* (subtle vital air) which shines like luminous vapour outside the orb of ego; it mixes with the astral body which is seated in the brain, wrapped in the five *tanmātrās* (subtle forms of the elements); it sustains, nourishes and irrigates the physical body that is constituted of five gross elements.

God encased the human soul successively in three bodies – the idea, or causal body; the subtle astral body, seat of man's mental and emotional natures; and the gross physical body. On earth a man is equipped with the physical senses. An astral being works with his consciousness and feelings and a body made of prāṇa. A causal-bodied being remains in the blissful realm of ideas.

Swami Śrī Yukteswar, from Paramhansa Yogananda, *Autobiography of a Yogi*

The Physical Body

The *annamāyā kośa* (the food sheath) is the physical sheath of the gross body, which is subject to birth, growth, disease, decay and death. It is called the food sheath because of its dependence on gross *prāṇa* in the form of food, water and air. *Prāṇa* is the vital life-energy, which sustains life and creation. *Prāṇa* permeates the whole of creation and exists in both the macrocosmos and the microcosmos. Without *prāṇa* there is no life. *Prāṇa* is the essential link between the astral and physical bodies. When this link or supply is cut off, then death takes place in the physical body. Both the *prāṇa* and the astral body depart from the physical body.

Using the analogy of the castle, the physical body is the main gateway for approaching the soul. This physical body is made up of five material elements (ether, air, fire, water and earth), and is born of past actions (*karma*). It offers gross services to the individual soul or *jīvātman*, lord of the castle.

The Astral Body

The subtle or astral body (*sūkshma sharīra*) is composed of five subtle elements – *ākāśa* (ether), *vāyu* (air), *tejas* (fire), *apās* (water), and *pṛithvī* (earth) – which produce the five gross elements on the physical plane.

The physical body does not have the energy to serve the soul. This energy comes from another body that pervades the whole physical body. This is the subtle or astral body, which is the conductor of the physical body. All actions of the physical body take place by the energy and the prompting of the astral body.

The subtle or astral body has three parts: *manomāyā kośa* (mind sheath) and *vijñānamāyā kośa* (intellect or intelligence sheath), and the *prāṇamāyā kośa* (vital air sheath).

The Manomāyā Kośa

The mind sheath is more subtle than the vital air sheath. It holds the food sheath and vital air sheath together as an integrated whole. The mind sheath functions as a messenger between each body, communicating the experiences and sensations of the external world to the intelligence sheath, and the influences of the causal and astral bodies to the physical body.

The real Self, being identified with the mind sheath, experiences the world of duality. It is the mind that is the cause of bondage, but also the means to liberation. The mind is subject to change and various modifications so it cannot be the real Self.

The Vijñānamāyā Kośa

The intelligence sheath, or discriminating faculty, functions as the knower and the doer, and being the subtlest of all the aspects of the mind, it reflects the radiance of soul-consciousness or the Self. It *appears* conscious because it reflects the intelligence of the Self. The focus of this reflection is the ego (I-consciousness).

This sheath is composed of the cognitive mind (*manas*), the intellect (*buddhi*) and ego (*ahaṁkāra*) conjoined with the five subtle sense organs of perception.

Both the *manomāyā kośa* and the *vijñānamāyā kośa* are especially important, because they are the means of individual as well as universal knowledge of all objects of creation, from the grossest to the most subtle.

The intellect sheath also cannot be the real Self, since it is subject to change – the fluctuations of ideas.

The Prāṇamāyā Kośa

This prāṇic body (the vital air or etheric sheath) provides energy and vitalizes the physical body. It is a channel for the manifestation of cosmic energy. It is approximately the same size and shape as the physical body. The vital sheath is a vehicle for the Self, but is not the real Self, since it too is subject to change and has a beginning and an end. The vital sheath is composed of five *prāṇas* (life-energies), which have distinct functions in the working of the physical body.

Prāṇa is a specific manifestation of cosmic *prāṇa* (the cosmic life-energy that pervades both the macrocosmic universe and the microcosmic unit of the body). This vital energy enters the body after its conception and leaves it at the time of its dissolution. The cosmic *prāṇa* enters the body through the medulla oblongata at the base of the brain. It then descends and ascends through the astral spine, where it is modified by the *chakras* and differentiated into the vital airs (*vāyus* – prāṇic air currents).

Vyāna, 'outward moving air', is the vital air that regulates the overall movements of the body, co-ordinating the other vital airs. It permeates the whole body.

Udāna, 'upward moving air', functions between the throat and the top of the head, activating the organs of sense: eyes, nose, ears, tongue. It has an upward movement that carries the *kuṇḍalinī śākti* (a person's potential spiritual energy or vital energy force, lying dormant at the base of the spine, in the *mūlādhāra chakra* or base energy centre). When awakened, this creative, vital energy force passes through the main subtle nerve channel (*suṣumnā nādi*) in the centre of the spinal cord, ascending to the crown *chakra* (*sahasrāra*).

At the time of death, *udāna* separates the astral body from the physical form.

Prāṇa, 'forward moving air', functions between the throat and the top of the diaphragm, activating the respiration. It also raises the *kuṇḍalinī śākti* to *udāna*.

Samāna, 'balancing air', functions in the abdominal area between the navel and the heart, activating and controlling the digestive system, the heart, and the circulatory system.

Apāna, 'air that moves away', functions from the region of the navel to the feet, activating expulsion and excretion. It has a downward movement, but carries the *kuṇḍalinī* upwards to unite with *prāṇa*.

These five airs (*vāyus*) are conjoined with the five subtle organs of action (speech, hands, legs, organs of evacuation and procreation), which have their counterparts in the physical body.

The Causal Body

When the gross physical receptacle is destroyed by the hammer of death, the other two coverings – astral and causal – still remain to prevent the soul from consciously joining the Omnipresent Life. When desirelessness is attained through wisdom, its power disintegrates the two remaining vessels. The tiny human soul emerges, free at last; it is one with the Measureless Amplitude.

Swami Śrī Yukteswar, from Paramhansa Yogananda, *Autobiography of a Yogi*

The causal body is known as the *kāraṇa śarīra* or the *linga śarīra*. It is even more subtle than the astral body. It has a finer and higher vibration and pervades the astral body, giving life to it. Although it gives energy to the astral body, its own vitality has a different abode, called the *ānandamāyā kośa* (bliss sheath). This is a body of light that reflects the blissfulness of the Self. It is the cause of both the subtle and gross bodies. Like the other sheaths, it too is a product of matter and is subject to change, and therefore cannot be the real Self.

The Soul

The soul is not inside the body. The soul projects itself as the body and the mind. It finds a location in space-time and broadcasts or telecasts itself *through the body.*

Deepak Chopra, *Power, Freedom and Grace*

The human being is a soul wearing a physical body. The soul is extremely subtle. It is even subtler than ether, mind and energy. Consciousness and intelligence are attributed to the soul not the gross body. Consciousness is evidence of the existence of the soul.

The bodies or sheaths obstruct true spiritual knowledge about the concealed soul or the kingdom of God within. When the obstruction veils are removed, the Self is realized. Knowledge of the soul is already present within us, but because of the entanglement into the twenty-four categories of *prakṛti* (material nature) due to *avidyā* (ignorance), it is forgotten. When these categories of *prakṛti* that bind the soul are transcended through the systematic practices of yoga, the true nature of the Self is realized and liberated from all suffering and bondage.

The individual soul or spirit resides within all three bodies, witnessing all of their activities. The soul is the ever-shining consciousness, perfect and complete, having no limits and without beginning or end. It is infinite and eternal. The light of knowledge that flows through *manas* (mind), *citta* (field of consciousness), *buddhi* (intellect), *ahaṁkāra* (ego) and then through the *indriyās* (senses) is called consciousness. The source of knowledge and intelligence, by which we know, exist and act, is our true Self. The realization of God's existence is inseparable from the knowledge of our Self. From this centre of consciousness the life-force flows in varying degrees. When a lamp has many shades, the light is very dim, but after removing the shades one by one, finally you find the centre of light whose radiance illumines them all. Similarly, the soul, the centre of consciousness, is covered by the three bodies.

The individual soul (*jīvātman*) is an image or reflection of the Supreme Soul (*Paramātman*). Just as the Sun can be reflected in different bowls of water, so also the Supreme Soul is reflected in different minds of different persons. All souls are the radiance of God, the one Self. All forms are God's expressions. The one consciousness has expanded and extended itself from its eternal pure-mind state to appear as countless individual living beings in a temporal universe of myriad forms. Each form possessing consciousness relates to the world as a subject to an object: 'I am the seer, and what I experience is the seen.'

These conscious soul-beings are forgetful of their true essential nature, identify with their body, ego-mind and senses, and regard themselves as being separate entities with specific desires and goals. Through lack of memory and unawareness of our true soul-identity we suffer unhappiness and feel there is something missing or incomplete in our life. Eventually we must all awaken to our true divine nature.

In the second chapter of the *Bhagavad Gītā,* Lord Krishna reminds us of our immortal and eternal true nature.

As we observe in life the change of a youthful body to an old one, so too after death, the soul adopts another body. Those who have understood the true nature of life are not deluded by these changes.

Bhagavad Gītā, 2: 13

The indwelling Self never takes birth and will never die. It has always existed and shall never cease to be. For it is birthless, eternal, immortal and unchangeable. It is not slain when the body is killed.

Bhagavad Gītā, 2: 20

As a person discards worn-out clothes and acquires new clothes, so also the embodied soul abandons a worn-out body and enters into another one which is new.

Bhagavad Gītā, 2: 22

The Self is beyond the power of any weapon to injure or of fire to burn it. It neither becomes moistened by water, nor dried by the winds.

Bhagavad Gītā, 2: 23

The Self is indivisible and indissoluble and cannot be transformed by fire or air. The soul is everlasting, omnipresent, unwaveringly steady and ever-existent.

Bhagavad Gītā, 2: 24

Realize that the soul, the spirit-self, is unmanifested, it is beyond the mind's ability to conceive and cannot be changed. Therefore, knowing this, transcend your unfounded anxieties and grief.

Bhagavad Gītā, 2: 25

Chapter 2

The Nature of Consciousness, Life and Death

Death

The physical body is subject to change, death and decay because it is born in time, is extended in space, and subject to the law of causation. Change is inherent in every fleeting moment and there can be no renewal without death. This law applies to the entire phenomenal universe, which also exists within time, space and causation, and is constantly changing. The law of causation is a universal law that keeps the inner harmony and the logical order of the universe – the sun shines, the rivers flow, the wind blows, the rain falls, trees blossom and bear fruit, one season follows another, night follows day – all phenomena of nature work in harmony and are governed by the one universal law of causation, which is also known as the law of *karma* – the eternal law of cause and effect.

At the time of physical death (which is not the end or annihilation of an individual being) the soul or the Self, which animates the body, withdraws from the physical form clothed in the astral and causal bodies. The lifeline which transmits life-energy to the physical and mental sheaths becomes severed; the consciousness frees itself from the limitations of the physical and becomes associated with the subtle body. The true Self is within and outside the body, and separate from it. This *ātman* is immortal, eternal, and is our permanent abode. Unlike the physical body, the *ātman* within is not subject to birth and death. Even after the destruction of the body we shall continue to exist. Death is only the habit of the body, not of the soul.

After death, the soul continues to exist in the vehicle of the astral body. This carries with it *saṁskāras* (past impressions) or *karma* of all one's actions, thoughts, desires, merits, demerits, good and evil tendencies and capacities. These are factors that determine the individual soul's journey beyond. Just as a person's inner attitudes and thoughts determine their life's course before death, so do they after their death.

Three Different Planes of Consciousness

The embodied self, the experiencer within, daily experiences three different states of consciousness – waking (*jāgrat*), dream (*svapna*), and dreamless deep sleep (*suṣupti*). These three states are variable but the self who is experiencing them remains constant; it continues unmodified throughout the three states, from birth to death and beyond. The person experiencing says, 'I wake,' 'I dream,' 'I sleep.' It is the same 'I' or experiencer in all three states of consciousness but it does not belong to any of them.

The Waking State

During the waking state the individual self, associated with the five sense-organs, five motor-organs, the five vital forces, and the mind, connects with the various external objects by means of the modifications of the mind, which constitute the limiting adjuncts of the soul, and apprehends these external objects and identifies itself with the physical body. The individual is aware of the external objects and also of the conscious mental states, but not aware of the hidden subconscious propensities.

The waking state and the dream state are projections of *Māyā* (cosmic illusion). As the reality experienced by the dreamer disappears on awakening, so too does the reality of the waking state disappear during the dream state. The waking state of consciousness does not exist in dream or sleep. It is therefore illusory. Reality always exists in all conditions or states.

The Dream State

During the dream state the experiencer of the dream is only conscious of internal objects. The senses are quiet and absorbed in the mind. The consciousness of the individual is withdrawn from the physical senses and becomes identified with the subtle body, the waking state temporarily disappears and the consciousness enters the dream state. In this dream state, the individual consciousness is restricted to the *antaḥkāraṇa*, the fourfold inner instrument, consisting of *manas* (deliberation), *buddhi* (determination), *ahaṁkāra* (egoism or I-ness) and *citta* (recollection). The dream state and images are projected inwardly upon the mental screen from impressions seen during the waking state. When these impressions and the external objects are modified and left in the mind the individual experiences dreams.

Differences between the waking state and the dream state

In the waking state, the mind depends on outward impressions, while in the dream state it creates and enjoys its own impressions. In dreams the objects exist only as long as there is the mind to dream them, and as long as the dream lasts. As soon as the mind returns to the waking state the dreams vanish.

Dreamless Sleep

In the dreamless deep-sleep state there is an absence of mental activity, there is no thinking, feeling, nor sensory perception. The individual is not conscious or aware of anything. But this is not negative, or a state of non-existence, for on waking we are happy and conscious of having slept a sound and restful sleep. We feel we existed even during sleep. In comparison to the waking and dreaming states of mental activity, whose characteristic is the presence of a knower and a known, or a thinker and a thought, in dreamless sleep the principle of consciousness remains and exists without its seeming to assume the duality of a conscious subject and object. Consciousness is continuous.

In deep dreamless sleep, the mental functions cease altogether, there is no thinker to think thoughts, there is no awareness of thoughts or 'I', there is no ego and no world. The Self recedes even from the mind. The five organs of perception and the mind remain hidden and latent, suspended in a state of ignorance (*ajñāna*), within the blissful sheath of the causal body.

During dreamless sleep the soul is united with consciousness, the nature of absolute bliss. But this is not the transcendental state, known as 'the fourth' or *turīya,* in which the consciousness merges into the *ātman*. This union is only apparent – it is only a reflection. It is not the true union or superconsciousness that follows the knowledge and realization of the Self. The sleeping individual returns to the consciousness of the waking state and returns to his conditioned personality, with the same habits, desires and attachments. The individual self-remembers that it had a happy and sound sleep. This recollection results from experience therefore there must be experience in the deep dreamless sleep. The causal body, which is of the nature of ignorance (*avidyā*) veils the luminous self without affecting its innate blissfulness. Happiness becomes self-manifest, being identical with consciousness that the Self is.

Differences between dreamless sleep and the transcendental state

In both deep sleep and transcendental consciousness there is no consciousness of objects. But this objective consciousness is present in an unmanifested seed form in deep sleep while it is completely transcended in *turīya*. In *turīya*, the mind is not simply withdrawn from objects but becomes one with Brahman.

The difference between sleep and death

In death there is a complete withdrawal of the organs into the heart-lotus or *ākāśa* of the heart. But in the dream state the organs are not absolutely withdrawn.

Sleep – A Perfect Model of Death

At night, as we begin to fall asleep, we initially move into the hypnagogic state, where we start to relax and alpha waves become predominant in the brain. This is the state of quiet reverie, where many images and memories flash before the mind. As we continue to fall asleep we move into the deep-sleep zone characterized by delta waves and further relaxation. In the next stage of sleep, the dream state, there is a deeper state of relaxation with rapid eye movement (REM), and this is characterized by higher-frequency alpha waves. The process of waking follows in the reverse order from REM sleep to deep sleep through the hypnagogic state to complete wakefulness.

Jāgrat (waking state) – conscious mind, beta waves
Svapna (dream state) – subconscious mind, alpha and theta waves
Suṣupti (deep sleep state) – unconscious mind, delta waves
Turīya (transcendental; superconsciousness) – unknown

In sleep or death we do not cease to exist, though all objective, individual experience has vanished. In sleep, the mind and its thoughts and mental modifications assume a subtle state.

Dissolution of the body is no more than sleep. Just as a person sleeps and wakes up, so are death and birth. Death is like sleep. Birth is like waking up. The domain of sleep is partly the same domain as the transition into death. In both cases you enter the astral plane, but in death, it is generally done with more conscious awareness.

When a person goes to bed at night, he lies down and pulls the bed covers up to his neck to feel comfortable and cosy. Before he begins to fall asleep his mind is busy and restless with the worldly thoughts of the day – work, relationships, family, finances and so on. After some time his mind begins to settle down. Slowly his consciousness begins to withdraw. First it is only aware of the four walls of the bedroom. As he begins to feel sleepy, his consciousness begins to withdraw further so he is only aware of the bed and the covers. There is an involuntary relaxation of energy from the motor and sensory nerves, which causes the consciousness to withdraw further; the bed and covers are forgotten, he is mainly aware of his limbs, hands and feet. As the consciousness continues to recede, he is only aware of the centres of consciousness, from the navel to the brain. Gradually the senses withdraw from their respective objects. The sense organs cannot perceive their respective objects unless the mind joins with them. Truly speaking, it is the Self that perceives the objects through the mind and the sense organs. Then, with his body lying still and relaxed, he becomes only aware of the thoughts in the mind. After a while the conscious thoughts and activities of the mind settle down and completely withdraw, leaving the person fast asleep.

Sleep is a perfect model for explaining death for the process is very similar. We die every night in our sleep. It is almost like a preparation for death. In deep sleep the sense organs enter into the mind, and the soul withdraws into the subtle body. In death the soul abandons its physical sheath and is carried within the inner subtle and causal bodies.

In sleep there is only sleep, not even 'I' who sleeps. You do not even know, 'I am asleep.' That is, there is no experiencer independent of the experience. When there is no dream, no thought, nothing – no world – that is a complete deep sleep. The world disappears in relation to us and we are not conscious of any phenomena around us. All the persons and all the possessions, power and ego to which we are attached vanish and are forgotten in the state of deep sleep.

During the waking state a person's organs of perception, mind, and the five *prāṇas,* though belonging to the subtle body, operate in the gross body. But in the dream state the organs of perception and the mind are withdrawn to the subtle body, and in dreamless sleep to the causal body. The five *prāṇas* continue to function in the gross body as in the waking state.

At death the organs, the mind, and the five *prāṇas* withdraw from the gross body and enter the subtle body, to which they belong. They all gather in the lotus-heart, where the subtle body in association with the Self is located.

In sleep, sleep alone exists, and therefore in sleep you are not aware that 'I am' – otherwise you are awake! The sleeping person is not at all dissatisfied with this state of sleep, nor is there evidence that he is satisfied either. There is no dissatisfaction with that sleep, and no desire to wake up again.

The message of sleep is that it is possible for a person to remain totally absorbed, integrated with the state in which one is, without even an effort to get out of it, without dissatisfaction arising from it, without a desire or craving for a state other than the one in which one is. When one is in that integrated state where there is no conflict or division within oneself, then there is neither pain nor suffering.

The Difference between Personality and Individuality

That which distinguishes a person from a thing or one person from another is personality. The term personality comes from the Latin word *persona,* 'the mask'. Personality is that particular consciousness which is ascribed to the physical body – descriptions of the physical status, name, character and emotional type, religion, profession – these labels are all attributed to the personality. They are the *persona,* 'the mask'.

Individuality is something that is beyond the gross body that is bound by time and space; it has no relation to the personality at all. Death destroys the personality but it cannot annihilate the individuality, the soul. It is beyond the body and has a separate and distinct existence. The individuality is the sense of 'I-consciousness' (the real Self) that has a continuous existence. It remains the same throughout childhood, youth and old age and continues beyond.

The personality changes but the individuality never changes. It will continue to exist even after death. Even in the dream and dreamless states you have the sense of 'I-consciousness' within. If you did not have the sense of 'I' in deep sleep you would not remember that you had a happy, sound sleep.

The individuality can only be lost when the individuality becomes one with the Supreme Self (Para Brahman) through deep meditation and the highest state of *samādhi* (superconsciousness), *nirvikalpa samādhi,* in which there is direct perception of the bliss of the soul or Self, and a total loss of any sense of duality. The soul is simultaneously conscious of Spirit within and of creation without. Just as a wave merges with the ocean. so the soul (a reflection of Spirit) becomes one with Spirit.

The reason why we find it so difficult to know the real Self is because we think in terms of describing it as an object, when we ourselves *are* it.

A man identifies himself about sixteen hours daily with his physical vehicle. Then he sleeps; if he dreams, he remains in his astral body, effortlessly creating any object even as do the astral beings. If man's sleep be deep and dreamless, for several hours he is able to transfer his consciousness, or sense of I-ness, to the causal body; such sleep is revivifying. A dreamer is contacting his astral and not his causal body; his sleep is not fully refreshing.

Swami Śrī Yukteswar, from Paramhansa Yogananda,
Autobiography of a Yogi

The Essence of Consciousness – Turīya ('The Fourth')

Beyond the three states of consciousness – waking, dream, and dreamless sleep – is *turīya*. This is the fourth state – Self-realization. Truly speaking, *turīya* is not a state at all, but the very nature and essence of our being, the Self. *Turīya* is present in all the states, it is Reality, pure consciousness in itself. The three states are subject to change, but the Self of an individual is distinct from all three states of existence; it is changeless. *Turīya,* the omnipresent consciousness, pervades all three states of existence; it is beyond time, space, and causation. The Self is the experiencer of the three states but remains unaffected by them. In the following verse from the *Māṇḍūkya Upaniṣad, turīya* is distinguished from the three states:

The Fourth [*turīya*], the wise say, is not inwardly cognitive [as in the dream state], nor outwardly cognitive [as in the waking state]; nor cognitive both ways [as in an intermediary state between waking and dreaming], neither is it an indefinite mass of cognition [as in dreamless sleep], nor collective cognition, nor unconsciousness. It is imperceivable, unrelated, inconceivable, uninferable, unimaginable, indescribable. It is the essence of the one self cognition common to all states of consciousness.

All phenomena cease in it. It is peace, it is bliss, it is non-dual. That is the Self [*ātmā*], and that is to be realized.'

The States of Consciousness

According to the *Māṇḍūkya Upaniṣad* the range of human consciousness begins with the waking state and ends with the absolute state of superconsciousness, where all objective relations and perceptions of duality are completely negated.

When the spirit is embodied in the universal aspect it is called macrocosm (universal consciousness). In the individual aspect it is called microcosm (individual consciousness).

The microcosmic individual consciousness (*puruṣa* or *ātman*) has four states of being:

Ātman – the omniscient, eternal Self.
Prajñā – 'knower', undivided consciousness, associated with *Iśvāra* (God), the source of all conscious souls.
Taijasa – 'luminous one', the manifestation of the individual in the subtle body, that develops a false identification of the self with ego.
Viśva – the individual self, the experiencer of the waking state bound and conditioned by matter, and associated with the phenomenal world and the gross body.

The macrocosmic universal consciousness (Brahman) also has four states:

Turīya or ***Avyakta*** – imperceptible and indescribable, absolute state beyond the three ordinary states of consciousness.
Īśvara – cosmic Lord or God, the omniscient source and cause of the universe. Associated with its own *māyā* (illusory power) and the causal body.

Hiraṇyagarbha – cosmic Self. Also known as *Sutrātma* (thread-soul of the universe) because it binds all the constituents of the universe together.

Virāt – universal cosmic form. The fully manifested macrocosm encompassing all the aggregates of the perceptible and tangible phenomenal universe.

The states of consciousness

State of consciousness	*Microscosmic or individual*	*Macrocosmic*
Waking state *Jāgrat*	*Viśva* Physical 'A' of Aum	*Virāt* Cosmic manifestation
Dream state *Svapna*	*Taijasa* Mental 'U' of Aum	*Hiraṇyagarbha* Universal mind
Sleep state *Suṣupti*	*Prajñā* Intellectual 'M' of Aum	*Īśvara* First cause or God
Transcendental *Turīya*	Beyond the three states of ordinary awareness yet pervading them all, is 'the fourth' (*turīya*), the *Brahman-ātman. Turīya* is not a 'state' like the others, since it is present in all the states and is actually the whole reality, pure consciousness in itself.	

Chapter 3

The Process of Death

When a person approaches death and is on the verge of expiring their last breath, first the functioning of the *prāṇas* (vital airs) in his or her body become disturbed. Their force is weakened and they begin to subside. As a result, a gradual numbness starts to spread throughout the body to the limbs, muscles and the breathing apparatus – heart, lungs and diaphragm. In the book *Karma and Reincarnation*, Paramhansa Yogananda says: 'When the heart begins to grow numb, there is a sense of suffocation, because without heart action the lungs cannot operate. This sense of suffocation is a little painful for about one to three seconds, and causes a great fear of death.'

Subsequently, the cognitive senses are disunited from the corresponding organs of perception. They begin to withdraw inward and become separated from the related sense organs. Then the association of the perception of objective things and cognition of forms of the external world becomes defunct. The principle of consciousness withdraws into the heart and the dying person falls into a state of subconsciousness.

In the next stage of death, there is a dissolution of the four gross elements in the dying person's body. The elements in the body begin to sink one after the other, in the order of earth, water, fire, and air. These elements correspond with the centres of consciousness (*chakras*). First, the earth element (the lowest *chakra* called *mūlādhāra*) loses its coherence as matter, resulting in a state of coma or loss of body consciousness.

Then the water element begins to dry out, causing the mouth and throat to be very dry. This makes swallowing difficult. This is followed by the fire element diminishing, causing the gross body to become cool. And finally, the air element ceases to function. The five vital airs leave the body. Of these five *prāṇas*, it is *udāna vāyu* that draws out the subtle body from the gross physical body at the time of death. The dying person becomes disorientated and there may be agonizing pauses between loud, laboured breaths. If there is fluid built up in the lungs, then that congestion will cause a sound known as the 'death rattle'. As the cells inside a person lose their connections, the person may start convulsing or having muscle spasms.

The hands and feet of the dying person may become blotchy and purplish. This mottling may slowly work its way up the arms and legs. The lips and nail beds become a pale bluish or purple colour. Blood pressure and body temperature are lowered. The pulse becomes irregular and perspiration increases.

The person usually becomes unresponsive and, as the light within him or her begins to diminish, the sense of sight disappears even though the eyes may be open or semi-open. The last sense to leave is the hearing.

As the person is dying, the *chakras* open and cords of energy flow out. The upper *chakras* open into great holes into other dimensions; the lower energy field begins to separate from the upper parts. The link between the subtle bodies and the physical body is disconnected and the life force ceases to flow into it. The soul abandons its physical sheath and is carried away into the subtle body. All physical pain and disease are left behind. The suffering is only on the mental level, when the mind realizes it cannot live in that body any longer. The physical consciousness disappears but all the experiences of that lifetime are recorded in the subconscious mind of the soul, as *saṁskāras* or impressions of past *karma*.

The human being is consciousness with a body, not a body

with consciousness. Like electricity expressed through a light bulb, consciousness or the real self is expressed through the physical body. And just as a light bulb has a limited and temporary life, so does the physical body. The sources of power and manifestation – the electricity that gives life to the light bulb and the consciousness that gives life to the physical body – do not die when the light bulb and the physical body are destroyed. Like electricity surviving innumerable light bulbs, consciousness survives innumerable bodies. Death does not end your self-consciousness, it merely opens the door to a higher form of life. Unlike the physical body, which is finite, the soul-consciousness is infinite, immeasurable, deathless and eternal. In reality no one comes and no one goes. Life is one continuous never-ending process. Birth and death are merely doors of entry and exit on the stage of this world. Just as as you move from one house to another house, every soul has to pass from one body to another to gain experience for its further evolution.

It is the nature of the body to disintegrate sooner or later, and it is the nature of consciousness to survive its body vehicle. The soul does not die, but passes over from one stage of life to another. There is a transition from one state of illusory consciousness to another dimension of greater awareness.

The last breath of the departing soul is expired as the life energy enters the *piṅgalā nāḍī* (one of the three subtle channels in the subtle spine) and flows deeply inward and back to the medulla oblongata, from where the soul leaves the body at death.

The departing soul journeys with great speed through a long and very peaceful dark tunnel, with a brilliant luminous light at the end. This tunnel experience is the soul ascending through the main power current channel of the subtle body through the inner spine (*suṣumnā*) and upward through the *chakras* and departing at the bright light of the medulla oblongata, the negative pole of the *ājñā chakra*.

The Near-Death Experience

There are many reported cases of people having a near-death experience (NDE) – a term which originated in 1975 in Dr Raymond Moody's book *Life After Life*. People who have begun the process of dying or who have been pronounced dead during an operation in a hospital may have an NDE. Although such people may have been pronounced as being clinically dead, they return to their physical bodies and are able to report an NDE. Many of those who have had an NDE also report an out-of-body experience (OBE).

These reported cases of NDEs appear to have some common characteristics, including a great feeling of peace and wellbeing, a sense of separation from the physical body, and a sensation of moving through a long dark tunnel to enter light at the end. Phrases like 'my whole life flashed before me' and 'I entered into a bright light' are also common to those who have had NDEs. The experience of travelling through a tunnel into a bright light is also an experience common in deep meditation, when energy is withdrawn from body consciousness and expanded into cosmic consciousness.

When the heartbeat and breath stop, the person is clinically dead. There is no circulation, and no new reserves of oxygen are reaching the cells. The brain requires a tremendous amount of oxygen but keeps very little in reserve, so any cut-off of oxygen to the brain will result in cell death within three to seven minutes; that is why a stroke can kill so quickly. However, clinical death also denotes that this is a point where the process is reversible, by means of CPR, a transfusion or a ventilator. The point of no return is biological death, which begins about four to six minutes after clinical death. After the heartbeat stops, it only takes that long for brain cells to begin dying from lack of oxygen.

Those people who have had an NDE commonly share the following traits:

Out-of-body experience – the person feels that they have left their body and, floating above it, can see their own body and the medical team working on it.

Entering a dark tunnel – the sensation of travelling at great speed through a long dark tunnel to a pure bright light at the end of it.

Entering the light – At the end of the tunnel the person enters an intense pure bright light. A sense of floating rather than walking into the light has been recorded by many of those people having NDEs.

Entering into another dimension – The person experiences a heavenly realm in the light, where there is peace and joy. Death to that person is no longer a skeleton bearing a sword to cut the thread of life, but rather an angel who has a golden key to unlock the door to a wider, fuller and happier existence.

Encounter with spirit beings – In this light they encounter subtle beings of light who act as their compassionate spirit guides. They experience a profound and comforting sense of peace and joy, and usually a reluctance to return. Some people see the spirit guides, while others are only aware of beings of light by their sides. Some subjects report being told to choose between going into the light or returning to their earthly body. Others feel they have been compelled to return to their body by a voiceless command, possibly coming from God.

Life review – In the tunnel or in the realm of light the person sees his or her entire life in a flashback, like a movie film played backwards. This can be very detailed or brief. At this time a spirit being may tell the person that it is not their time yet and command them to return to their earthly or physical body. Others may have the choice either to enter the light or return to their earthly body.

What this NDE means is that the return to the physical body is always because the soul mission has not yet been accomplished. This results in the returning soul having a personality and life transformation brought about by the event.

The Warning Signs of Impending Death

There are certain ancient texts from India that describe the premonitory signs and symptoms of coming death. One of the most ancient medical texts in the world, the *Charāka-Samhita*, describes various indications of impending death in its *Indriyā* volume. These are observed in the patient or in natural phenomena by employing the three means of knowledge – perception, inference and authority – wherever appropriate. The signs, symptoms and indications are listed below:

1. Discolouration in nails, eyes, face, urine, faeces, hands, feet or lips, with diminished strength and sense functions.
2. Sudden change to abnormal colour in a patient going downhill.
3. Sudden change of voice to a feeble, subdued and indistinct variety.
4. Appearance of desirable or undesirable odours suddenly and without apparent cause.
5. Sudden appearance of loathsome or sweet smells in a deteriorating patient, which repel or attract insects.
6. Loss of a pulse in body parts which had one earlier, coldness of parts which were warm, hardness of what was soft, instability of joints, and wasting particularly of muscle and blood.
7. Very deep or very shallow respiration, absence of a pulse in the neck, teeth displaced and white concretions, matted eyelashes, sunken, unequal, glassy and permanently open or closed eyes, aberrant vision with the perception of intense and

varied colours, discolouration of the abdominal wall, severe pallor or bluish hue of nails, absence of cracking sound when fingers are bent.

8. Mask-like face, fatigue, anxiety, confusion, restlessness, profound weakness, loss of appetite, urticaria, irritability, severe thirst and fainting in patients with insanity.
9. Jaws, neck, eyes become stiff and the back becomes arched and rigid.

However, the Ayurvedic sage Charaka says that it must be kept in mind that death may not always follow the appearance of premonitory signs just like a fruit may not always succeed the flower; but death seldom occurs without warning signs.

Another ancient text, *Śivasvarodāya* (a scripture in the form of a dialogue between Śiva and Śākti which begins by discussing the nature of the universe and the essential knowledge on living a happy, healthy and inspired life), one of the major tantric texts on the science of breath rhythms called *svāra* (pronounced as 'swara'), describes the premonitory signs that indicate impending death within one year to the immediate future.

Svāra Yoga is the ancient science of prāṇic body rhythms which explains how the movement of *prāṇa* can be controlled by manipulation of the breath. The Svāra Yoga practices related to the breath were used to understand the governing forces of life, the nature of the universe, and effects of the elements on the body and mind by observing the different patterns of breath.

Do not confuse Svāra Yoga with *prāṇāyāma* (breath control). Although they both deal with *prāṇa,* there is a difference in purpose. Svāra Yoga is a precise science. It has an emphasis on the analysis of the breath and the significance of prāṇic rhythms: the flow of *prāṇā,* a very subtle and vital aspect of the breath. *Prāṇāyāma* is more concerned with techniques to redirect, store and control *prāṇā.*

The state of our health, body and mind is reflected in the alternation of the *svāra* cycles. These alternating cycles correspond to the alternating breath in the left and right nostrils, which in turn affect the *nāḍīs* (subtle pathways). The specific functions of the cerebral cortex of the brain (the twin hemispheres) correlate with the activities of *iḍā* and *piṅgalā nāḍīs,* which connect respectively with the left and right nostrils. When the left nostril is operating, the mental energy or *citta* predominates and prāṇic energy is weak. When the right nostril is operating, the prāṇic forces are stronger and the mental aspect is at a low ebb. When both nostrils are operating simultaneously, spiritual energy flows freely and the *ātma* is in control. For instance, before the onset of a disease in a person, the flow of *svāra* becomes disturbed. If one is aware of this then the imbalance can be rectified and the illness averted.

The nostrils are alternately active, each one dominating in turn for an hour or an hour and twenty minutes. This rhythm regulates all our psychological and physiological processes. An irregular *svāra* indicates that something is not functioning correctly in the body.

The *Śivasvarodāya* describes the premonitory signs that indicate impending death in verses 321–69. A few of the verses are shown below:

When the flow of one *svāra* is continuous night and day, death will come in three years. (331)

When *piṅgalā* flows constantly with full force day and night, then it is said two years are left to live. (332)

When the same *nāḍī* flows continuously up to three nights, one year is left to live. (333)

When the lunar *svāra* flows continuously at night and the solar *svāra* in the day, death will come in six months. (334)

Preparatory Stage Before Death

In most cases of the preparatory stage close to death, the dying person is visited by loved ones on the subtle planes. They are compassionate spiritual helpers or guides in their subtle forms, who come to explain to the dying what will happen when they make the transition from the earthly realm to the subtle plane. This explains why those people dying from terminal diseases are often heard 'talking to themselves' or seem to be seeing others who are not physically there.

Physical death is attended by the disappearance of breath and the disintegration of fleshly cells. Astral death consists of the dispersements of lifetrons, those manifest units of energy which constitute the life of astral beings. At physical death a being loses his consciousness of flesh and becomes aware of his subtle body in the astral world. Experiencing astral death in due time, a being thus passes from the consciousness of astral birth and death to that of physical birth and death. These recurrent cycles of astral and physical encasements are the ineluctable destiny of all unenlightened beings.

Swami Śrī Yukteswar, in Paramhansa Yogananda,
Autobiography of a Yogi

After-death Intermediate State

After death, and preceding rebirth into a new life, there is usually an interlude period in which the departed soul remains resting in a healing state within the subtle and causal bodies. The duration of this depends on the latent impressions (*saṁskāras*), actions (*karma*) and desires of the soul in the life it has just departed from. This interlude state is like a prolonged state of dreaming, experiencing mixed feelings of pleasure and pain. All the merits and demerits that one has committed in one's life must be faced and accepted. It is a time of introspection for the person to affirm positive intentions to correct the errors of their past deeds. The incarnating soul meets with its spirit guides and its tasks are considered to determine its next life circumstances – the tasks that it needs to accomplish to grow spiritually; the *karma* it needs to meet and deal with; and the negative belief systems it needs to clear. Parents are chosen who will provide the needed environment and physical experience for rebirth in the soul's next life.

It is not a Day of Judgement as in the concept of God sitting on a throne in the clouds, sternly looking down upon us, a God who keeps an account of every sin and every good deed we have committed, so that an individual may be punished with damnation in hell or rewarded in heaven. This concept is steeped in ignorance. In fact there is a verse in the *Bhagavad Gītā* that firmly denies this concept of a judgemental God.

The All-pervading [God] is not concerned about people's sins or virtues. Wisdom (though it is the natural state of every individual) is eclipsed by cosmic delusion. Mankind thus becomes bewildered [as to the difference between right and wrong].

Bhagavad Gītā, 5: 15

Swami Kriyānanda (a direct disciple of Paramhansa Yogananda) explains the above verse in the commentary from his book *The Essence of the Bhagavad Gītā*:

Yogananda often said, 'God is not worried about your mistakes. All he wants from you is your love, and that you love Him evermore deeply.'

. . . God (it should go without saying) is not touched by human wrongs. What is sin? It is nothing but error! Because it springs from delusion, it does not really exist. The thought that God could be 'angry' with anyone is itself an error – indeed an absurd one! How could the ocean depths be affected by even the most violent storm at the surface?

Rebirth

The caterpillar dies to become a chrysalis. In the slumber of the chrysalis, the energies incubate and rearrange themselves, and a butterfly is born. Is the caterpillar the same being as the chrysalis or the butterfly? It is the same intelligence that has become something else. And in that something else, every cell is different, every expression of the energy in its body is different. Nothing has really died; it has only transformed.

Deepak Chopra, *Power, Freedom and Grace*

Death is nothing but a change of body. The soul throws the body off like a used garment. Human life is purged and perfected in order to attain the final bliss. This takes place through myriads of births. All change is only change of embodiment and environment. The soul is without form and is changeless and immortal.

Just as we move from one house to another, the soul takes one form after another on account of its own actions or *karma*. As the soul passes from one body to another it is enveloped by the subtle parts of the elements which are the seeds of the new body.

A soul, being invisible by nature, can be distinguished only by the presence of its body or bodies. The mere presence of a body signifies that its existence is made possible by unfulfilled desires. So long as the soul of man is encased in one, two, or three body-containers, sealed tightly with the corks of ignorance and desires, he cannot merge with the sea of Spirit. When the gross physical receptacle is destroyed by the hammer of death, the other two coverings – astral and causal – still remain to prevent the soul from consciously joining the Omnipresent Life. When desirelessness is attained through wisdom, its power disintegrates the two remaining vessels. The tiny human soul emerges, free at last; it is one with the Measureless Amplitude.

Swami Śrī Yukteswar, in Paramhansa Yogananda,
Autobiography of a Yogi

When a transmigrating soul is ready for reincarnation on the human plane the *saṁskāras* of its *karma* guide it to the parents from whom it can secure the genetic and environmental materials for its physical body. Led by its *karma,* the transmigrating soul moves into the body of the male parent suitable for its purpose, and enters into the requisite sperm, which turns into a potent seed for its development as an individual. The seed being united with the requisite ovum in the female parent turns into the zygote (fertilized egg) and becomes ready for germination. Behind this fusion of the sperm and ovum to create a new physical body is the universal law of cause and effect (*karma*).

Whatever the world to which an individual soul is granted admission to be reborn, the individual soul immediately rushes there to enter the womb that has been reserved for it. As the parents' sperm and ovum meet, there is a flash of light on the astral plane. The soul seeking to be reborn, clothed in the subtle and causal bodies, accompanied with its unpaid balance of past *karma* and unfulfilled desires, enters the womb to begin yet another life in a new body. As the soul begins its new life with a new identity, it forgets everything that was acquired in its previous life. All memory of the past life and the identity of that self is lost. The only thing that is *not* lost is the old legacy of karmic deeds and desires carried over from the previous life in the form of *saṁskāras*.

Saṁskāras and Karma

Saṁskāras are the dormant impressions or imprints of our past lives. The desires (*vāsanās*) are stored in the mind as *saṁskāras* until they mature into action (*karma*). The *saṁskāras* are linked to the soul with the subconscious mind. Our past *saṁskāras* motivate our present actions by producing thoughts, desires, tendencies and images, creating an inclination toward the external choices we make.

Karma comes from the root *kri*, meaning 'to do', 'to make', 'to act'. Not only is *karma* the cause and seed for the continuation of the life process after death (in rebirth), but even in this present life, our actions or *karma* produce results, having a decisive influence on our present character and destiny.

The soul is subject to three types of *karma*:

sañcita karma – those actions that have accumulated in several previous lifetimes.

prārabdha karma – results of past actions which are producing fruit in the present. This is also called *ripe karma*, because it is a debt which is overdue and it is time that it should be paid in the form of sorrow and suffering, gain and loss, whether we like it or not.

āgāmi karma – the actions which are being done in this present life that will bear fruit in a future life. It is this *karma* which preserves our free will, with certain limitations, and ensures our future success.

The *sañcita* and *āgāmi karma* are destroyed by attaining Self-realization/God-realization, but *prārabdha karma* can only be exhausted by experiencing its fruits in the present life.

We are all born with *saṁskāras*. The mind is not like a blank sheet of paper. It contains the impressions of thoughts and actions of our previous births. A human being's birth and environment is determined according to the nature of his or her desires. *Prārabdha karma* places a person in such suitable environments as are favourable for the gratification of his or her desires. A woman may be born in Africa as a poor village girl. If she longs to become a multi-millionaire, she may get her next birth in the USA. This is *karma* – the eternal law of cause and effect. This law of *karma* governs on the plane of human life and consciousness with the same exactness as do the laws of cause and effect in physics. *Karma* is not a fatalistic idea, it is the expression of the rule of perfect justice within us. There is nothing arbitrary about *karma;* nothing happens by accident or chance. No supernatural power determines the events of a person's life. There is no scope for chance in human existence. It is not blind nature that motivates human actions. *Karma* is ever associated with self-determination. No volitional action is possible without self-awareness. Whatever happens is both the result of previous choices and actions and is necessary for completing the experience of the individual. Every thought and action reaps its own corresponding rewards.

The doctrine of predestination is a dogmatic version of fatalism. According to this all that happens to human beings is predetermined by God; some are fore-ordained to everlasting happiness and others to everlasting misery. It makes God responsible for the human individual's vices and sufferings. How can God be conceived as all-just and all-merciful in such a case?

As my guru, Paramhansa Yogananda, said:

Souls are 'made' in the image of God. Even the greatest of all sinners cannot be damned forever. A finite cause cannot have an infinite effect. Due to the misuse of his free will, a person might imagine himself to be evil, but within he is a son of God. A king's son might, under the influence of alcohol or a bad dream, think himself poor, but as soon as he recovers from his state of intoxication, or as soon as he awakens, he forgets that delusion. The perfect soul, ever sinless, eventually wakes up in God when it remembers its real, eternally good, nature.

A benign father could never eternally burn a soul made in his own image for its temporary mistakes on earth. The idea of eternal punishment is illogical. A soul is forever made in the image of God. Even a million years of sin could not change its essential, divine character. Man's unforgiving wrath against the evil actions of his brethren has created this misconception of eternal hell-fire.

Paramhansa Yogananda, *Karma and Reincarnation – The Wisdom of Yogananda*

The Individual's Free Will to Choose

Every circumstance in our lives, every characteristic, every habit, however much we now repudiate it, was something we ourselves created, whether recently or in the distant past. Each one is due to our misuse of the free choice God first bestowed on us . . .

Blame no one for the evils that beset you. Accept responsibility for your own life, and for whatever misfortunes you encounter. Do your best, with firm resolution, to eliminate the harmful tendencies in your nature.

Paramhansa Yogananda, *Karma and Reincarnation – The Wisdom of Yogananda*

Every individual is constantly accumulating within himself the subtle impressions of the diverse *karma* he performs. These are the factors that build his inner nature and character, and also serve as retributive forces leading to a favourable or unfavourable situation in this life or in the next.

Freedom of action is a special privilege of human life, but there is a penalty of the privilege – moral responsibility. We are accountable for our own actions; in every moment of our life we have free will or the freedom to choose our course of action. Whatever thoughts and actions we set into motion, we have to be prepared to take the full consequences of them. 'We reap what we sow' is the karmic law of cause and effect. The example of a bowman is sometimes used as an analogy to show how the law of *karma* affects an individual. The archer has no control over the arrows which he has already released from his bow. They represent his past *karma, prārabdha karma*. The arrow that is now loaded in his bow and is ready to shoot can be aimed where he chooses to do so. This is *āgāmi karma,* action which will bear fruit in a future life. The archer can also choose to discard the whole quiver of arrows. This is *sañcita karma,* actions that have accumulated in several previous lifetimes.

A farmer reaps rich harvests only when he labours in his field for a long time. Unless he cares to plough the ground, sow the seed, and nourish it with water and manure, he will not be in a position to enjoy the fruit of his toil. What he sows today he will reap tomorrow. This is an immutable law. To think that an individual's capacity for fresh effort is paralysed by their past actions is as futile as to think that because one sowed yesterday, one cannot sow fresh seeds today.

Free will is never stifled and prevented by any past action. The only limitation is that a person cannot achieve what he or she wants all at once, and without delay. The karmic law pays every person according to his or her need and in due time. The law of *karma* runs its own course. The results of past thoughts, feelings and actions appear to us as effects we set in motion by our own free choice. Similarly, we have free will to choose a line of action which is certain to bring its fruit in due time. Although we have free will, we are conditioned to think and act in certain ways, and as a consequence we suffer or are happy because of this conditioning of our mind.

Collective Karma

The collective *karma* of a race or nation is as much a fact in the law of nature as an individual one. The same principles underlying the karmic laws apply, without much difference, to national and collective *karma*. History, as recorded, shows nations rising and falling, states whose kings, queens, emperors and dictators flourish and are then brought down. The immutable law of *karma* operates everywhere on the physical and mental planes. No event can occur without having a positive, definite cause behind it. Earthquakes, floods, volcanic eruptions, outbreaks of war and conflict, famine, diseases of the body, jet airliner crashes – all these have definite causes. There is no such thing as chance or accident.

Freedom from Karma

Freedom is our birthright. Freedom is *Sat-chit-ānanda* (ever-existing, ever-conscious, ever-new bliss). Freedom is immortality and peace.

Consciously or unconsciously we are all attempting to attain this freedom from our own ignorance. Each and every person is the creator of their own happiness or suffering.

We cannot possibly live without creating thoughts and doing actions. When we perform actions, whether good or bad, we reap the fruit of those actions. The reaping of the fruits causes one to go on doing further actions and reaping the fruits again. The cause and effect cycle continues. We are caught in the bondage of *karma*.

One cannot gain freedom from activity by abstaining from action. Nor can one achieve perfection by merely ceasing to act.

Bhagavad Gītā, 3: 4

How do we find freedom from *karma,* from the bonds of cause and effect? Freedom is not attained by inaction or action, but by surrendering the fruits of one's actions. This means to perform actions skilfully and selflessly so that *karma* no longer remains a bondage. Unskilful and selfish actions lead to suffering and bondage. Freedom from activity does not mean inactivity but the absence of any sense of personal doership. Non-action is action without the ego-sense of 'I', whereas both deliberate action and deliberate inaction include the sense of personal doership.

Actions performed for selfish gain are karmically binding. Therefore, O son of Kunti (that is to say, of dispassion), perform your duty without attachment in a spirit of religious self-offering.

Bhagavad Gītā, 3: 9.

Our actions are determined and governed by our thoughts, by the thinking process, either at the conscious or the unconscious level. The subtle impressions carried from past lives in the subconscious mind motivate our desires. These desires in turn produce thoughts that lead to actions, which determine our happiness or sorrow.

To attain true knowledge and inner freedom, first we need to know and understand the true nature of the mind in order to become aware of our ignorance. We also need to practise introspection so that we can change our ingrained mental patterns and the habits that keep us in karmic bondage, thus transforming our conditioned character and personality to its true nature. If the faculties of the mind are not integrated it will not be able to perform skilful actions, because the ego and the field of consciousness with its *saṁskāras* and desires will remain obstacles in the path of freedom.

The mind can be understood by understanding *vṛttis* (waves of feeling and thought that create the disturbances of the mind). By controlling the *vṛttis* we can gain control over the *saṁskāras*, the subtle impressions stored in the *citta*, where all unconscious memories and emotions are stored. Thus by controlling the *vṛttis* we can gain control over our *karma*.

The word *vṛtti* means 'to revolve', or 'whirlpool', connoting the waves of feeling and circling thoughts that create the disturbances or fluctuations of the mind. These waves of feeling create our likes and dislikes, which in turn create *karma*.

Without the *vṛttis* the mind has no existence. The *vṛttis* are created when the reflection of the Self in *buddhi* (intellect) is mixed together with the reflection of an object in the *buddhi*. *Vṛttis* create *saṁskāras* from our experience in the outer world, and *saṁskāras* create *vṛttis* in our mental world within – together they create the cycle of *karma*.

According to Patañjali in his *Yoga Sūtras,* yoga is the 'Neutralizing of the waves of feeling in the mind.' Patañjali states that when the waves of feeling are neutralized, 'Then the seer [Self] is established in its own essential nature.' He then goes on to say that, 'At other times [when the waves of feeling are not neutralized and brought to stillness] one identifies with the feelings and thought waves [*vṛttis*] in the mind.'

Thus through yoga and meditation we can attain freedom from *karma*.

Contemplate the monotonous recurrence of death and rebirth. While still in this body, work to destroy the seeds of your past karmas. Remember, roasted seeds will not germinate. People who in deep meditation roast their karmic seeds in the fires of wisdom will never again need to reincarnate on earth.

Paramhansa Yogananda

Chapter 4

The Chakras: The Body's Energy System

What Are the Chakras?

Chakra is a Sanskrit word meaning 'wheel', 'circle', or 'revolving disc'. Some people are able to see the *chakras*, by observing the aura (a rainbow of light surrounding the body) or luminous energy field within the 'subtle' or astral spine. They are seen in cross-section as fast-moving whirlpools or vortices of energy containing colours, each taking the form of a luminous funnel-shaped structure, somewhat like a convolvulus flower. Each *chakra* has its own specific plane and direction of rotation. The first and third *chakras* rotate in a clockwise direction; all the other *chakras* rotate counterclockwise. Kuṇḍalinī Yoga, Laya Yoga, Tantric Yoga, and Kriyā Yoga are the main branches of yoga that specifically concentrate on the *chakras*.

The yoga traditions recognize seven major *chakras*, confluences of consciousness and energy, distributed along the midline of the body, located above the crown of the head, at the forehead, the throat, the chest, the navel, the genital area, and at the base of the spine. In the texts of Hātha Yoga and Kuṇḍalinī Yoga the *chakras* are represented and visualized as luminous lotus flowers or *pādmas* with various numbers of petals, *bīja* (seed-syllable) *mantras* inscribed in each petal, and symbols within the centres of the lotuses.

These representations of the *chakras* are images of energetic experiences in symbolic form. The petals, radiating light, are small rotating vortices whirling at very high speeds. Each vortex metabolizes an energy vibration that resonates at its particular whirling frequency. The colours in each *chakra* are related to the frequency of energy being metabolized at its particular rate.

The lotus, a beautiful and captivating symbol of the *chakras*, represents to us the nature of the *chakra* as a living force. The lotus (Latin – *Nelumbo nucifera;* Sanskrit – *pādma* or *kokanada rakta-kāmāla* – reddish lotus; *pundarika* – white lotus) which can be seen growing in lakes and ponds throughout Asia in such countries as India, Sri Lanka, Thailand, China and Japan, is very beautiful to observe. The lotus flower grows from the bottoms of streams, muddy ponds and lakes to rise above the water and bloom. Its roots are deeply buried in the mud far below the surface, but its petals are not soiled by mud, which just rolls off them. The leaves are coated with a film, upon which water forms magnificent, glittering droplets. The flower stalk rises above the leaves, ending in large, sweet-perfumed, white or pink blooms, which appear one at a time. Symbolically the lotus flower can be related to the human condition, being fully grounded in earth, with its density and heaviness, yet reflecting the upward aspiration of human consciousness toward the light and the divine. And just like the lotus, the *chakra* can be closed, in bud, opening or blossoming.

Do not go to the garden of flowers!
O friend! go not there;
In your body is the garden of flowers.
Take your seat on the thousand petals of the lotus, and there gaze on the infinite beauty.

Kabir (15th-century Indian mystic and poet)

The petals of the lotus symbolize subtle nerves (*nāḍīs*) which resonate to a specific sound vibration. If the hue of the petal is muddy or dull, the sensitivity to sound is decreased. Improving the purity of the sounds through spiritual practice energizes the petals so that they turn and point upwards. This increases the smoothness with which the *chakra* rotates. The rhythm of the rotation is perfect when the lotus petals are pointing upward and in full bloom.

Essentially, *chakras* are energy centres situated within the astral body – the subtle body that mirrors the physical body's informational and energy content. The *chakras* energetically connect the five sheaths (*kośas*) that embody the soul, to the functions of the physical body, primarily through the endocrine glands and the nerve plexuses in the spine. They also access all emotional, mental and spiritual states of our being.

The *chakras* act as dynamos of cosmic energy, which allow our energy bodies to plug in to the universal power source. They serve as transformers and act as regulators to receive, assimilate and distribute energy (prāṇic life-force) to the subtle body, which then distribute the energy to the spinal nerve plexuses where it is in turn transferred to the blood circulation and organs of the physical body.

Chakras and Energy

The human body is surrounded by a halo of conscious Cosmic Energy. Through vibrations of Cosmic Energy, God's intelligence supplies our bodies with Life Force. The medulla oblongata, the 'mouth of God', is the antenna that receives energy from Cosmic Consciousness.

Paramhansa Yogananda

Ultimately even our bodies are nothing but energy. The body is composed of cells, which are composed of atoms, which in turn are made up of particles (including leptons, quarks and mesons) that spin around at incredible speeds in largely empty spaces. It is all a ceaselessly changing pattern of energy. Think of the body as a pattern of intelligence in a field of pure consciousness.

The subtle prāṇic life-force enters the body at the base of the brain (medulla oblongata) and flows to the higher brain centres. Then it filters downward through the six major *chakras* or energy centres. As this energy and light force filters and spirals down through each *chakra*, it becomes increasingly dense. At the lowest *chakra* at the base of the spine (*mūlādhāra chakra*), the vibrational frequency is slower than in those above it. The higher the *chakra*, the more subtle and finer the vibrational frequency. These higher *chakras* are closely related to the innermost sheaths and higher levels of consciousness.

The energy that filters down through the *chakras* ultimately spirals down from cosmic energy, produced from cosmic light, which is created by the will and energy of God – the Ultimate Reality.

Consciousness moving becomes energy. As consciousness descends in a spiralling movement of energy, it subdivides and stretches out, and when the movement is slowed down, it becomes matter. As it condenses into matter it forms the five elements: ether, air, fire, water and earth – first the subtle elements, then the gross elements. The difference between one element and the other is a difference in their vibratory wavelengths and frequencies.

As consciousness descends and moves in space, it becomes air. When air moves there is friction and therefore fire, and when the gases collide and fire is generated, water is also generated; and then water condenses into solid substances (earth). These elemental stages describe the stages of the descent of soul-consciousness into matter.

The process of yoga is a reversal of this descent into matter. Through definite stages of spiritual awakening in our awareness of our true identity as the Self, the soul-consciousness can return from matter to the freedom and oneness in Spirit.

Chakras and the Elements

The elements associated with the *chakras* should not be confused with the chemical elements known to modern science. In their pure states the elements are not visible and are known as *mahābhūtas* (generic gross elements) which evolve in this specific order: *ākāśa* (ether), *vāyu* (air), *tejas* or *agni* (fire), *apās* (water) and *pṛithvī* (earth), which have evolved out of the five *tanmātrās*, which evolve in this specific order: *śabda* (sound), *sparśa* (touch), *rūpa* (colour / form), *rasa* (taste), and *gandha* (smell). Each of the *mahābhūtas* is a compound of all the five *tanmātrās*, one of them dominating in each. Sound dominates in ether, touch in air, form in fire, taste in water, and smell in earth.

The earth centre (*mūlādhāra chakra*) is that part of your anatomy which comes into contact with the earth. A little above there is the water element (*svādhiṣṭhāna chakra*), the next subtle element, located where water collects. At the navel centre (*maṇipūra chakra*) is the fire region – when we talk about digestion, we think of the gastric fire there. Above the navel is the heart region (*anāhata chakra*), which represents air – the region in which the lungs and oxygenation operate. Above the heart is the throat region (*viśuddha chakra*) – a little space (ether) in the throat. Higher still is the Spiritual Eye (*ājñā chakra*), at the midpoint between the eyebrows, which represents the mind.

Characteristics of the Chakras

The *chakras* vibrate at different frequencies as they transmit energy. Each is associated with a vibrational frequency, a characteristic colour, a petal sound, a seed-syllable (*bīja*) *mantra,* an element, a planet, a spiritual quality, a presiding deity, a symbolic animal, a sense organ, and an endocrine gland.

Besides the *chakras* manifesting the specific sounds of the *bīja mantras,* they also manifest the following inner astral sounds, which can be heard by meditating deeply on the *chakras*:

ājñā chakra – *Oṁ*
viśuddha chakra – roar of the ocean
anāhata chakra – long drawn out deep bell sound; deep gong
maṇipūra chakra – harp
svādhiṣṭhāna chakra – flute
mūlādhāra chakra – humming sound, like a bumble bee

All of these subtle sounds are manifestations of the Cosmic Vibration of *Oṁ.* These six subtle sounds can be heard in meditation by listening with deep concentration in the right ear. The inner *Oṁ* sound is heard in meditation with the inward gaze at the Spiritual Eye mentally chanting *Oṁ,* while simultaneously listening with deep concentration.

As the various vital centres [*chakras*] begin to open up, different sounds are perceived inwardly and the devotee comes to feel the sounds of conches, bells, flutes, etc. all merging in the cosmic rhythm of one great voice of infinite silence. At that stage no thought or object of the outside world can distract his attention. As he advances, his being gets dissolved in the bottomless depth of that blissful music that pervades the whole universe, and he finds eternal repose.'

Śrī Ānandamayī Mā, *Life and Teaching of Śrī Ānandamāyī Mā*

Functions of the Chakras

Every *chakra* governs a specific kind of energy related to various human attributes. For example the heart *chakra* is the centre of consciousness, of the mind, feeling and emotions. If the heart *chakra* is functioning in a balanced way, the person will be able to relate to others in a caring, understanding and unselfish manner. Love and the ability to forgive are attributes of a balanced heart *chakra*. Conversely, those persons who tend to close themselves off from others or who are dominated by emotions may have energy blockages in the heart *chakra*.

Essentially, the *chakras* relate to our individual growth and development. The first three *chakras*, the lower centres of consciousness, are primarily concerned with the primal issues of survival and self-preservation, sexuality and power, while the upper *chakras* are concerned with issues of personal expression, spiritual insight and spiritual realization. We begin individual growth and development at the first *chakra* or 'root' *chakra* (*mūlādhāra*) in infancy and develop our upper *chakras* as we mature into adulthood.

The lower *chakras* give us firmness and stability in life. This foundation becomes unreliable when we hold fears and misconceptions in our consciousness, creating blockages in the flow of energy to and from the *chakra*. We need to understand that the *chakras* are conduits that conduct and transform subtle energy (*prāṇa*) into matter. If the channels are blocked then imbalances will occur.

Although the higher *chakras* reflect the aspiration of human consciousness towards Self-realization, all the *chakras* remain important to a person's overall state of health and wellbeing. One should not think, for example, that development of the sixth *chakra* (*ājñā chakra*), the centre of insight and intuition, is more important than development of the second or sacral *chakra* (*svādhiṣṭhāna chakra*), the centre of procreation, creative instincts, and self-fulfilment. In fact, the balanced development of the second *chakra* is an important step for the development of the sixth *chakra*. For instance, in some cases, there are persons who have taken vows of celibacy on entering a spiritual community, an ashram, a convent or a monastery, who have an unbalanced second *chakra* through suppressing their sexual energy rather than naturally transforming and redirecting it into other areas of creativity. This causes a blockage in the second *chakra*, causing the person to become unbalanced in their energy and attitude toward sexuality. A person's sexual energy is connected to their life-force; it is a source of vitality. If the energy in that *chakra* is blocked it will have the unhealthy effect of lowering physical and natural sexual vitality.

In the traditions of Kuṇḍalinī Yoga, Tantric Yoga, Hāṭha Yoga, and Kriyā Yoga, there are spiritual practices that involve *āsana, prāṇāyāma, mantra* and meditation to transform and redirect the sexual energy through different energy channels. The energy is directed upwards through the central channel and power current of the inner spine to the higher *chakras* and brain centres, to be transformed into higher vibratory energy.

Chakras and the Endocrine System

On the physical level each *chakra* is related to and has a significant effect on a ductless gland. The *chakras* function as transmitters of energy, distributing prāṇic energy to the physical body. The *chakras* absorb the universal or cosmic energy, break it up into component parts, and distribute it via a network of channels (*nāḍīs*) to the nervous system, the endocrine glands, and then the blood circulatory system to nourish the body. The endocrine system, which regulates different mechanisms in the body, plays a vital role in health and wellbeing.

When there is a balance between the astral and the physical systems, the life-current energy becomes harmoniously connected and synchronized. However, if the flow of energy is blocked and unbalanced in the *chakras*, the corresponding endocrine gland will be affected, causing malfunction in the physical body, with mental and emotional changes.

The endocrine system is a collection of glands and cells that secrete hormones directly into the circulation. Hormones are complex chemical substances that regulate body functions such as the metabolism, growth and sexual reproduction. The control centre of hormone secretion is in a part of the brain called the hypothalamus, which secretes 'releasing factors', which in turn, control the secretion of hormones from the pituitary gland.

The Endocrine Glands

The **pineal gland** or epiphysis is a small pine-cone-shaped structure about 1 cm long, and weighing little more than 0.1 g. It is located on the midline, attached to the posterior end of the roof of the third ventricle in the brain. The pineal gland contains a complete map of the visual field of the eyes. There is a pathway from the retinas in the eyes to the hypothalamus, called the retinohypothalamic tract. This transmits information about light and dark cycles to a region of the hypothalamus called the suprachiasmatic nucleus (SCN). From the SCN, nerve impulses travel via the pineal nerve (sympathetic nervous system) to the pineal gland. These impulses control the production of melatonin. When these impulses stop, when light at night is no longer stimulating the hypothalamus, pineal inhibition ceases and melatonin is released. The pineal gland's production of melatonin is dramatically increased during the night hours and decreases during the day. Also, melatonin levels are much higher in children under the age of seven than in adolescents and are lower still in adults. The reason for the higher level of melatonin in children is because it acts to keep a child's body from reaching sexual maturity, since sex hormones such as luteotropin, which play a role in the development of sexual organs, emerge only after melatonin levels have declined.

The pineal gland is a photosensitive organ and an important timekeeper. The melatonin it produces governs circadian rhythms and sleep–wake cycles, and is implicated in seasonal affective disorder. The light-transducing ability of the pineal gland has inspired mystics to call the pineal the 'third eye', the organ of spiritual vision. The pineal gland is the sense organ of the sixth *chakra* and the organ of action for the seventh *chakra*. When the pineal gland is awakened by connecting to a higher frequency in deep meditation, the meditator feels a pressure at the base of the brain.

The **pituitary gland** (hypophysis) is sometimes called the 'master gland', because it controls the activities of many other endocrine glands and cells in the body. The pituitary gland is situated inside the brain. It is a very small structure with a stalk; it looks like a tiny fig, and weighs about 0.5 g. It is made up of two parts – an anterior (front) lobe and a posterior lobe. The anterior lobe, in Latin called the pars distalis, contains cells that produce six major hormones for secretion into the bloodstream. The posterior lobe, called the pars nervosa, stores two of the hormones produced in the hypothalamus, which are also secreted into the bloodstream.

The **thyroid gland** is located in the front of the neck, partially surrounding the trachea, and is composed of two lobes joined by a segment called the isthmus. It plays an important role in regulating the body's metabolism. Behind the thyroid are four smaller glands called the parathyroid glands, which regulate calcium levels in the blood. The thyroid is the only endocrine gland in the body that contains a stored supply of its hormone, usually sufficient for the body's needs for three months. Thyroid hormone is important for the development of the brain and the bones in the foetus and infant. At the cellular level, thyroid hormone increases oxygen consumption and protein synthesis within the cells.

The **adrenals** are small triangular-shaped structures attached to the upper poles of the kidneys. Within the gland are two layers: an outer layer – the adrenal cortex, which secretes steroid hormones – and an inner layer called the adrenal medulla, which secretes the hormone adrenaline. The adrenals play a role in regulating the body's response to stress, and balancing the metabolism and the immune system.

The **pancreas** has a dual function. It is both an exocrine and an endocrine gland. The exocrine gland secretes digestive enzymes into the pancreatic duct, which drains into the duodenum. The endocrine gland mainly secretes two hormones – insulin and glucagon – directly into the bloodstream. These hormones are secreted from the endocrine cells in structures called the islets of Langerhans. These are groups of cells scattered throughout the exocrine tissue of the pancreas. These hormones are needed for regulating blood-sugar levels and the metabolism.

The **gonads** (testes and ovaries) secrete the sex hormones testosterone in men and women, and oestrogen and progesterone in women, which are essential to sexual development and fertility.

Relationship between the chakras and the endocrine glands

Chakra		*Endocrine gland*
Sahasrāra	crown centre	pituitary
Ājñā	brow centre	pineal
Viśuddha	throat centre	thyroid / parathyroids
Anāhata	heart centre	thymus
Maṇipūra	navel centre	adrenals
Svādhiṣṭhāna	sacral centre	testes / ovaries
Mūlādhāra	root centre	perineal body

Chakras and the Nerve Plexuses

Where branches of one spinal nerve interconnect in an area with other nerves to form a network of nerves, this is called a plexus. These are located along the physical spinal cord. The *chakras* are related to the nerve plexuses and appear to be attached by their 'stems' very close to the major nerve plexuses. Each nerve plexus is like a computer. It receives information from the senses and the internal organs (input), processes the information within the brain (data processing), and transmits nervous impulses and energy to the various body parts (output). This in turn causes the activation of the various organs in the body, such as muscles and glands, by the nerves leading to them.

Nerve Cells

The basic unit of the nervous system is a nerve cell called a neuron. Neurons form connections with each other and with various body organs. Neurons have long fibre-like extensions, known as axons and dendrites, which have short, branch-like processes attached to the cell body. Axons carry nerve impulses away from the cell and dendrites receive impulses from other neurons. Throughout human life, the number of neurons progressively decreases. Neurons are unable to divide or replicate, so when a neuron dies it is not replaced. However, under certain circumstances, when neurons are damaged the nervous system can create new connections between the remaining neurons to restore at least some of the impaired function.

Billions of electrical and chemical signals are constantly active in the brain and body. One neuron can establish connections with thousands of other neurons. The way this is achieved is by a chemical transmitter substance. This passes across from the end of the axon of one neuron to stimulate the dendrite or cell body of another neuron, which alters the electrical charge in its axon. The electrical charge on the inside of the cell membrane changes from negative to positive, and a nerve impulse travels down the fibre to a synaptic knob at its end, triggering the release of neurotransmitter chemicals that cross the gap between the neuron and the target cell, stimulating a response in the target.

Nervous System

The nervous system is divided into two main systems:

1. The **Central Nervous System** (CNS), which is made up of the brain and spinal cord.
2. The **Autonomic Nervous System** (ANS), which is that part of the peripheral nervous system that controls the functions of the internal organs of the body.

The autonomic nervous system has sensory input pathways that transmit information from the internal organs to the brain, and outgoing pathways from the brain back to the body, which transmit signals that control and regulate the function of internal organs, including non-somatic structures such as blood vessels, throughout the body, and sweat glands in the skin.

The outgoing pathways are divided into sympathetic and parasympathetic pathways. In general, the **sympathetic nerves** activate the body's organs and blood vessels during periods of stress. The sympathetic nerves arise mainly in the thoracic (chest) segments of the spinal cord.

The **parasympathetic nerves** are activated mainly during quiet, restful states, and their activity predominates during sleep. Nerve cells in the brain do not rest during sleep; they are still active but in a different way from that of the waking hours. The parasympathetic nerves arise in the brain stem, and the lower spinal cord in the region of the sacrum.

Spinal Nerves

There are 31 pairs of peripheral spinal nerves that emerge from the spinal cord and pass through apertures in the sides of the spinal column, between the vertebrae, to various parts and organs of the body. Each nerve attached to the spinal cord divides into two branches: anterior (front), containing axons of motor nerves that serve the front of the body; and posterior (back) containing axons from sensory nerves that serve the back of the body.

Relationship between the chakras and the nerve plexuses

Chakra		*Nerve plexus*
Sahasrāra	crown centre	None
Ājñā	brow centre	Medullary plexus
Viśuddha	throat centre	Cervical plexus
Anāhata	heart centre	Cardiac plexus
Maṇipūra	navel centre	Solar plexus
Svādhiṣṭhāna	sacral centre	Sacral plexus
Mūlādhāra	root centre	Coccygeal plexus

The *sahasrāra chakra* is associated with the cerebral cortex and the pineal gland.

Chapter 5

Nāḍīs

The anatomy and physiology of the gross physical body is patterned from the blueprint or template of the subtler etheric body (between the astral and physical bodies) composed of a luminous matrix of web-like lines of force in constant motion, scintillating with a bluish or white light. The etheric body acts as a receiver, assimilator and transmitter of life-energy.

The etheric body channels the flow of life-energy (*prāṇa*) to create and sustain the physical body through a vast network of fine subtle channels called *nāḍīs* (*nāḍī* literally means 'flow' or 'motion'), astral nerve conductors of *prāṇa*. Any mental or emotional disturbances that a person experiences in life will create blocks to this flow of life-energy, which will be registered in the astral body, and stored in the *chakras* – the main energy centres of the astral body. This in turn will influence the energies of the physical body and will have an effect on the health and wellbeing of the individual.

The physical spine and the ganglia of the sympathetic nervous system alongside the spine, correspond to the astral spine (*suṣumnā*) with its *nāḍīs* of the *iḍā* on the left side, and *piṅgalā* on the right side of the central astral channel (*suṣumnā*).

The *suṣumnā,* which corresponds with the central nervous system, consists of the *śirobrahman* (cerebrum) contained within the cranium, the *suṣumnā śirśakam* (medulla oblongata), and the *suṣumnā kandam* (spinal cord within the vertebral canal).

The *parisariya nāḍī maṇḍalam* (the peripheral nervous system) consists of a series of nerves by which the *suṣumnā* is connected with the various tissues of the body. The autonomic nervous system is called *iḍā,* corresponding with the parasympathetic nervous system, and *piṅgalā,* corresponding with the sympathetic nervous system.

The source of the *nāḍīs* in the astral body is an egg-shaped centre of nerves called the *kanda,* which is located between the anus and the root of the reproductive organs, just above the *mūlādhāra chakra.* From this source 72,000 *nāḍīs* with 14 main channels according to the *Darśana Upaniṣad* (or 350,000, with 14 main channels, according to the *Śiva Samhita*) flow out to the entire subtle circuitry of the astral body. The *kanda* is the junction where the *nāḍī* that passes through the spinal column is connected to the *mūlādhāra chakra* at the base of the spine. Corresponding to this centre in the physical body is the cauda equina ('horse's tail'), a fibrous network at the base of the spinal cord, that tapers off to a fine silk-like thread.

There are two views regarding the origin of *nāḍīs* – one belief is that the origin lies in the *kanda sthāna* and the other is that it is in the solar plexus near the navel. The *Jābāla-darśanopaniṣad* text states that the centre is nine finger-breadths above the *mūlādhāra* in the navel region. But the *Yogi Yājñavalkya-Saṁhitā* (4: 16–17) gives its location as being nine finger-breadths, above the navel, and that it is egg-shaped, and four fingers in breadth, width and height. The *Yogaśikh-opaniṣad* states that the navel encircled by the *vilamba nāḍī* (a particular prāṇic channel) as the *nābhi* (navel) *chakra,* is egg-shaped, and it is from here that the *nāḍīs* originate.

The solar plexus is the main storage battery of *prāṇa* and large amounts of *prāṇa* can be held there to give vitality to the physical body, through the practice of *prāṇāyāma.* The *nāḍīs* can be purified by this practice, particularly through *nāḍī śodhana* or *anuloma viloma prāṇāyāma* (alternate nostril breathing). If the *nāḍīs* are not purified, then the *prāṇa* cannot flow into the *suṣumnā.*

The life-energy which flows through the *nāḍīs* is used by the soul in its expression through the physical and astral manifestations. Without light of the in-dwelling Self or soul, the brain, mind, body organs, senses, and even *prāṇa* cannot function. It is the Self that sustains the body by agency of *prāṇa*.

Fourteen Important Nāḍīs

1. ***Suṣumnā*** – carries the *kuṇḍalinī śākti.*
2. ***Iḍā*** – carries the mental energy.
3. ***Piṅgalā*** – carries the prāṇic energy.
4. ***Gāndhārī*** – is situated by the side of *iḍā nāḍī* and helps to support it. *Gāndhārī nāḍī* stretches from below the corner of the left eye to the big toe of the left foot. Affects the excretory system.
5. ***Hastijihvā*** – is a complementary *nāḍī* to *iḍā. Gāndhārī, iḍā,* and *hastijihvā* form the left channel. The *hastijihvā nāḍī* stretches from below the corner of the right eye to the big toe. Affects the excretory system.
6. ***Kuhū*** – originates from the throat and terminates at the genitals. Affects the liver, and when this *nāḍī* is balanced, it keeps the stomach and the blood circulation functioning well.
7. ***Sarasvatī*** – is seated on the tongue and runs parallel to the *suṣumnā nāḍī.* Affects the spleen, and controls the temperature of the stomach.
8. ***Pūṣā*** – extends from the left big toe to the right ear. This *nāḍī,* along with *yaśasvinī nāḍī,* forms the right channel and is complementary to *piṅgalā.*
9. ***Śaṅkhini*** – originates from the throat and passes between *sarasvatī* and *gāndhārī nāḍīs* on the left side of *suṣumnā nāḍī,* terminating in the anus. Affects the kidneys; its main functions are purification of the blood and urinary excretion.

10. ***Payasvinī*** – flows between *pūṣā nāḍī* and *sarasvatī nāḍī*. *Pūṣā* is complementary to *piṅgalā* on the right side of the *suṣumnā,* and to *sarasvatī* on the left. Directly linked to the gallbladder, it controls the level of bile in the body and affects the digestion.
11. ***Vāruṇī*** – situated between *yaśasvinī* and *kuhū nāḍīs*. *Vāruṇī nāḍī* assists in keeping *apāna vāyu* free of toxins. Together they help each other in the body's process of excretion.
12. ***Alambuṣā*** – begins at the anus and terminates at the mouth. It affects the mind and the metabolic system. This is an important *nāḍī* because all feelings of the senses are conveyed to the *suṣumnā* through it, and are then carried to the brain. It affects the mind and the metabolic system.
13. ***Viśvodarī*** – flows between *kuhū* and *hastijihvā nāḍīs* and is located in the area of the navel. *Viśvodarī nāḍī* is related to the adrenal glands and the pancreas; it affects the intestines, and controls the metabolism and catabolism. *Viśvodarī,* working together with *vāruṇī nāḍī,* improves the distribution and flow of *prāṇa* throughout the body, especially the *prāṇa* rising through the *suṣumnā*. The yoga practices of *uḍḍīyāna bandha* and *nauli kriyā* energize the *viśvodarī nāḍī.*
14. ***Yaśasvinī*** – extends from the right big toe to the left ear. It affects the excretory system.

Three Main Nāḍīs

The *Brihadāranyaka Upaniṣad,* one of the oldest *Upaniṣads,* dating from about 800 BCE, states that the *nāḍīs* are as fine as a hair split into a thousand parts. Out of the network of 72,000 *nāḍīs* ten are regarded as important *nāḍīs*. These ten *nāḍīs* are the main channels of the distribution of life-energy and consciousness to the whole body. Of these ten *nāḍīs,* three – *iḍā, piṅgalā* and *suṣumnā* – are seen as specially important, because they control the complete network of the 72,000 *nāḍīs*.

Iḍā nāḍī, the left-hand current, transmits mental energy (*citta śākti*) and controls all the mental processes. *Piṅgalā*, the right-hand current, transits the vital life-force (*prāṇa śākti*) and controls all the vital and physiological processes. The central channel, *suṣumnā*, is for the awakening of spiritual consciousness; it transmits spiritual power (*ātma śākti*). Both *iḍā* and *piṅgalā* control our normal consciousness and are constantly active, even during sleep. The *suṣumnā nāḍī* is mainly dormant in the majority of people who are not consciously and actively engaged in spiritual development through such practices as yoga and meditation. Their consciousness is limited to the lower *chakra*s on the worldly plane; they have not yet spiritually awakened.

The Spinal Cord

In the physical body the central nervous system consists of the brain and the spinal cord, the cerebro-spinal centre. The spinal cord is a continuation of the brain. It extends from the top of the spinal canal to the second vertebra of the coccygeal region where it tapers off into the cauda equina.

The spinal cord continues into the brain stem before it reaches the brain. The brain stem contains important centres that regulate several vital functions for survival, including heartbeat, respiration, blood, pressure, digestion, and the reflex actions of swallowing and vomiting. The brain stem includes the mid-brain (controls visual and auditory reflexes), the pons (controls the functions of facial expression and eye movement), and the medulla oblongata (controls regulation of heart rate and breathing rate). The bulb-shaped medulla oblongata, below the pons, is a connecting medium between the brain and the spinal cord.

The spinal cord contains two types of tissue: white and grey matter. The grey matter within the centre of the cord is butterfly-shaped. It contains the cell bodies of the motor tracts, the sensory tracts, and the autonomic nerves. The outer white matter serves as a pathway for nerve tracts passing impulses to and from the spinal cord and the brain.

Suṣumnā

The *suṣumnā* ('most gracious'), the major central *nāḍī* in the astral spine corresponding to the spinal cord in the physical body, is also called *brahma nāḍī* ('Path to God'), *brahma daṇḍa* (God's staff), *divya-mārga* (divine path) and *meru daṇḍa* (Mount Meru is *axis mundi*, the supporting pillar of the earth, running from the underworlds to the heavens). Most of the Vedic and yoga texts consider the *mūlādhāra* at the base of the spine to be its origin, and the *brahmarandhra* at the crown of the head to be where it terminates. *Suṣumnā* corresponds with the sacred river *Sarasvatī*.

The *mūlādhāra chakra* is located and experienced between the genital root and the anus in males, and at the cervix, or base of the uterus, in women. From the *mūlādhāra chakra*, the *suṣumnā nāḍī* ascends slightly backward and upward to the second energy centre, *svādhiṣṭhāna chakra*, located at the point in front of the coccyx where the *suṣumnā nāḍī* enters the spinal column. From the *svādiṣṭhāna chakra* the *suṣumnā* continues upwards through the spinal column, through the navel centre (*maṇipūra chakra*), heart centre (*anāhata chakra*), throat centre (*viśuddha chakra*), the point at the base of the brain where the spinal column ends, and passes through *ājñā chakra* (the psychic passage which runs from the eyebrow centre to the medulla oblongata at the back of the head). *Suṣumnā* terminates at *sahasrāra* (the Gate of Brahman) at the crown of the head.

Suṣumnā nāḍī is composed of three subtle currents of force, concentric tubes arranged one within the other. The innermost channel is *citriṇī* (pale like the moon), and has a sattvic (pure) nature. The second inner channel is the active and forceful *vajriṇī* (sunlike), and the outer channel is the *suṣumnā* itself. When *kuṇḍalinī* energy, the psycho-spiritual power, is awakened, it passes through the *brahma nāḍī*, a very fine canal inside the *citriṇī nāḍī*. It enters through the 'door of Brahman' (*brahma dvāra*) at *mūlādhāra chakra* (at the base of the spine) and blissfully ascends to *sahasrāra chakra*, the thousand-petalled lotus of supreme consciousness at the crown of the head. In a general sense the *suṣumnā nāḍī* itself can be called the *brahma nāḍī*.

Iḍā and Piṅgalā

The Sanskrit word *iḍā* means 'comfort'. The *iḍā nāḍī*, also called *chandra nāḍī*, is the 'comforting' channel due to its cooling effect on the body. *Iḍā* is associated with feminine and lunar energy, which are also seen as possessing cooling qualities. *Iḍā* corresponds with the sacred river Gaṅgā (Ganges), which is nourishing and purifying. *Iḍā* controls all the mental processes, and is sattvic in nature.

The origins of the subtle *prāṇa* and the breath lie in the astral body. When there is an upward movement of *prāṇa* in the *iḍā nāḍī* this is astral inhalation. Astral exhalation is when there is a downward movement through the *piṅgalā nāḍī*.

In Svāra Yoga, *iḍā* represents the breath flowing in and out of the left nostril. During the ascending moon cycle, from the new moon to the full moon, *iḍā nāḍī* is dominant for nine days in the fortnight at the time of sunrise and sunset. There are some yogis who follow Svāra Yoga, who create a sattvic balance in body and mind by keeping the flow of breath in the left nostril during the day. This balances the solar energy that is received during the daylight hours.

In Sanskrit *piṅgalā* means 'tawny-red', which is derived from the word *tan* symbolizing the action of the Sun. The *piṅgalā nāḍī*, also called *sūrya nāḍī*, is associated with masculine and solar energy, possessing heating qualities. *Piṅgalā* corresponds with the sacred river Yamunā, and controls all the vital processes. *Piṅgalā* represents the breath flowing in and out of the right nostril. *Piṅgalā* is more active during the descending moon cycle, from the full moon to the new moon, and operates for nine days in the fortnight at the time of sunrise and sunset.

The Svāra Yoga practice of keeping the right nostril open at night, when solar energy is less strong, is said to maintain a balance in a healthy body. This can be achieved in sleep by lying on the left side of the body at night. Keeping the left nostril open and predominant during the day, and the right nostril open and active at night, increases vitality and longevity.

The two *nāḍīs* run up either side of the spine – *iḍā* on the left side, and *piṅgalā* on the right side of the *suṣumnā*. *Iḍā* and *piṅgalā* correspond with the sympathetic nerve ganglion on either side of the spine, while *suṣumnā* runs between them in a position corresponding to the spinal cord. At certain locations along the spine, these three energies converge into whirling vortices – the *chakras*.

Iḍā and *piṅgalā* emerge from *mūlādhāra chakra* at the coccygeal point of the base of the spine. This junction where the three *nāḍīs* meet is known as *yukta triveni (yukta,* 'combined'; *tri,* 'three'; *veni,* 'streams') the point at which three rivers converge – Gaṅgā, Yamunā, and Sarasvāti – corresponding respectively with *piṅgalā, iḍā,* and *suṣumnā nāḍīs*. (In India these three rivers meet at a place called Prayag [also known as Allahabad].) From *mūlādhāra,* the base *chakra, piṅgalā* emerges from the right side of the spine in a semi-circular curve, and crosses the *suṣumnā* at *svādiṣṭhāna chakra* (sacral plexus). It then curves up on the left side, joining the *suṣumnā* at *maṇipūra chakra* (solar plexus). Continuing in a series of curves crossing back and forth over the *suṣumnā, piṅgalā* goes to the right and *iḍā* goes to the left. *Iḍā* and *piṅgalā* continue to move in opposite directions, and cross each other at the *chakras,* finally meeting at the sixth *chakra, ājñā chakra.* This meeting point of the three streams is called *mukti triveni* (*mukta,* 'liberated'). *Iḍā* and *piṅgalā* end in the left and right nostrils, respectively.

The spiral patterned movement is likened to the double helix of our DNA, or a pair of intertwined serpents as seen in the symbol of the caduceus of medicine. The caduceus is a winged staff, with two serpents, and is carried by the Greek god Hermes, who is said to be the messenger of the gods. Together, *iḍā* and *piṅgalā* form the two serpents or snakes of the caduceus, while *suṣumnā* forms the staff. The snakes intersect at the *chakras*, as do the *nāḍīs*. At the *ājñā chakra*, the midpoint between the eyebrows, there are two petals, one on either side, just as there are two wings at the top of the caduceus. Although the caduceus symbol was only adopted as a Western symbol for medicine about a century ago, we can see the representation of the entire system of *kuṇḍalinī śākti*.

Relationship of Iḍā and Piṅgalā with the Hemispheres of the Brain

In the physical body the cerebrum, the largest part of the brain, is made up of two halves, called hemispheres. The hemispheres are known as the left and right cerebral hemispheres. These halves are interconnected by a pathway of nerve fibres along which information continuously passes. The cerebrum is divided into four lobes paired according to the skull bones next to them: frontal, parietal, temporal, and occipital lobes. The grey matter of the cerebrum is located in the outer layers of the brain, known as the cortex, as well as in 'islands' of grey matter within the white matter.

The cortex of each hemisphere controls the opposite side of the body and contains various centres – motor centres that control the voluntary muscles, sensory centres for receiving skin sensations, visual centres that processes stimuli arriving from the eye, and hearing centres.

The specific functions of the two hemispheres of the cerebrum correlate with the activities of *iḍā* and *piṅgalā nāḍīs*. *Iḍā* is connected to the right hemisphere, which governs the left side of the body. *Piṅgalā* is connected to the left hemisphere and governs the right side of the body.

The right hemisphere (non-dominant hemisphere), in relation to *iḍā*, contains centres for spatial orientation, extrasensory perception, intuition, and creative, artistic and musical abilities. The right brain moves from whole to parts, holistically. It reviews the big picture first, not the details. It is also random; its tendency is to jump from one track to another.

The left hemisphere (dominant hemisphere), in relation to *piṅgalā*, is concerned with logical, rational and analytical abilities. Information is processed in a linear, sequential and logical manner. It processes from part to whole. It takes parts, lines them up, and arranges them in a logical order; then derives conclusions.

Mind and *prāṇa* are interrelated and interdependent. When the *prāṇas* are disturbed the mind also becomes disturbed and, vice versa, when the mind is disturbed the *prāṇas* become disturbed. The practices of Hātha Yoga, Svāra Yoga and Rāja Yoga help bring a balance between the alternating activities of the *iḍā* and *piṅgalā nāḍīs*, ensuring that they operate in rhythm with the movements of the external sun and moon.

There is one particular Hātha Yoga practice called *nāḍī śodhana* (alternate nostril breathing) that is the best technique to calm the mind and nervous system. *Nāḍī śodhana* purifies the *nāḍīs*. The exercise also produces optimum function to both sides of the brain – optimum creativity and optimum logical and verbal activity. This creates a more balanced person, since both hemispheres of the brain are functioning properly.

Prāṇa and the Nāḍīs

Prāṇa is the life-force that links the physical with the mental, and the mental with the spiritual. The word *prāṇa* comes from two Sanskrit roots. *Prā* means 'first', and *ṇa* is the 'smallest unit of energy'. *Prāṇa* is therefore the first breath, the primal or atomic beginning of the flow of energy. Out of this first unit of energy manifest all aspects and levels of the human being. It is one and the same as *kuṇḍalinī śākti.*

The *nāḍīs* are channels or pathways for carrying *prāṇa* into the *chakras* situated along the spinal column in the astral spine. Consciously to activate a *chakra* one can either direct *prāṇa* to the *chakra* or, using mental visualization, concentrate on its location and form.

Kuṇḍalinī

Kuṇḍalinī is the primordial energy of consciousness (*caitanya śākti*) that lies dormant at the base of the spine in the causal body of all beings, and in every atom of the universe. It is the spiritual potential force of the Cosmic Power. *Kuṇḍalinī* maintains the individual soul through the subtle *prāṇa.* The subtle *prāṇa* is connected with the subtle *nāḍīs* and *chakras,* and the *nāḍīs* are connected with the mind, which is linked to all the parts of the body. When *kuṇḍalinī śākti* is dormant or is active only in the lower three *chakras,* a person has only a finite experience. When *kuṇḍalinī* is aroused and ascends upward, she withdraws into herself the moving powers of creation, and unites with pure consciousness (*Śiva*). This is the reverse process of the evolution of the mind and the five gross elements. In reality *kuṇḍalinī* has no form, but the mind and intellect require a particular form on which to concentrate initially, so the subtle, formless *kuṇḍalinī* has symbolically taken the form of a coiled serpent or snake. In the *mūlādhāra chakra* there is a self-existent point, at which the *suṣumnā nāḍī* is attached to the *kanda*. The sleeping *kuṇḍalinī* serpent lies face downwards at the mouth of *suṣumnā nāḍī* on the head of this point. She is coiled like a serpent with three and a half coils around the *svayambhu* ('self-born') *lingam.* The unawakened *kuṇḍalinī śākti* remains coiled around the *lingam* with her tail in her mouth. The three coils represent the *kuṇḍalinī* energy within us, compressed like a spring, ready to change from potential static energy (dormant) into kinetic manifestation (awakening). The half coil represents the state of transcendence. There are also other meanings: the three coils also represent the three *gunas* of *prakṛti – sattva, rajas* and *tamas* (equilibrium, activity and inertia); the three states of consciousness (waking, sleeping, dreaming); and the three syllables of Aum (*Oṁ*).

Kuṇḍalinī comes from the Sanskrit word *kuṇḍal,* which means 'coiled'. But a more correct meaning of *kuṇḍalinī* is derived from the word *kuṇḍa,* which means 'pit'or 'cavity'. *Kuṇḍa* refers to the concave cavity in which the brain, resembling a coiled, sleeping serpent, nestles. Prāṇic energy and consciousness (*caitanya śākti*) are the two forms of *kuṇḍalinī.* Prāṇic energy is the cause of action, and *caitanya śākti* gives rise to knowledge and wisdom. When *kuṇḍalinī* is activated these two energies are activated in all the brain centres.

Kuṇḍalinī Awakening

The kuṇḍalinī , in its latent form is coiled like a serpent. One who causes that Śākti to move [from the *mūlādhāra* upwards] will attain liberation.

Hāṭha Yoga Pradīpikā, 3: 108

In Tantra Yoga *kuṇḍalinī* is an aspect of Śākti, the divine female energy and consort of Śiva. The one Consciousness is polarized into static (Śiva) and dynamic (Śākti) aspects for the purpose of manifestation. The object of Kuṇḍalinī Yoga is to awaken the latent coiled-up cosmic energy (Śākti) in the spine and unite it with Pure Consciousness (Śiva). The consummation of the blissful union between Śākti and Śiva in the *sahasrāra chakra* is the union of the individual self (*jīva*) with the supreme Self, or Divine Consciousness. The duality becomes one.

If the positive and negative forces of the *iḍā* and *piṅgalā nāḍīs* are completely balanced, an awakening can occur which activates the latent *kuṇḍalinī* to rise from its dormant state. There are degrees of awakening – sometimes there may only be a mild awakening in which *kuṇḍalinī* rises as far as *svādhiṣṭhāna chakra* and then drops back to *mūlādhāra*, the root support. That is why it is important to purify and balance the *nāḍīs* through the Hāṭha Yoga practice of *prāṇāyāma*. The *chakras* also need to be purified and in balance.

When activated, the *kuṇḍalinī* energy, which was lying dormant and static in the *mūlādhāra chakra*, becomes kinetic and dynamic. It travels up the psychic pathway in the *suṣumnā nāḍī*, the central axis, criss-crossed in a helix by the *iḍā* and *piṅgalā*. As the *kuṇḍalinī* climbs up on its spiritual ascent towards the *sahasrāra chakra*, the seat of consciousness at the crown of the head, it activates all the *chakras* in the subtle body in succession. They are stimulated into intense activity by the force of the *kuṇḍalinī* as it travels upwards. Layer after layer of the mind becomes fully opened, causing the yogi to experience visions, powers, knowledge and bliss. But for the vast majority of people, whose minds operate only in the lower levels of consciousness, the *suṣumnā* is generally closed at the base of the spine.

Kuṇḍalinī can also be awakened in an individual *chakra*. For instance, if *kuṇḍalinī* is awakened in the second *chakra* (*svādhiṣṭhāna*) it ascends directly to *sahasrāra chakra*. Similarly, if *kuṇḍalinī* is awakened in the third *chakra* (*maṇipūra*) it ascends straight to *sahasrāra chakra*.

After having made its ascent through the six centres of consciousness to the awakening at *sahasrāra*, the *kuṇḍalinī* descends back down through the *chakras* to its root support at the *mūlādhāra chakra*. The luminous ascent through the *chakras* is a reabsorption (*laya*) of all the cosmic powers into *kuṇḍalinī*, culminating in a freedom that transcends the phenomenal world in which consciousness is bound and conditioned by space, time and causation. As *kuṇḍalinī* makes the return journey or descent to her root support at the base of the spine, she revivifies and illumines what she had previously absorbed.

The latent force of *kuṇḍalinī* may be activated through various means such as: birth, *mantra* (a method used in Bhakti Yoga), austerity (*tapasyā*), meditation, *prāṇāyāma*, Kriyā Yoga, Rāja Yoga, *śāktipāt* (the transmission of spiritual power from the guru to the disciple), Karma Yoga, Bhakti Yoga and Jñāna Yoga.

In some circumstances, *kuṇḍalinī* can even occur without yoga practice, for instance due to a shock or an accident, but in this kind of circumstance the person has no conscious control over the power, and so there is no guarantee of true spiritual awakening.

The Three Psychic Knots – Obstacles to Kuṇḍalinī Awakening

Within the *suṣumnā nāḍī* there are three psychic knots of energy known as *granthis*. The Sanskrit word *granthi* means a 'knot', a tied-up force, or an obstacle to one's spiritual growth. These knots restrict human life to instinctive, emotional and intellectual levels. If lower desires become dominant in a person, the flow of *prāṇa* gets obstructed and short-circuited at the first knot or *Brahma granthi*, diminishing the flow of energy to the higher centres. The path of the *kuṇḍalinī* is obstructed, preventing its upward movement to the *sahasrāra chakra*.

When *kuṇḍalinī* is activated it rises upward through the *chakras*, and pierces successive veils of ignorance in the form of *granthis*, which change the perception of reality and consciousness.

The *granthis* are a protective mechanism, like safety valves or circuit breakers, that effectively prevent premature entrance of the *kuṇḍalinī* energy into the *chakras* above the *svādhiṣṭhāna chakra*. The three knots are named after the presiding deities of these knots: *Brahma granthi, Viṣṇu granthi* and *Rudra* (*Śiva*) *granthi,* which are respectively the creative, preservative and transforming forces involved in the presence of any object.

For the spiritual aspirant or yogi it is important to loosen these knots and make the *iḍā* and *piṅgalā* function smoothly so that they are in balance, with a clear flow of *prāṇa*. The *nāḍīs* need to be purified and strengthened to allow the strong surge of energy to rise up the spine.

Brahma Granthi

The first knot is located at the root *chakra* (*mūlādhāra*), and is related to the physical body. This knot is connected with our entanglement in the world of names and forms. It creates instinctive drives and strong, demanding, sensual desires with attachment.

Viṣṇu Granthi

The second knot is located at the heart *chakra* (*anāhata*), and is related to the astral body. This is associated with emotional life, attachment, and understanding ourselves through the concept of ego.

Rudra granthi

The third knot is located in the *ājñā chakra* or Spiritual Eye, and is related to the causal body. This is the point where the *iḍā* and *piṅgalā* cross over. *Rudra granthi* is concerned with intellectual obsessions, and attachments to psychic phenomena and psychic powers, and our mortal insecurity. When the *kuṇḍalinī* loosens this knot, it can continue its upward journey to the crown *chakra* (*sahasrāra*), enabling the yogi to attain transcendental bliss.

Chapter 6

The Seven Major Chakras

Just as you find that earth, water, fire, air and the space beyond the atmosphere, interpenetrate one another, so also these . . . main centres lie inside the body apparently one above the other, but functioning in mutual interdependence as one vital chain. A little reflection will convince you that the play of life goes on in the upper centres [*chakras*] of your body when your thoughts are pure and full of bliss.'

Śrī Ānandamayī Mā, *Life and Teaching of Śrī Ānandamāyī Mā*

Now each *chakra* will be explained in detail. The *chakras* are specific life-energy centres that control the living formative forces or *tattvas,* without which our physical bodies could not be animated. The *chakras* are the link between the physical realm and the spiritual dimensions of existence. Each *chakra* facilitates the flow and interchange of energies from the subtle dimensions by stepping them down, so that they can be utilized by the physical body. The frequency of energies can also be stepped up so they can be used at the subtle realm. To become aware of the more subtle levels of our spiritual existence, meditation on the *chakras* can help us to transcend our identification with the impermanent physical body.

In the yoga and tantric traditions the *chakras* have been represented as diagrams or *yantras* in the form of lotuses (*pādmas*) with various symbols, colours, *mantras* and deities, representing the different energies and consciousness of each centre. In reality the *chakras* do not actually look like this: the *yantras* are visual metaphors, corresponding to the inner states of human consciousness through which we can discover our inner spiritual identity. *Yantras* function as revelatory symbols of spiritual truths; they are instruments or maps for visualization and meditation that can help the spiritual aspirant to transcend the *tattvas* (elemental nature or quality), which dominate the five basic centres from *mūlādhāra* to *viśuddha*. Considering the *chakras* in the form of diagrammatic *yantras* helps the meditator to concentrate the mind on the spiritual reality symbolized by the form. Through the form the meditator reaches the Formless, and as a result the meditator feels the presence of the Omnipresent Being. Knowledge about the *chakras* can help an individual to develop a deep inner experience in meditation and in life. The dormant powers and energy in these *chakras* can be purified, balanced, strengthened and activated.

Each *chakra* appears as a lotus with a particular number of petals with a Sanskrit letter for each petal. The number of petals in each *chakra* is determined by the number and position of the *nāḍīs* around the *chakras*. The entire fifty letters of the Sanskrit alphabet are present in the fifty petals of the lotuses. Each letter represents the sound vibration produced by its petal. These *mantras* can be manifested and their vibrations experienced during meditation.

When the *kuṇḍalinī* is lying dormant at the *mūlādhāra chakra,* the petals of the *chakras* hang downward. When *kuṇḍalinī śākti* is awakened, the petals turn upward towards the head.

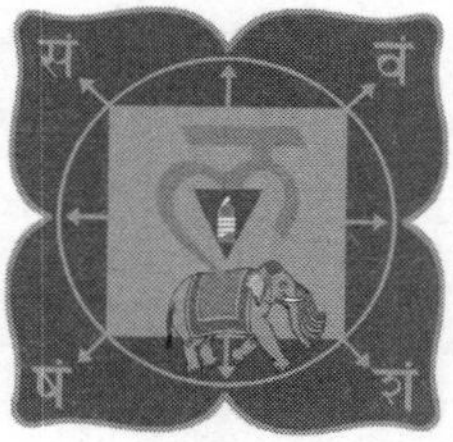

Mūlādhāra Chakra – Four-Petalled Lotus

Now we come to the Ādhāra Lotus [*mūlādhāra chakra*]. It is attached to the mouth of the suṣumnā, and is placed below the genitals and above the anus. It has four petals of crimson hue. Its head [mouth] hangs downwards. On its petals are the four letters from va to sa, of the shining colour of gold.

Ṣaṭ-cakra-nirūpaṇa, verse 4*

The upward journey of *kuṇḍalinī śākti* begins at the root support centre, the foundation for the development of our personality, and the basis from which the possibility of higher realization arises.

The *mūlādhāra chakra* is located between the origin of the reproductive organ and the anus. It is just below the *kanda* and the junction where *iḍā, piṅgalā* and *suṣumnā nāḍīs* meet. In the male the seat of *mūlādhāra* is situated slightly inside the perineum, midway between the scrotum and the anus. In the female, it is located on the posterior side of the cervix.

Mūlādhāra chakra corresponds to the physical earth plane. It is our base in the physical world that provides the instinctual drives and energy necessary for meeting the basic survival needs of security, food and shelter. It represents the primitive instinctive drive and will to survive, with its associated feelings of fear, defensiveness, aggression, gratification of the senses, and the instinct to have sex and reproduce. It is not

---

* The *Ṣaṭ-cakra-nirūpaṇa* is a part of the sixth *patala* of the *Śrī-tattva-cintāmani*, a tantric work composed in Sanskrit in CE 1577 by the tantric *sadhaka*, Pūrnaṇānda, who attained spiritual perfection.

surprising that the glands associated with this *chakra* are the adrenals, which produce several hormones that influence the body's metabolism and are involved in the 'fight-or-flight' response that is triggered by stress. An example of the most basic survival instincts and energy centred in *mūlādhāra chakra* is the animal living in the wild with its primitive responses to life-threatening situations. It hunts and kills another animal to eat it, or it fears being hunted itself. The animal also has the most basic first *chakra* instinct to mate and reproduce. It is through this first *chakra* that life is brought into being, preserved, and reproduced.

The first seven years of a child's life are the formative years for an all-round healthy, balanced development. During these years the child will be self-centred and concerned with his own physical survival. The child will have the desire for more experience and information, which acts as a motivating force for its individual development.

If the first *chakra* is underdeveloped, the individual may show signs of insecurity, nervousness, loss of confidence and low self-esteem, and engage in self-destructive behaviour. Conversely, if the first *chakra* becomes overactive, it can result in self-obsessed behaviour and greed for wealth, power and sex.

Concerning sexuality, if an individual adopts highly restricting attitudes towards sex and represses the energy, the first *chakra* may become blocked. Over-activity of the first *chakra* can also be harmful, as it can lead to sexual addiction.

The positive attitudes of *mūlādhāra chakra* are vitality and growth. The negative qualities are inertia, laziness, self-centredness, greed, rigidity and intolerance. It is here, also in *mūlādhāra chakra*, that our lowest *saṁskāras* and *karma* are embedded.

Mūlādhāra represents the earth principle (*pṛithvī tattva*) symbolized by a yellow square. It is concerned with the physical body and the material plane. It has the qualities of solidity and inertia. This *chakra* is also the seat of *annamāyā*

Colouring bookmarks
4/8

Detail from Japanese Patterns

Share your colouring:
#BDcolouring
@bookdepository

View full set:
bookdepository.com/bookmarks

Image courtesy of
Michael O'Mara Books

O'Mara Books

kośa, the sheath of nourishment, connected with the absorption of food and elimination of fecal matter.

Four important *nāḍīs,* symbolized as petals, radiate out from this *chakra*. The subtle vibrations produced by each *nāḍī* are represented by the Sanskrit letters *va, śa, ṣa,* and *sa*. The four petals of the lotus are described in the yoga and tantric *yantras* of the *chakras* as being deep crimson-red in colour. Enclosed within the lotus is a yellow square, representing the earth element. Radiating out in eight directions from the yellow square are eight golden spears. The spear that guards the base represents earth, while the other seven represent the seven great mountains. The yellow square earth element is supported by the elephant Airavata. Indra, the god of the firmament, rides upon its back. The elephant has seven trunks, giving stability, solidity and power. The seven trunks represent the seven main constituents that are vital to physical functioning or the seven tissues of the body (*sapta dhātus*) as given in Ayurveda.

In the centre of the yellow square is a deep red inverted triangle, symbolizing creative energy or *śākti.* Within the triangle is a smoke-coloured *śivaliṅga* (representing the astral body), around which the *kuṇḍalinī* serpent or snake, representing the ego, is coiled three and a half times. In the centre of the triangle is the *bīja* (seed-syllable) *mantra 'laṁ'*. Above the inverted triangle are the *deva* (god) Gaṇeśa and the four-armed *devi* (goddess) Ḍākinī. She is the carrier of the 'ever pure intelligence'. Bāla Brahma, the presiding deity of the first *chakra* also appears, who is depicted as a radiant child (*bāla*) with four heads and four arms.

Svādhiṣṭhāna Chakra – Six-Petalled Lotus

There is another Lotus [*svādhiṣṭhāna chakra*] placed inside the suṣumnā at the root of the genitals, of a beautiful vermilion colour. On its six petals are the letters from Ba to Puraṁdara [the letter *la*], with the Bindu superposed, of the shining colour of lightning.

Ṣaṭ-cakra-nirūpaṇa, verse 14

We began our journey through the *chakras* at the *mūlādhāra chakra,* now we arrive at *svādhiṣṭhāna,* where we can start to express ourselves creatively. The evolution of consciousness towards Pure Consciousness begins in *svādhiṣṭhāna chakra.*

The Sanskrit word *svā* means 'one's own' and *ādhiṣṭhāna* means 'dwelling place', so *svādhiṣṭhāna* means 'one's own place'. It has been suggested by some yogis that this refers to a distant time when the seat of *kuṇḍalinī* lay dormant within *svādhiṣṭhāna chakra,* but for some reason there was a fall and *kuṇḍalinī* came to rest in *mūlādhāra chakra.*

Svādhiṣṭhāna is the second *chakra,* located in the sacral region of the spine at the level of the coccyx, behind the sexual organs. It is associated with *apās tattva,* the element of water, and physiologically related to the urinary system, and reproductive system. The glands that *svādhiṣṭhāna* is linked to are the testicles in the male and the ovaries in the female. *Svādhiṣṭhāna* is concerned with creativity in all forms, and with procreation and the life-sustaining energy behind the sexual impulse, and is often referred to as the centre of self-expression and joy.

This *chakra* corresponds with the astral plane. It is the seat of the subconscious mind where all our life experiences and impressions from the past are stored. The development period for males in this *chakra* is between the ages of 7 and 14, and for females it is between 6 and 12. This is when the child begins to assert its ego and reaches out to others for physical contact. The ego manifests as our awareness develops, distinguishing childhood from infancy. It is a vital part of one's early learning and social training, when the infant is dependent on the family for satisfying its needs. The expression of the sense of I-ness is a crucial element in personality development in our formative years. It becomes necessary in order to provide a datum for establishing our relationships with the physical, material world around us and with other people. It also ensures the continuity of memory and beingness. From the age of 12 expansion of personality begins. A new awareness of the physical body develops as the child enters puberty, and with it comes sensuality.

The association of this *chakra* with the water element is to do with 'flow'. When a river's flow of water is blocked it stagnates. Similarly, our energy stagnates when our flow of consciousness becomes blocked and contractive, causing feelings of separation, isolation and fear. Sensuality and sexuality may be suppressed or rejected due to guilt feelings associated with sex. Or it may cause sensual over-indulgence, and escape into fantasy. Water is soft and fluid, but also has immense power like a tidal wave or tsunami out of control. Similarly, when negative emotions arise from the subconscious to the conscious, we can be thrown off balance.

In the positive aspect of the sacral *chakra*, we need to have a more fluid consciousness, to flow in balance with life naturally, to be willing to change and flow with life's changes, and be open to new ideas and inspiration. If we flow with life in this way our vitality, sensitivity and creative abilities will expand. When an individual's consciousness has been purified of negative qualities, awakening of *svādhiṣṭhāna chakra* brings clarity and development of the personality.

Svādhiṣṭhāna chakra is the storehouse of *sañcita karmas* (stored actions of many births) and *kriyamāṇa karmas* (the actions being worked out in the present). *Karmas* remain dormant in this *chakra* awaiting to give birth some time in the future. The *mūlādhāra chakra* also has *karmas* which are in an active state, related to the present (*prārabdha karma*). That is why this *svādhiṣṭhāna chakra* can be an obstacle in the awakening of *kuṇḍalinī śākti* because, when the *kuṇḍalinī* is activated and it rises from *mūlādhāra* to *svādhiṣṭhāna*, the stored *karmas* become operative and prevent the *kuṇḍalinī śākti* from ascending to the third centre, *maṇipūra chakra*. When the *svādhiṣṭhāna* is awakened in an individual, the person is often confused and disturbed by the amount of the unconscious material that erupts. This is when the *kuṇḍalinī* can fall back down to *mūlādhāra*. For the successful ascent from *svādhiṣṭhāna* there must be detachment (*vairāgya*) from sensual desires and pleasures, which are very prominent in this *chakra*. These desires may be in a suppressed state and can manifest at any stage.

Svādhiṣṭhāna chakra is depicted as a vermilion or orange-red lotus (the colour of sunrise, symbolic of the rising consciousness, activity and purity) with six petals. The lotus petals represent the flow of energy from six *nāḍīs*. Six passions are associated with the six petals: lust, anger, greed, deceit, pride and envy. The sound vibrations that are produced by the *nāḍīs* are represented by the Sanskrit letters *ba, bha, ma, ya, ra, la*. Inside the six petals is a white coloured *yantra*, a circle symbolizing the water element, within which there is a crescent moon, which shows the relationship between the moon and water. The crescent moon is formed by two circles which create two further *yantras*. The outer boundary of this white *yantra* has eight petals that point upwards, and the inner boundary has eight petals pointing inwards. These symbolize respectively the conscious and subconscious.

Inside the crescent moon is a white crocodile (*makāra*), which is the vehicle of karmic tendencies, and is associated with laziness, insensitivity and sensuality, depicting the sensuous nature of a person who is stuck at this level. At the centre of the inner lotus is the *bīja mantra 'vaṁ'*. Seated on it are the deities: Viṣṇu, who has four arms, and is the lord of preservation; the *devi* presiding over the subtle body is the two-headed goddess Rākinī, who is an aspect of Sarasvatī, the goddess of wisdom and creativity, and the consort of Brahma.

Maṇipūra Chakra – Ten-Petalled Lotus

Above it [*svādhiṣṭhāna*], and at the root of the navel, is the shining Lotus of ten petals [*maṇipūra chakra*], of the colour of heavy-laden rain clouds. Within it are the letters Ḍa to Pha, of the colour of the blue lotus with the Nada and Bindu above them. Meditate there on the region of Fire, triangular in form and shining like the rising sun. Outside it are three svastika marks, and within, the bīja of Vahni himself.

Ṣaṭ-cakra-nirūpaṇa, verse 19

On our journey upwards from the inert stability of *mūlādhāra chakra*, and the fluidity and adaptiveness of *svādhiṣṭhāna chakra*, we now rise to the dynamic fire of *maṇipūra chakra*. This third centre radiates its fiery energy like a bright sun. The element of this *chakra* is fire. The first two lower *chakras* are predominantly tamasic (lethargic and negative), but *maṇipūra,* the third lower *chakra* is predominantly rajasic (active, intense). Both *svādhiṣṭhāna* and *maṇipūra* are the seat of *prāṇayama kośa*.

The literal meaning of *maṇipūra* is the 'city of jewels' – *maṇi* means 'jewel' and *pūra* means 'city'. *Maṇipūra* contains many precious jewels with the qualities of self-confidence, self-assurance, the ability to make right decisions, clarity, wisdom and knowledge.

Maṇipūra chakra (also called *nābhi chakra* – navel plexus) is the third *chakra* above the *mūlādhāra*. It is located directly behind the navel within the *suṣumnā nāḍī*. It has its corresponding centre in the physical body at the solar plexus, which controls the digestive fire and heat regulation. *Maṇipūra* is associated with the cortex of the adrenal gland.

Maṇipūra is very important because it is the centre of willpower, energy, vitality and achievement. It generates and distributes prāṇic energy throughout the whole body, and controls our energy balance, vitality and strength. The foetus born into the womb receives nourishment to sustain development from this centre; thus by entering into the body through this centre one can attain knowledge of the entire body. Patañjali states in his *Yoga Sutras*, 3: 26: 'By meditating on the navel centre one attains knowledge of the whole body.'

The development period for males in this *chakra* is between the ages of 14 and 21, and for females it is between 12 and 18. As the youth grows in thinking and feeling about themselves and about their family and friends, so develops their sense of I-ness as an individual and as a part of the family group. When they reach the stage of making their own decisions and making their own way in the world, then the roots of self-centred egoism begin to take hold. The energy of this third *chakra* develops the ego, motivating a person to find their own identity. If a person is dominated by the energy of this *chakra*, they will be competitive and strive for personal power, recognition and fame. They may embrace materialistic ambition as their career ladder to the top, to the detriment of their own spiritual ideals, and of giving service to others. They may let religious faith or spiritual ideals take over part of their developing personality, so reducing their area of personal responsibility, or they may use religion as part of their ego to boost their ambitions in the world.

This *chakra* is concerned with assertiveness and personal power. Domination or control of others is very strong. The fire in this centre fuels the ego, which can manifest as anger, rage, aggression, intolerance, lack of consideration or disregard for others, bitterness, resentment, harshness and cruelty. In this *chakra* we have both the fire of desire and the power of the emotions to deal with.

If the energy is flowing through *maṇipūra chakra* in a positive way, then the energy can be channelled into dynamic enthusiasm and willingness for self-improvement and for giving consideration to others and helping them. When this *chakra* is in balance and functions in a right and positive way, reason and emotions are balanced, and then, instead of competing, dominating and controlling others, our personal power and willingness can be used to cooperate and help others.

The sense organ associated with *maṇipūra chakra* is the eye. Light is an aspect of the fire element for which the eyes are receptors. It is the light through the fire in the eyes that we can use to express warmth, enthusiasm and love.

According to many tantric texts the spiritual activation of *kuṇḍalinī* takes place in the m*aṇipūra chakra*, which is the junction or meeting point of two vital forces, *prāṇa* and *apāna*. In normal respiration when one inhales, the *prāṇa* rises from the navel to the throat and the *apāna* rises from the *mūlādhāra chakra* to the navel. The reverse process happens when we exhale. Changing this normal process is the activation of *maṇipūra chakra*. The three lower *chakras* work together. The seat of *kuṇḍalinī* is in *mūlādhāra chakra;* the *kuṇḍalinī*'s abode is in *svādhiṣṭhāna;* and the activation of *kuṇḍalinī* is in *maṇipūra chakra*.

From *maṇipūra chakra* emanate ten *nāḍīs* appearing like the petals of a lotus. The lotus is yellow and the petals depict the ten *prāṇas*, the vital forces, which control and nourish all the functions of the body. On each petal is inscribed a letter in blue, giving the sound vibrations produced by the ten *nāḍīs*: *ḍa, ḍha, na, ta, tha, da, dha, na, pa, pha*. Inside the yellow lotus is an inverted red triangle-shaped *yantra*, representing the fire element, and the spreading of energy. The inverted triangle also suggests the movement of energy downward. On its three sides the triangle has *svastika* signs shaped like a 'T', representing the formative force of fire (*tejas tattva*). At the lower end of the inverted triangle is a symbolic animal, a ram, representing dynamism and endurance. The ram is the vehicle of Agni (the fire god) and on it is inscribed the *bīja mantra 'rāṁ'*, which lies latent. This is the symbol of the Divine Intelligence presiding over fire.

Above the inverted triangle is the storm-god Rudra (Śiva), portrayed as an old Śiva, daubed with white ashes, who represents the power of destruction. Presiding over the subtle body, seated beside Rudra, is his consort, the three-headed, four-armed goddess of fire, Lakini.

Anāhata Chakra – Twelve-Petalled Lotus

Above that, in the heart, is the charming Lotus [*anāhata chakra*], of the shining colour of the Bandhūka flower, with the twelve letters beginning with Ka, of the colour of vermilion, placed therein. It is known by its name of Anāhata, and is like the celestial wishing-tree (Kalpa-taru), bestowing even more than [the supplicant's] desire. The Region of Vāyu, beautiful and with six corners [interlacing triangles], which is like the colour of smoke.

Ṣaṭ-cakra-nirūpaṇa, verse 22

From the *maṇipūra chakra* we rise above the limitations of perception in the two lower centres and we ascend to the fourth centre of consciousness, *anāhata chakra*. The three lower *chakra*s relate primarily to the physical body, the *anāhata chakra* takes us beyond the limits of the ego-self. The development period for men in this *chakra* is between the ages of 21 and 28, and for women it is between 18 and 24. The individual becomes aware of his or her *karma* and life actions. It is also the time of forming deeper relationships.

The heart *chakra* is the seat of the emotional heart-mind that stores our emotions and experiences. It represents pure, unconditional love. Through this *chakra*, we can reach beyond the egoic mind and connect and commune with the hearts and minds of others. When this *chakra* is open and balanced there is the ability to give and receive selflessly, and love and compassion become a natural expression of feeling from the heart. The path towards higher consciousness begins at this level.

The heart *chakra* is the pivotal point of transition, the plane of balance between the three lower *chakras* – related to the world of body, mind and senses, and associated with survival, security, sensuality, sex and power – and the *chakras* above, related to a higher and more evolved consciousness. When the *kuṇḍalinī* ascends to *anāhata chakra*, it is almost completely beyond the worldly associations of the three lower *chakras*. Almost, because the gravitational field of latent *saṁskāras* can still pull us back down to the lower three *chakras*. Like a space rocket rising through the earth's gravity into outer space, we need to accelerate towards spiritual consciousness through inner space, by rising above the gravitational field of worldly passion, so that we are no longer dragged down by the lower *chakras'* magnetic forces. If our consciousness sinks down to the levels of worldly passion, our emotions become confused and unbalanced, and the negative emotions of desire, jealousy, envy, anger, sadness and despair overwhelm us.

The *anāhata chakra* is the fourth centre of consciousness, located at the level of the heart, behind the centre of the chest. It is related to the thymus gland, situated in the upper anterior chest cavity, between the sternum and the pericardium. The thymus is composed of lymphatic tissue (mainly lymphocytes), and plays a crucial role in the development and maturation of the immune system. The heart *chakra* is also related to the sense of touch. The organ of this sense is the skin. The Sanskrit word *anāhata* literally means 'unstruck'. It refers to the inner subtle sound vibration (*nāda*) experienced in meditation. It is called 'unstruck' because it is not created by physical action.

There are two kinds of *nāda*: *ahat nāda* – all external or struck sounds, such as when musical instruments are played, and *anāhata nāda* – all sounds which do not have any external source and are 'unstruck' sound.

The *anāhata chakra* is also the seat of the subtle life-force (*prāṇa*). Within this subtle heart resides the individual soul (*jīvātman*), together with mind (*citta*) and ego-principle (*ahamkāra*). Various scriptures affirm that the heart is the seat of the individual soul:

God is seated in the hearts of all beings. His cosmic delusion [*māyā*] causes them to revolve as though they had been mounted on a machine.

Bhagavad Gītā, 18: 61.

By meditation upon the heart the Ātman is realized.

Patañjali, *Yoga Sutras*, 3: 34.

'Which is the self?' This Omnipresent Being [*Puruṣa*] that is identified with buddhi and is in the midst of the organs, the [self-effulgent] light within the heart.

Brihadāranyaka Upaniṣad, 4: 3.7.

According to the *Chandogya Upaniṣad* the location of the self is in the heart. The physical body is referred to as Brahmapuram (the city of Brahman), because Brahman resides here as the internal ruler with a retinue of attendants, such as the ten organs and the mind. His abode is the small lotus of the heart. Nondual Brahman (Pure Consciousness) who is immanent in the universe, is the all-pervading Being (Puruṣa). But His direct manifestation in the phenomenal world is the innermost self of every individual, shining as the central principle of consciousness in the centre of the heart.

In this city of Brahman there is a small lotus, an abode. Inside this there is a tiny space [*ākāśa*]. That which is within this one should seek and yearn.

Chandogya Upaniṣad, 8:1.1.

Most people when they refer to themselves with strong or affirmative feeling as 'I' or 'me' automatically and spontaneously bring their hand or point their finger to their heart. The heart is instinctively recognized as being the place where the soul resides.

Anāhata chakra is represented by the air element (*vāyu tattva*), which has the qualities of expansiveness and freedom. In this *chakra* one's consciousness can expand into infinity. Its awakening brings a feeling of unselfish, unlimited, unconditional, universal love for all beings. True unconditional love is free of selfish motives, it does not involve bargaining, and it expects nothing in return.

Paramhansa Yogananda's guru, Swami Śrī Yukteswar, said: 'Until one develops the natural love of the heart. It is impossible to take a single step on the spiritual path.'

In the consciousness of one who is immersed in divine love of God, there is no deception, no narrowness of caste or creed, no boundaries of any kind. When you experience that divine love, you will see no difference between flower and beast, between one human being and another. You will commune with all nature, and you will love equally all mankind.

Paramhansa Yogananda, 'Where There is Light'

The *anāhata chakra* is symbolized as a light blue lotus, the colour of the sky. The lotus has twelve petals, representing the expansion of energy in twelve directions and the divine qualities of the heart, such as love, peace, harmony, bliss, understanding, empathy, compassion, unity, clarity, purity, kindness and forgiveness. The sound vibrations inscribed on these twelve petals are *ka, kha, ga, gha, ṅa, ca, cha, ja, jha, ña, ṭa* and *ṭha*. Within the centre of the twelve-petalled lotus is a dark smokey-grey hexagonal *yantra* representing the air element (*vāyu tattva*). The hexagram is composed of two intersecting triangles: one pointing upward, representing consciousness, the other pointing down, representing creative energy.

The vehicle at the lower end of the hexagram is a black antelope leaping with joy. The antelope symbolizes alertness, attentiveness and the lightness of the air element. In the centre of the hexagon is the radiant gold coloured *bīja mantra* '*yaṁ*', symbolizing the Divine Intelligence presiding over air. Within the *bindu* of the *bīja mantra* '*yaṁ*' are the god Īśa, (from Īśvāra, which means 'lord' or 'master') who is Rudra, an aspect of Śiva, and the goddess Kākinī, a representative of *kuṇḍalinī*, who embodies the swift air element, and like air, is all-pervading. She is also the benefactor of devotion. At the very centre of this *chakra* is a small inverted triangle in which is a divine light – a steady, inextinguishable flame, that burns eternally. Within it is a radiant, golden *bāṇa liṅga* (symbol of Śiva) representing the soul, along with a lunar crescent that serves as a basin to catch the nectar.

Closely associated with the main *anāhata chakra,* and below it, there is a smaller eight-petalled lotus with red petals. Streams of shapes and colours flow out from it to the whole astral body. The most important flow to the *chakras,* traverse their petals and regulate their whirling. From the tips of the petals they then move out into space. Contained within the eight-petalled lotus, is a divine wish-fulfilling sacred tree called *kalpa vrikśa.* When you wish for a desire to be fulfilled concentrate on it in the inner shrine of your heart. The purer your *anāhata chakra,* the more swiftly your wish will be fulfilled.

Viśuddha Chakra – Sixteen-Petalled Lotus

In the throat is the Lotus called Viśuddha, which is pure and of a smoky purple hue. All the shining vowels on its petals, of a crimson hue, are distinctly visible to him whose mind is illumined. In the pericarp of this lotus there is the ethereal region, circular in shape, and white like the full moon. On the elephant white as snow is seated the Bīja of Aṁbara, who is white of colour.

Ṣaṭ-cakra-nirūpaṇa, verse 28.

The word *viśuddha* means 'pure'. *Viśuddhi* means 'purity'. *Viśuddha* is derived from the Sanskrit words *visha* 'impurity' and *śuddhi* 'to purify'. It is the centre of purity. Another name for this *chakra* is *Bharatisthana* (the god of speech). *Viśuddha chakra* is the starting point of *udāna prāṇa* (one of the five vital energies operating above the throat), which functions to purify the body of toxic substances during respiration. The name of the *chakra* is derived from this function. Purification occurs in the mind as well as the body.

The fifth centre of consciousness, *viśuddha chakra,* is located in the cervical plexus, directly behind the base of the throat. On the physical level it is related to the throat, neck, thyroid and parathyroid glands, vocal cords and auditory system, pharyngeal and laryngeal nerve plexuses. *Viśuddha* is associated with the sense of hearing and listening. Communication involves listening with attention and understanding, as well as speaking. Speech is of no relevance if there is no listener. The fifth *chakra* is the centre for communication, creativity, self-expression, non-attachment and learning to accept and receive. When this *chakra* is balanced and open the powers of communication and creativity become awakened. If the energy in this *chakra* is out of balance, communication between the heart and mind is affected, blocking the feelings of the heart.

It is at this level of consciousness, at the throat *chakra,* that thinking and feeling are connected most intimately, forming the foundation upon which we make the next two steps toward the seventh level, *sahasrāra chakra,* above the crown of the head. In the raising of consciousness, *viśuddha chakra* is an important bridge from the *anāhata chakra* to the higher *chakras* above, belonging to the mind principle.

The age of development in this *chakra* for men is 28–35; and for women is 24–30. The fifth *chakra* is also associated with the dream state.

The element of *viśuddha chakra* is *ākāśa* (ether, space). In the fifth *chakra* an alchemy takes place. All the *tattvas*: earth, water, fire and air – of the lower four *chakras* are purified and dissolved into their purest manifestation, *ākāśa*. Only the *tanmātrās* (subtle frequencies of the elements) remain. Earth dissolves into water, water evaporates into fire, fire transforms into air, and the air element of the fourth *chakra* enters into the ether / space element and becomes pure sound.

It is through space that sound can be transmitted. Without space there cannot be sound.

The organs of action associated with this *chakra* are the vocal cords. Sound is important to the throat *chakra*. The quality of our speech, negative or positive, indicates the state of this *chakra*. Learning to develop and express the voice brings the *viśuddha chakra* into full expression. It is through the voice – through music, singing, chanting, speaking and poetry – that we can touch the hearts of others. The voice is a reflection of our personality, our thoughts, feelings, and emotions. It can reflect both positive and negative vibrations. When it is positive, and we strike a chord that resounds in the heart of the listener, the voice can be like a magnet that attracts others. Sound and its vibrations are inseparable and can result in powerful emotional responses. It is important to be aware of when and how we use our voice and speech. There are many people who can use their voice to talk excessively, preach and make a noise, but nothing superficial can bring us fulfilment when the energy is nervously or restlessly directed outwardly in this way. The inner qualities of *viśuddha chakra* are calmness and expansion. When we quieten mental restlessness by directing the energy inward and upward in meditation, we reach a deep level of inner calmness and an expansion of consciousness. Even-minded calmness is clarity of perception and intuition, calmness is the enjoyable experience of the Self. Until we learn to think, talk and act with calmness and even-minded attitude, we cannot make our life productive. Paramhansa Yogananda said that calmness is more dynamic and more powerful than peace, because calmness gives one the power to overcome all the obstacles in one's life.

The practice of silence is a very great help for acquiring calmness and evenness of mind. All spiritual vision and deeper understanding are unfolded in silence, in meditation and contemplation. The practice of silence, however, does not mean merely refraining from speech. It means stilling the vital energies so that there is a cessation of all inner and outer activity. In silence we are able to think clearly and concentrate, and we are able to express our ideas through our outer actions more effectively.

When the fifth *chakra* is in balance you will feel in harmony with your aims, and will be able to translate them effectively into reality and communicate them to others. You will acquire good listening and communication skills, receptiveness, attentiveness, patience and discernment.

Vāk siddhi can be realized in this *chakra,* which is the extraordinary ability to have the words that one speaks come true.

Viśuddha chakra is represented by a 16-petalled lotus. The vibrations produced by the 16 *nāḍīs* associated with this *chakra,* and represented by these petals, are inscribed with Sanskrit letters in crimson: *a, ā, i, ī, u, ū, r, ṝ, l, ḹ, e, ai, o, au, aṃ, aḥ*. There are 14 vowels and two aspirated vowels, *aṃ* and *aḥ,* in this *chakra*. The vowels occur exclusively in the vocal or laryngeal organ.

In the centre of the lavender-grey or smokey purple-coloured lotus is a silver crescent, the lunar symbol of *nāda,* pure cosmic sound (symbolic of purity) within a white full-moon-shaped *yantra*. Within the moon shape, on the lower part of the *yantra,* is a white elephant (Airavata) with seven trunks, which is a vehicle of consciousness and also symbolizes the ether element. Carried on the back of the elephant is the *bīja mantra 'haṁ'*, which is the colour white.

The deities presiding in the fifth *chakra* are the five-headed, four-armed god Sadāśiva and the five-headed, four-armed goddess Sākinī.

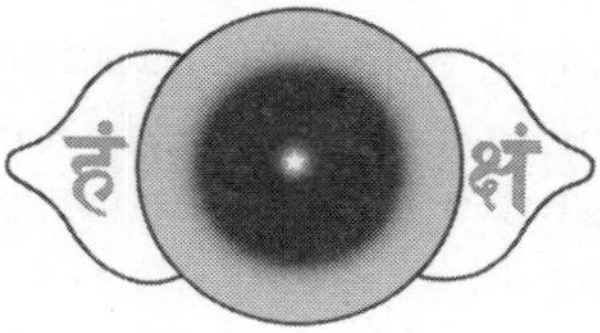

Ājñā Chakra – Two-Petalled Lotus

The Lotus named Ājñā is like the moon [beautifully white]. On its two petals are the letters Ha and Kṣa, which are also white and enhance its beauty. It shines with the glory of Dhyāna. Inside it is the Śākti Hākinī, whose six faces are like so many moons. She has six arms, in one of which She holds a book; two others are lifted up in the gestures of dispelling fear and granting boons, and with the rest She holds a skull, a small drum [*damaru*], and a rosary [*japā* beads]. Her mind is pure [*śuddha-citta*].

Ṣaṭ-cakra-nirūpaṇa, verse 32

The Sanskrit word *ājñā* (pronounced as 'agya') literally means 'command' or 'to obey, and to know'. It is the seat of the mind-space and 'inner Master', indicating that wisdom and knowledge are realized in all actions. The *ājñā chakra* is the instruction and command centre that guides the other *chakras*.

The fifth *chakra* is also known as the 'guru *chakra*'. This is because in astrology *ājñā chakra* is the centre of Jupiter, represented by Brihaspati, the guru of the gods. In deep states of meditation while concentrating on *ājñā chakra*, the directions of the inner guru are communicated and heard in this *chakra*.

Ājñā chakra is the *chakra* of the mind and the seat of concentration. It represents a higher level of awareness. It is the centre of extrasensory perception, intuition, clarity and wisdom, and it forms the boundary between human and Divine consciousness.

Ājñā chakra is the sixth centre of consciousness. It is located in the *suṣumnā nāḍī*. *Ājñā chakra* has two poles – positive and negative. The negative pole of self-consciousness is located in the medulla oblongata of the brain stem, just below the base of the brain at the back. It is here at the medulla that the prāṇic life-force enters the physical body and flows into the network of *nāḍīs* and is distributed throughout the body. The medulla oblongata has the vital function of regulating the breath and the heartbeat.

The negative pole is the seat of the ego (*ahaṁkāra*), the sense of 'I, me, mine', the 'I-thought'. Ego is the identifying principle, that causes the real Self to appear as identical with the body, the senses or the mind. Paramhansa Yogananda defined the ego as the soul identified with the body.

The positive pole, the centre of the higher expression of Self-consciousness of the *ājñā chakra*, is located at the midpoint between the eyebrows, and is called the Spiritual Eye, Third Eye or Christ-Consciousness Centre. It is the seat of Self-realization, divine perception, intuition, concentration and willpower.

It is at this point that the three main *nāḍīs*: *iḍā* (lunar current), *piṅgalā* (solar current) and *suṣumnā* (central neutral current) unite in one stream of consciousness. As we have seen, it is also represented in the caduceus in the Western tradition, and in addition is evident in Egyptian images of the head of Pharaoh, in which we see the snake or serpent at the third eye. The snake was placed so that its tail touched the medulla oblongata and drew the energy of the spine into the pituitary gland and then upward to the pineal gland. Its purpose was to keep the life-force sublimated to the higher *chakras*.

The age of development in this *chakra* for men is 35–42, and for women is 30–36. Intuition may be fully developed.

The total of the lotus petals in the five lower *chakras* is 48. When these are synthesized into the two-petalled lotus (*ājñā chakra*) the number fifty is formed, which is the number of the perfected personality.

Ājñā chakra has two luminescent-white petals and the vibrations of these *nāḍīs* are represented by the Sanskrit letters *ha* and *kṣa (ha* is seen on the left petal – *iḍā nāḍī*, as seen by the observer, and *kṣa* on the right petal – *piṅgalā nāḍī).* These two sounds *ha* and *kṣa* represent the cosmic creative forces on the wings of time.

The sense organ of the sixth *chakra* is associated with the pituitary gland (the 'master gland' which controls many other endocrine glands) and the sense of intuition.

Inside the two-petalled lotus is a circle, and within the circle is an inverted triangle representing *śākti* (creativity and manifestation). Within the inverted triangle is the *bīja mantra 'Oṁ'*, the sound vibration for the sixth *chakra*.

In the white circle of the *ājñā chakra* is the third *śivaliṅga* (a symbol of the astral body), known as the *itara liṇga* ('the remaining'). This *śivaliṅga* represents Ardhanārīśvāra (Śiva – pure consciousness, and Śākti – creative energy, united in one form), signifying the eternal relation of *puruṣa* and *prakṛti* (spirit and nature). This means that in *ājñā chakra* consciousness and nature are already united, but have still not merged into total unity.

The residing deities are Śiva in the highest form, Parāmśiva (in the form of *haṁsa*, which means 'swan'; *haṁ* is Śākti, and *sa* is Śiva), and the six-headed, four-armed Śākti Hākinī. Above the golden inverted triangle is a crescent moon with a golden dot (*bindu*), a concentrated point of energy, above it.

When the devotee reaches beyond the highest vital centre which is situated between the eyebrows, his mental powers merge in the supra-mental, his ego dissolves in Mahābhāva [highest ecstasy, supreme love for God] and he finds his eternal refuge in Svarūpa [his own true Self]. He then goes into samādhi, a state of perpetual bliss.

Śrī Ānandamāyī Mā.

The Spiritual Eye

Stop beholding only the little toy show of this world; close your physical eyes and plunge behind the screen of darkness. Lift the veil of silence, and behold the magic of soothing, rolling fires of planets, of trillions of multi-coloured dancing atoms. Behold life-force dancing in the hall of electrons. Behold one layer of light lying within another. Behold consciousness dancing in the sphere of living light. Behold the Bliss-God and His blessed angels dancing in the thought fashioned, wisdom lighted Eternal Chamber of Perpetual, ever-new Bliss. Lift all curtains of light and behold God in the glory of bliss. The Spiritual Eye is the tunnel through all veils of light, leading straight to God.

Paramhansa Yogananda, *Super Advanced Course Number 1*

Ājñā chakra has two poles: a positive and a negative. The positive pole is the 'Spiritual Eye' or 'Christ centre' as Paramhansa Yogananda referred to it, which is located at the midpoint between the eyebrows (ruled by the sun). It is associated with Divine joy. The negative pole is the medulla oblongata (ruled by the moon), located in the brain stem of the spinal cord at the base of the skull. It is the seat of the ego. The moon is a symbol of the ego. The moon has no light of its own; it only reflects the light of the sun. Similarly, the ego having no reality of its own, reflects the light of the Self. The mind reflects the object on which it meditates, and takes on the qualities of that object, as a mirror takes on the qualities reflected in it. In other words we see the mind's activity by the light of the Self. Neither the mind nor the intellect has the ability to illumine the Self. The source of light does not need another light to illumine it; similarly the Self needs no other knowledge to make itself known, as its nature is Knowledge itself. The ego-mind is differentiated from the luminous Self in the same way that the physical body, sense-organs and external objects are. In respect to this, Patañjali, in his *Yoga*

Sutras 4.19, states: 'The mind is not self-luminous, because of its nature as the [visible] object of inner perception.' The mind in itself is not perceivable.

Both the Spiritual Eye and the physical eye are reflections of the medulla oblongata. By concentrating on the point between the eyebrows (Spiritual Eye) one can see the medulla reflected as one light. This is the meaning behind Jesus Christ saying: 'If, therefore, thine eye be single, thy whole body shall be full of light' (Luke 11: 34–35). When the two physical eyes manifest the single Spiritual Eye, then one can perceive, by continuous spiritual development, the physical body as filled with the illumination of the astral body.

The medulla oblongata (the negative pole of *ājñā chakra*) is where the Conscious Cosmic Energy (life-force; *prāṇa*) primarily enters into the body, and remains concentrated in the brain as the thousand-rayed lotus.

It is also interesting to note that images of Śiva show the moon symbol resting in his hair at the crown of the head (*sahasrāra chakra*), showing that his ego-consciousness is totally one with the Cosmic Consciousness.

When we are meditating with deep calm concentration at that point between the eyebrows, with a feeling of joyous aspiration, it is possible to see the Spiritual Eye. This inner eye of luminous light is seen as a circular sphere of blue light, haloed with a ring of gold, and at its centre is a white star with five rays of luminous scintillating light.

Suṣumnā is comprised of three astral tubes or currents of life-energy, like an electrical wire with two or three coverings to insulate it. The outermost covering or sheath is the *suṣumnā* itself. The second 'tube' is the sun-like *vajriṇī nāḍī*, which covers the third astral tube, the moon-like *citriṇī nāḍī*. Within the *citriṇī nāḍī* is a very fine astral current called the *brahma nāḍī*. The Spiritual Eye is a cross-section of the *suṣumnā*, showing the various coverings for the energy in the spine. The *nāḍīs* are reflected in the Spiritual Eye. The sun-like *vajriṇī nāḍī* is reflected in the Spiritual Eye as a halo of gold light, which the meditating yogi experiences as the Cosmic Vibration, *Oṁ*. The Spiritual Eye elongates first into a golden tunnel, and then into a tunnel of blue as the yogi's consciousness enters into the blue sphere of light (the moon-like *citriṇī nāḍī*), giving the experience of Christ-Consciousness or *Kūtastha Caitanya*. Finally at the end of the tunnel of blue is a silvery-white star with five rays of luminous, scintillating light (*Brahma nāḍī*) representing the Kingdom of God beyond all creation. Here the meditating yogi enters the light uniting his or her consciousness with Cosmic Consciousness.

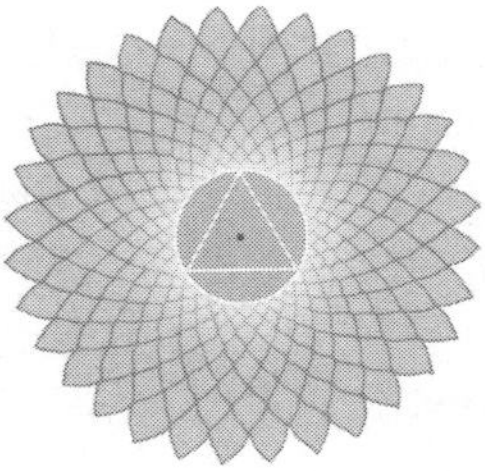

Sahasrāra Chakra – Thousand-Petalled Lotus

Above all these, in the vacant space [*Parama-vyoma*, the supreme ether] wherein is Śaṅkhini Nāḍī, and below Visarga is the lotus of a thousand petals. This lotus, lustrous and whiter than the full moon, has its head turned downward. It charms. Its clustered filaments are tinged with the colour of the young sun. Its body is luminous with the letters beginning with A, and it is the absolute bliss [Brahman bliss].

Ṣaṭ-cakra-nirūpaṇa, verse 40

The Sanskrit word *sahasra* means one thousand; *sahasrāra* means 'thousand-petalled'. The *sahasrāra chakra* is also called the crown *chakra* or crown centre and is known as *Nira-lambapuri* ('dwelling place without support') and *Brahma-randhra* ('the Door of God').

The *sahasrāra chakra,* the seventh centre, strictly speaking is not actually a *chakra,* as it does not belong to the planes of consciousness of the mind and body. It is an extended field of consciousness that is experienced above the head as the highest centre of Pure Consciousness. *Sahasrāra* is the abode of higher consciousness and expanded awareness. It corresponds with the plane of the Absolute. According to the Indian scriptures (*śatras*), *sahasrāra* is the seat of the Self.

The attainment of super-conscious awareness of the Self as the Infinite at the *sahasrāra* is symbolically shown in many religious paintings as a halo of light above the crown of the head. Jesus Christ and many saints in Christian paintings are portrayed with a golden disc or golden halo of light just a few inches from the crown of the head, or surrounding the head. The Theosophist Alice Bailey described the light in the head in her book *A Treatise on White Magic*: 'The soul light penetrates into the region of the pineal gland, there it produces an irradiation of the ethers of the head. Frequently students speak of a diffused light or glow; later they may speak of seeing what appears to be like a sun.' This is evident in some Christian paintings. Carlo Crivelli's 'Annunciation with St Emidius' (1486), in the National Gallery, London, shows the Virgin kneeling with a line of golden light beaming down from above into her crown centre. We can see a courtyard outside the Virgin's room, in which is clearly shown the Archangel Gabriel wearing the symbols of *sahasrāra* (as a gold disc above the crown) and *ājñā chakra* (as a serpent-shaped feather attached to an emblem at his forehead). In the same painting is also the symbol of a white dove from which the golden ray of light is beamed down into the Virgin's crown centre. The white dove represents the omnipresence of the Holy Ghost ('the Comforter'), which is the Vibratory Cosmic Sound *Oṁ,* vitalizing the individual life-force in the body. It is the Supreme Cosmic Consciousness of the Transcendent 'God the Father' (Iśvāra) that manifests within the Holy Ghost as the 'Son of God', the Christ-Consciousness. As was said earlier, the 'Son of Man' refers to the physical body, and the 'Son of God' refers to the Christ-Consciousness, that is attainable by all God-seeking souls. We can all become sons of God as was Jesus.

The *sahasrāra* lotus has one thousand *nāḍīs* symbolized as petals emanating from it. The thousand petals of *sahasrāra* carry the total sound-potential represented by all fifty letters of the Sanskrit alphabet. The 50 letters are repeated 20 times, 50 in each layer.

Sahasrāra chakra is a shining moonlike white lotus of a thousand petals and the light of a thousand suns. It lies about three inches (8 cm) above the crown of the head with its face or petals pointing downwards. This differentiates it from the other six *chakras*. *Sahasrāra* has no associated element, colour or sound as the other six *chakra*s have, but it synchronizes all colours, encompasses all senses and all functions, and is all-pervading in its power. It is the centre of quintessential consciousness, where integration of all polarities is experienced.

In *ājñā chakra* there was still the experience of a Self apparently differentiated from the 'object' of God, but in *sahasrāra* the experience, the experienced and the experiencer become one and the same. They all become unified and liberated. The illusion of individual self is dissolved.

When the *kuṇḍalinī śākti* (creative energy-power) awakens, she ascends to unite in one form above the crown of the head with Śiva (Pure Consciousness), whose manifest energy she is through the *chakras*. Śākti merges with Śiva in Laya Yoga (Absorption).

Through deep meditation the yogi finally attains the goal of yoga by uniting his or her consciousness in *nirvikalpa samādhi* (the highest level of superconsciousness, *samādhi*) at the *sahasrāra chakra*. All the *vṛttis* of the mind come to complete stillness, and the yogi attains fulfilment and liberation in the union of knowledge, the knower, and the object of knowledge. To reach this divine union in *sahasrāra chakra* we must first awaken the *ājñā chakra*, which is the gateway to it. In the first six *chakras* – *mūlādhāra* to *ājñā* – the ego has not been transcended. Transcendence begins at *ājñā chakra* with *savikalpa samādhi*, which has fluctuations and has four stages: *vitarka* (reasoning; gross thought), *vichāra* (reflection, analytical thought process, subtle thought), *ānanda* (bliss) and *asmitā* (pure 'I-am-ness', sense of individuality), which is consciousness reflecting on the mirror of the mind. The *citta* (mind) gains a true and absolute knowledge of the real source of the consciousness pervading it.

Self-realization takes place at the *ājñā chakra*. Here you have the first union with God in the blissful state of *savikalpa samādhi*. And finally comes the highest experience, which is identification with the Absolute in *nirvikalpa samādhi*, which liberates the Self. Liberation (*kaivalya*) takes place in the *sahasrāra chakra*. First *samprajñāta-samādhi* is established, then it develops into *asamprajñāta-samādhi*, finally culminating in *kaivalya* (these terms are explained below). *Samādhi* is attained by faith, energy, memory, meditation, and the awakening of wisdom.

To give you some idea of what *asamprajñāta-samādhi* is, think about the following comparisons of time that a meditator can concentrate for: concentration on an object for 12 seconds is called *dhāranā*.

If the period of concentration is increased to 12 times that of *dhāranā*, to 144 seconds, it is called *dhyāna*. And if the concentration lasts for 12 times the period of *dhyāna*, to 1,728 seconds (28 minutes 48 seconds), it is called *asamprajñāta-samādhi*.

Samādhi is that state in which everything external is gone. The senses no longer function; the eyes, even if they are open, don't see. All consciousness has gone within. The eyes are not able to see if consciousness is not behind them. Anything that becomes the instrument of knowledge has to have some consciousness behind it. In each of us, consciousness has become spread over the whole body. That is why if someone touches my skin anywhere I know that I have been touched. But in the state of *samādhi*, consciousness is withdrawn from everything external and is centred on the bliss of God within. Only Pure Consciousness remains, revealing Itself to Itself.

Śrī Ānandamayī Mā (1896–1982), the Bliss-Permeated Mother, as Paramhansa Yogananda called her (Yogananda visited her in Calcutta in 1936), was constantly in the ecstatic blissful state of *samādhi*. According to one of her loyal devotees named Bhāijī, Ānandamayī Mā could not only transcend the need for food whenever she so desired, but she could often be seen in the breathless state of *samādhi*. He described one of these instances: 'Her face glowed with a crimson hue due to the intensity of inner *ānandam* [bliss]. Her cheeks shone with a heavenly light, her forehead looked bright and serene with a divine calm. All her physical expressions were suspended; yet from every pore of her body radiated an uncommon glow – a mute eloquence of silent, inner speech. Everybody present felt that Mother was sinking into the depths of divine communion. Thus passed some ten to twelve hours . . .'

For half a year Ānandamayī Mā lived on a daily diet of only six grains of boiled rice and two or three ripe fruits, which – she insisted – must have fallen from trees. If no fruit had fallen off in a natural way, she would forgo eating fruit on that day. Being conscious of the Oneness underlying the multiple manifestation, she was able to extract whatever she needed out of the air. Her followers claim that she was continuously in the highest state of *samādhi*. Even as she looked at you, you were aware of the fact that she was with you and yet far beyond you, that she had a dual vision encompassing the manifest and the transcendent. As her name – Ānandamayī Mā – indicates, she is considered the very incarnation of bliss.

Samprajñāta-samādhi

Samprajñāta-samādhi (superconsciousness absorption with wisdom (*prajñā*) or perfect knowledge) is the first category of *samādhi* in which the mind needs an object (gross or subtle) or supportive factor (*ālambana*) in concentration, until *dharma-megha samādhi* is reached. *Dharma-megha samādhi* ('raincloud of virtues') is the supportless *samādhi*, the higher stage of the *asmitā*-accompanied *samādhi* in which the mind dwells in itself by itself, and it is the initial stage of the acognitive *samprajñāta-samādhi*. *Dharma-megha samādhi* acts as a bridge between *samprajñāta-samādhi* and *asamprajñāta-samādhi*.

Samprajñāta samādhi (*samādhi* with support) occurs at four levels: *savitarka samādhi*, which relies on gross thoughts and objects knowable through the senses; *savichāra*, which relies on the same gross thoughts turned subtle, aspects of the physical object with reference to space, time and causation; *sānanda samādhi*, which relies on a more subtle support accompanied by bliss; *sāsmitā samādhi* in which there is only self-awareness (awareness of the 'I-existence'). As each stage becomes complete, the subtle aspect of the object of concentration becomes the supportive factor for the next level of concentration. When these four levels are achieved in gradual succession, wisdom and knowledge are attained in their perfect expansion (*samprajñāta* – complete higher consciousness). Each level attained is purer and more refined than the previous level because of the increased *sattva guṇa* (pure quality of consciousness).

Asamprajñāta-samādhi

Asamprajñāta-samādhi (superconsciousness absorption beyond perfect knowledge) is the second and higher category of *samādhi* that is without support. This is the state where the awareness of *Puruṣa* is no longer connected to any external object. The mind is not supported by any active thought, there is a cessation of *vṛttis* (thought waves). This includes all mental activities that arise in the *citta*, including the object of meditation. There is no mind-field, only Self-awareness. The seer abides in the Self.

To attain liberation (*kaivalya*) the yogi first has to bring the rajasic and tamasic *vṛttis* under control (*nirodha*) by means of practice (*abhyāsa*) and dispassion (*vairāgya*). Then the yogi has gradually to progress through each of the different refined and subtle *samprajñāta-samādhi* levels from *savitarka* to *sāsmitā*, until Self-realization is attained, in which there is true and direct realized knowledge of the 'real' and dispassion for the 'unreal'. Complete cessation of fluctuations of the mind emanates from the constant practice of *paravairāgya* (supreme detachment) which is free from any material cogitation. Both the knowledge of non-self and the knower of non-self (the 'I-sense') disappears. *Paravairāgya* produces no *saṁskāras* in the mind-field other than its own latent impressions of dispassion. And no other *saṁskāras* can replace these because there is no higher stage. Without the seeds of *saṁskāras*, there cannot be *kleśas* (afflictions), *karma* (action), and *vipāka* (fruition of action).

Chapter 7

Descent and Ascent of the Soul

The Descent

The higher state of consciousness, with its different levels, has to be realized here on earth, where we are able to perceive God through direct experience. God-realization is not attained merely by dying, thinking that our faith will take us to heaven to meet God. Higher consciousness is not something we have to find, or develop, acquire, possess, or to build up, because it is always present here and now. It is not out there or up there somewhere. The kingdom of God is within you. It is here, and is available at all times, but because we are not giving any attention and awareness to it, the Truth/Reality remains hidden from us. The belief that one is the ego obscures the realization of the reality of the Self. The constant identification with the body–mind–ego complex keeps us in bondage. The ego deals in form and definition, so it is unable to comprehend the Self, which is beyond all form. The sun is always shining brightly until the clouds cover it, or so it seems. Moving away the clouds does not cause the sun to shine but merely reveals that which was temporarily obscured. Similarly, the higher conscious Reality or Infinite Presence is always present. Its realization occurs of itself when the obstacles to it are removed. The Self is awareness itself, and behind this luminous Self, the individual consciousness, is the one effulgent ocean of reality, Supreme Consciousness.

Everybody in this world has descended from the subtle causal state to the gross physical state. The majority of the souls here on earth have no conscious awareness or knowledge of the divine nature of the being that dwells within their own material form of mind–body. We feel finite, separate from the Divine Reality we call God, separate from one another, and more identified with this physical form.

God is one Supreme Being undivided and unrelated to creation, and yet the same God is also made up of an infinite number of individual shining souls. Just as there is a boundless ocean of water behind each and every wave, similarly the Supreme Consciousness is behind each and every individual consciousness. The one Supreme Consciousness has extended Itself from Its eternal pure-mind state to appear as innumerable individual souls living in a temporal universe of forms.

Through different stages of the process of involution, the divine, infinite and undivided God has descended into the human physical form to manifest as individual souls. God is in the heart and soul of every being. This is the all-pervasiveness of God as He manifests as innumerable individual souls. And yet God remains undivided; the Supreme Being never loses Itself by becoming many. Just as water can be taken from the ocean and divided into numerous cups, without losing its quality of water, similarly, the ocean of God's presence behind the wave of your consciousness always retains its original nature.

From the *sahasrāra chakra* Divinity descends to the *ājñā chakra*, located at the junction of the eyebrows. Here the soul makes its entry into the physical body through the negative pole, the medulla oblongata, of the *ājñā chakra*. It is here that the individual soul has come into existence, distinct from God. The soul has not forgotten God, but there is a separation, a duality.

As the soul descends from *ājñā chakra* in the astral spine, to the fifth centre, *viśuddha chakra*, at the level of the throat, the soul is no longer in union with God, as it was in the *ājñā chakra*. The soul still feels God's presence; there is still an intensity of feeling for God but it is not very clear.

The soul continues its journey downward in the spine to the level of the heart, *anāhata chakra*. At this level of the descent, the soul has awareness of God but the intensity of feeling for God is lessened.

God is still within the heart and soul of the individual being as it descends through the *chakras*, but as it descends further below the three highest *chakras*, the soul's awareness becomes more and more obscured. Below the level of the heart the soul enters the next centre at the navel, *maṇipūra chakra*. Here identification with the body–mind–ego is beginning to take effect, and the awareness of God is fading.

The soul then passes deeper downward in the spine through the *svādhiṣṭhāna chakra*, becoming more entangled in bondage to matter. Finally, the soul reaches the lowest centre at the base of the spine, *mūlādhāra chakra*. In this last stage of the downward journey through the *chakras* the soul comes to rest. Now the soul has become more aware and identified with gross matter, with the material form of the body and the mind. It has also forgotten God. Clothed in the physical form, the individual soul forgets its real identity. The soul is now identified with the three lower centres of consciousness and in its relationship to the world functions and operates from those *chakras*.

The primal life-force known as *kuṇḍalinī śākti* now lies latent and 'coiled up' waiting at the base of the spine in the *mūlādhāra chakra*. The physical, astral and causal bodies in which the soul is clothed are integrated and work together. The coiled knot in the *mūlādhāra chakra* prevents the soul from being released from material bondage. Due to ignorance (*avidyā*) the soul becomes oblivious to its eternal, ever perfect and immutable divine nature. And as a result, the world of objectivity and duality becomes more pronounced, and demands more and more attention of the individual soul.

The Ascent

Now if we made our home or remained at the level of these lower centres of consciousness, particularly the *mūlādhāra*, and *svādhiṣṭhāna chakras*, the soul would essentially be conscious only of eating, sleeping and procreation. If a human being is functioning from these lower planes of consciousness, then he or she is behaving essentially like an animal. How do animals live? They are preoccupied with eating, sleeping and procreating. Of course that is normal for an animal, but it is not normal for the human being to live in that way. One of the main differences between the animal and the human being is that the consciousness of the human being is more highly evolved. The human has the power to discriminate between the real and the unreal.

The human being's real nature is divine, and the aim of human life is to realize this divine nature: that you are *sat-chid-ānanda* (ever-existing, ever-conscious, ever-new joy). It is joy we seek, because joy is our true nature. The instinct for knowing our own real nature is inherent and self-evident; it needs no proof. Everybody will eventually awaken to some degree to that divine consciousness present in their lives. We may call it God, or we may call it Self; but when you know God through inner discovery and direct experience, you will know the Self as well, for they are one. As souls we may turn to God, or as the Self we may turn within to our own identity; in both we experience the one Light, the one Pure Consciousness.

Under the power of Nature (*Prakṛti*) and its conditions, the human soul identifying with the active mind and senses becomes confused and tired of the frustrations and suffering of life, and because of these obstacles, the soul cannot become conscious of the God within, whose power gives us the power to act. Thus, the embodied soul conditioned by Nature feels enslaved and limited to the gross physical form. A person cannot be spiritually minded until he or she realizes the futility of worldly desires. When a person understands this truth and recognizes the limitation of what the worldly desires can fulfill, he or she develops the insight that the one supreme purpose of life and complete fulfilment in life is to realize God. Eventually there comes a time when the soul becomes aware of its higher nature and spiritual ideas begin to enter the mind. The human soul begins to think, 'There must be more to life than just eating, sleeping, procreating and enjoying the senses.' 'Who am I?', 'Where did I come from?', 'What happens after death?', 'What is my true purpose and what is the meaning of life?', 'Who or what is God? What is the Ultimate Reality?'

As we become more and more disillusioned with the nature of the world we begin to understand the inherent limitation of this life. You will come to know that, however wonderful and fascinating this world may be, it cannot fulfil your inner yearning for complete freedom from all bondage and suffering. We live in a world of dualities – life and death, growth and decay, knowledge and ignorance, happiness and sorrow, health and disease, success and failure – these opposites coexist. The world cannot be made perfect, but it can be used as an instrument, as a means to perfection. Jesus Christ said: 'Know the truth and the truth shall make you free.' Know the truth of your essential nature, the Divine Self, the fountain of Infinite Joy within you, then you will find freedom.

Now there is a glimmer of light, there is some hope. The individual soul aspires to something higher than what it has experienced in the lower states of the lower *chakras*. The soul tries to remove the veil of ignorance by meditating on God. When the mind turns towards God, the spiritual ascent begins. *Kuṇḍalinī* begins to wake up. Now the soul becomes more and more disidentified with the mental–physical form and rises above the three lower *chakras* to the subtle state. Through deep God-conscious meditation the soul ascends through the same path it descended in the astral spine, reversing the primal life force and consciousness from matter, and retracing its steps back to Supreme Consciousness.

In its upward journey, when the soul reaches the heart level of the *anāhata chakra,* it has left the world of darkness and has entered into the world of inner light, giving the individual soul a wonderful sense of relief and freedom as it moves towards the innermost consciousness. But at this level of the heart something of our attachment to the world is still left. There is still the danger of falling to a lower stage. The *anāhata chakra* is the crossroads between the lower and higher *chakras,* so the spiritual aspirant needs to be cautious. That is why the next stage of the journey upward to *viśuddha,* the throat *chakra,* is said to be the most strenuous. It is only by constant, persistent effort of spiritual practice, by withdrawing the mind from the objects of the senses in deep meditation, and concentrating on God within, that you make the soul rise higher.

When the soul in its journey upwards advances to the level of the *viśuddha chakra* it is secure. It may fall down a little, but it will never fall below the *anāhata chakra.* Here the mind is no longer limited or bound by time and space. The mind is transformed from the lower to a higher consciousness, into a finer state, transcending the seeker's negative and material vibrations. In *viśuddha* all the elements are purified and transmuted into their refined essence of *ākāśa.* It is then that the individual soul is established in pure consciousness.

The next stage of the soul's ascent is from *viśuddha* to *ājñā chakra,* the sixth centre of consciousness at the midpoint between the eyebrows. At *ājñā chakra,* you have the first union with God in *samādhi,* in which the finite self as the meditator, the process of meditation, and the object of meditation – the Supreme Self (God) – become one. Consciousness of the body, and the sense of 'I' or ego-consciousness disappears, and knowledge of the external world is lost. In this *samādhi* state which is called *savikalpa samādhi,* the meditator's individual consciousness merges with the Cosmic Consciousness, and experiences ever-new joy (bliss). Like a wave dissolving into the ocean, the individual soul is merged in an effulgent ocean of bliss.

The last stage of the soul's upward journey through the astral pathway in the spine is to the thousand-ray lotus at the *sahasrāra chakra,* the pinnacle of consciousness. Reaching this plane of inner consciousness, there is a Divine awakening of the highest experience in *nirvikalpa samādhi,* which is identification with the Absolute. The individual soul and the Supreme Soul become one. The finite self becomes absorbed in the Supreme Self and the identity of the two as Pure Consciousness is realized. The forms or attributes of God disappear; God is experienced as the ultimate One, as undivided Pure Consciousness. The soul is resurrected from delusion and regains its Divinity. The individual soul becomes identified with the limitless Supreme Self – the two vanish, and one integral, undivided consciousness, beyond subject–object relationships, alone shines.

The Supreme Being is not perceived by the eye nor expressed by the organ of speech, nor apprehended through any other organ, nor is this attainable through austerity or by the performance of deeds. When one becomes purified in mind through the clarity of understanding then one can realize that indivisible Self through meditation.

Mundaka Upaniṣad, 3: 1.8

Meditation is the means to the attainment of the ultimate One. The direct experience of the Supreme Being is not possible by any other method. From the scriptural texts and from words of the seers and sages we can know much about God, yet we remain ignorant of Him because they do not reveal God to us. Similarly, by logical reasoning we can have only partial knowledge of the Absolute God or ultimate Reality, which is indefinite and indecisive. Once the seeker realizes the Supreme Being through direct experience in *savikalpa* or in *nirvikalpa samādhi* he or she does not lose sight of God any more.

Yoga, Chakras and Kuṇḍalinī in the Bible

Know the Truth, and the Truth shall set you free.

John 8: 32

Behold, the Kingdom of God is within you.

Luke 17: 21

Be still, and know that I am God.

Psalms 46: 10

The Father is in me and I am in the Father.

John 10: 34, 38

I [inner self] and the Father [Supreme Self] are One.

John 10: 30

The Bible, both in the Old and New Testaments, has many hidden meanings relating to the teachings of yoga. Above are a few Bible quotes that relate to the yoga teachings; there are more that can be revealed, if one can take the time to search and study the Bible in the light of yoga for these spiritual insights. The deeper levels of meaning in the scriptures are revealed to those people who are spiritually ready to understand them. Jesus revealed the hidden meaning of his teachings only to his closest disciples: 'The secret of the kingdom of God has been given to you. But to those on the outside everything is given in parables' (Mark 4: 11). When Jesus wanted to get across the deeper meanings of his words he would always say: 'He who has ears to hear, let him hear' (Matthew 11: 15). In other words, those whose minds are purified will understand the true significance of the inner teachings. To those outside the inner circle of his disciples his inspired teachings were given to them on a basic level of morals and ethics, using parables. 'Jesus spoke to the crowds in parables; indeed, he would never speak to them except in parables' (Matthew 13: 34). 'He spoke the words to them [the crowds] as far as they were capable of understanding it . . . but he explained everything to his disciples when they were alone' (Mark 4: 33–34). Jesus gives this reason for speaking in parables to the public: 'Though seeing, they do not see; though hearing, they do not hear or understand' (Matthew 13: 13). Jesus knew that if people heard the truth without proper preparation and purification of the mind and heart, they would misuse it for egoistic purposes. He knew that among the masses of people, there were very few who were ready to seek Self-realization. As Krishna says in the *Bhagavad Gītā*: 'Maybe one among thousands seeks spiritual perfection. And even among those who seek and attain perfection, perhaps one will come to know Me as I truly am' (*Bhagavad Gītā*, 7: 3).

The New Testament is a complete description of the transformation from the lower stages to the higher stages of consciousness. In the writings of the Bible, the symbol of the wheel or seal is used to represent the *chakras* in the subtle bodies.

Then I saw in the right hand of him who sat on the throne a scroll written on both sides, and on the backside [in the spine], sealed with seven seals.

Revelation 5: 1

When he opened the seventh seal, there was silence in heaven for about half an hour.

Revelation 8: 1

In the Gospel of John and in the Book of Revelation (a record of what the Apostle John saw and heard, in which constant use is made of symbols) it is significant that John places these seals on the back of the book of life. Each of the churches of the Book of Revelation represents one of the seven major *chakras* in the astral spine:

Church of Ephesus	*mūlādhāra chakra*
Church of Pergamos	*svādhiṣṭhāna chakra*
Church of Smyrna	*maṇipūra chakra*
Church of Thyatira	*anāhata chakra*
Church of Sardis	*viśuddha chakra*
Church of Philadelphia	*ājñā chakra*
Church of Laodicea	*sahasrāra chakra*

The seeker's journey to Pure Consciousness begins from *mūlādhāra chakra* at the base of the spine, where the first seal resides, and upwards to *sahasrāra chakra* in the brain, where the seventh seal resides (the ultimate state of oneness with the eternal Father).

So Jesus said, 'When you have lifted up the Son of man [to Divine Consciousness], then you will know that I am He.'

John 8: 28.

Revelation 1, 10–20 gives a record of spiritual experience and description of the astral anatomy. John also refers to the three main *nāḍīs*: *iḍā, piṅgalā* and *suṣumnā,* and the *chakras*:

And there appeared a great wonder in heaven; a woman [*kuṇḍalinī*], clothed with the sun [*piṅgalā*], and the moon [*iḍā*] under her feet, and upon her head a crown of twelve stars [the six *chakras* up and down].

Revelation 12: 1

And there appeared another wonder in heaven; and behold a great red dragon, having seven heads [seven *chakras*] and ten horns [the five organs of action and the five organs of knowledge], and seven crowns [seven *chakras* and associated vibrations] upon his head.

Revelation 12: 3

Blessed are they that do his commandments, that they may have right to the tree of life [the spine], and may enter in through the gates [*chakras*] into the city.

Revelation 22: 1.

The three astral *nādis,* and the seven main *chakras* are also referred to in the Old Testament, in Zechariah:

Then the angel who talked with me returned and wakened me, as a man wakened from sleep. He asked me, 'What do you see?'

I answered, 'I see a solid gold lamp-stand [*suṣumnā*] with a bowl at the top [*sahasrāra*] and seven lights on it, with seven channels to the lights. And there are two olive trees by it [*iḍā* and *piṅgalā*], one on the right of the bowl and the other on its left.'

Zechariah 4: 2,3

As noted earlier Carlo Crivelli's 'Annunciation' shows a golden bowl turned downwards just above the head of the Archangel Gabriel, representing the *sahasrāra.*

In his right hand he held seven stars, and out of his mouth [medulla oblongata, the negative pole of the *ājñā chakra*] came a sharp double-edged sword. His face was like the sun shining in all its brilliance [the concentrated energy in the head].

Revelation 1: 16

The mystery of the seven stars that you saw in my right hand and of the seven golden candlesticks [*chakras*] is this: The seven stars are the angels of the seven churches, and the seven candlesticks are the seven churches.

Revelation 1: 20

The seven *chakras* are thus symbolized in the book of Revelation as candlesticks, churches and seven seals. The seven stars are the radiating currents and vibrations of the *chakras* that create the elements (*tattvas*).

The Key to Opening the Seals

The scientific interior process of Kriyā Yoga meditation is the key to opening the seals (*chakras*). The meditator, regulating his mind and heart through self-discipline, disconnects the mind from the outward senses and their objects of distraction. He interiorizes his attention within and deeply concentrates on the Spiritual Eye; he withdraws his bodily consciousness and life force from the lower *chakras*, and directs it upwards through the astral spine to the thousand-rayed lotus in the *sahasrāra chakra*. There the individual soul is freed and united in blissful superconsciousness in oneness with God.

And no one has ascended up to heaven, except he who came down from heaven. And as Moses lifted up the serpent in the wilderness, even so must the Son of man be lifted up in order that all who believe may have eternal life in him

John 3: 13–14

In this verse, the term 'Son of man' refers not to Jesus but is a metaphor for the physical body consciousness. The 'serpent' is the *kuṇḍalinī* 'serpent force' that must be 'lifted up'. The individual soul-consciousness and life force must be raised up in the spinal passage through deep Kriyā Yoga meditation to unite in the Supreme Consciousness at the *sahasrāra chakra*.

The serpent power, *kuṇḍalinī*, is also referred to in the Old Testament:

And the Lord said to Moses, 'Make a serpent [downward-moving *kuṇḍalinī*] and put it up on a pole; anyone who is bitten [by delusion of worldliness] can look at it and live.' So Moses made a bronze serpent and put it on a pole. Then when anyone was bitten by a serpent and looked at the bronze serpent [the radiant light of the upward-moving *kuṇḍalinī*], he lived.

Numbers 21: 8, 9

Again the *suṣumnā, iḍā* and *piṅgalā* are referred to by St John in the last chapter of Revelation:

Then the angel showed me the river of water of life, as clear as crystal, flowing from the throne of God and of the Lamb [Christ Consciousness within] down the middle of the great street of the city. On each side of the river [*suṣumnā*] stood the tree of life [*iḍā* and *piṅgalā*], bearing twelve crops of fruits [the positive and negative poles of the six *chakras*, produced by the upward and downward currents in *iḍā* and *piṅgalā*], yielding its fruit every month. And the leaves [vibrations and rhythms] of the tree [consciousness] are for the healing of the nations [whole body].

Revelation 22: 1–2

The *ājñā chakra* is also mentioned in both the Old and New Testaments:

The light of the body is the eye; if therefore thine eye be single, thy whole body shall be full of light.

Matthew 6: 22

My guru, Paramhansa Yogananda, referred to the *ājñā chakra* as the Christ centre. This centre has two poles – the medulla oblongata (negative pole) and the Spiritual Eye (positive pole). The verse from Matthew is referring to the Spiritual Eye, which is seen during deep meditation, when concentrating deeply at the forehead, midpoint between the eyebrows. The Spiritual Eye is seen as a deep blue circular field, surrounded by a circle of golden light, and in the centre of the blue field radiates a scintillating five-rayed silvery-white star. This is the same star that the Three Wise Men saw 'in the east'.

When the two eye currents are concentrated and thrown back in the medulla by focusing the eyes on the point between the eyebrows, they are perceived as one single Spiritual Eye of light. When the two physical eyes manifest the Spiritual Eye, then one can perceive, by continuous spiritual development, the physical body as filled with the super-lights of the supersensuous astral body.

Paramhansa Yogananda

Afterwards he brought me to the gate, even the gate that looketh toward the east: and, behold, the glory of the God of Israel came from the way of the east: and his voice was like a noise of many waters: and the earth shined with his glory.

Ezekiel 43: 1–2

In his *Autobiography of a Yogi* Paramhansa Yogananda explains this further:

Through the divine eye in the forehead [east], the yogi sails his consciousness into omnipresence, hearing the Word or Aum, divine sound of many waters or vibrations which is the sole reality of creation.'

Yogananda also described his divine experience of the Spiritual Eye, when his guru, Lahiri Mahasaya, initiated him into Kriyā Yoga meditation.

He touched my forehead. Masses of whirling light appeared; the radiance gradually formed itself into the opal-blue Spiritual Eye, ringed in gold and centred with a white pentagonal star.

'Penetrate your consciousness through the star into the kingdom of the Infinite.' My guru's voice had a new note, soft like distant music.

Vision after vision broke as oceanic surf on the shores of my soul. The panoramic spheres finally melted in a sea of bliss. I lost myself in ever-surging blessedness. When I returned hours later to awareness of this world, the master gave me the technique of Kriyā Yoga.

Paramhansa Yogananda, *Autobiography of a Yogi*

Chapter 8

Hāṭha Yoga: The First Steps Towards Rāja Yoga

The various āsanas, kumbhakas, and the various mudrās of Hāṭha Yoga should all be practised, till the fruit – Rāja Yoga – is obtained.'

Hāṭha Yoga Pradīpikā, 1: 67

Hāṭha Yoga, the skilful training and mastering of the physical body, is the first step towards training and mastering the mind. A healthy and balanced mind can only exist in a strong, healthy body. For this reason, Hāṭha Yoga is the first step to the training of the mind or Rāja Yoga. The aim and goal of Hāṭha Yoga is to recondition the physical system, both the mind and the body. The skilful techniques of Hāṭha Yoga (*āsana, kriyā, prāṇāyāma, mudrā, yantra, mantra* and *laya* (absorption), purify, strengthen, balance, and remove any obstructions or obstacles, so that the mind and body can become fit vehicles toward Self-realization.

Purification is accomplished by the six acts; the yogi becomes strong through postures [*āsana*]; stability is acquired through the seals [*mudrā*] and calmness through sense-withdrawal [*pratyāhāra*]. Lightness results from breath control [*prāṇāyāma*], perception of the Self from meditation [*dhyāna*], and the untainted state from ecstasy [*samādhi*]; this last state is undoubtedly liberation [*mukti*].

Gheraṇḍa Saṁhitā, 1: 10–11

The purpose of the Hāṭha Yoga scientific approach is to give you the knowledge and means of controlling the two energies (the two syllables of *Hāṭha)*: *hā* and *ṭha,* which represent sun and moon, and *prāṇa* and *apāṇa,* respectively. Hāṭha Yoga subdues the current of thought that creates the fluctuating waves (*vṛttis*) of feeling in the mind and heart by subduing the *prāṇa.* Without this knowledge (*vidya*) it is very difficult to gain control over the mind. Hāṭha Yoga is a very practical way to control the mind through control of the prāṇic energy.

Hāṭha Yoga also aims to awaken the prāṇic energy in the spine and *chakras,* to prepare oneself for Rāja Yoga, which leads to the highest state of Self- and God-realization.

I salute Adīśvara [the first Lord, Śiva], who taught to Parvati [Śiva's consort] the Hāṭha Vidya, that is a step to attaining the higher pinnacle of Rāja Yoga.

Hāṭha Yoga Pradīpikā, 1: 1

I salute Adīśvara who taught first the science of Hāṭha Yoga – a science that stands out as a ladder that leads to the higher heights of Rāja Yoga.

Gheraṇḍa Saṁhitā, opening verse

Hāṭha Yoga cannot be obtained without Rāja Yoga, nor can Rāja Yoga be attained without Hāṭha Yoga. Therefore, the Yogi should first learn Hāṭha Yoga from the the instructions of a wise guru.

He who, while living in this physical body, does not practise Yoga, is living merely for the sake of sensual enjoyments [*bhoga*].

Śiva Saṁhitā, 5: 181–2.

Chapter 9

Yoga and the Chakras

Most of the yogic practices such as *āsanas, prāṇayama, kriyās, mudrās* ('seals' to awaken and direct the flow of prāṇic energy), *bandhas* (psychic energy locks) and *yoga nidrā* (psychic sleep) are described in the ancient *tantras* which precede both Patañjali's *Yoga Sutras* and the *Upaniṣads* by many centuries. The Natha Siddha yogis (*c.* 9th–12th centuries CE) Gorakhnātha and Matsyendranātha integrated the *Upaniṣad* philosophy with the practices of the *tantras* to create the system of yoga.

Hāṭha Yoga can be considered as a preliminary to the practice of Kuṇḍalinī Yoga, Kriyā Yoga, and Rāja Yoga. This is because Hāṭha Yoga purifies, tunes and stimulates the *chakras* in preparation for the higher Kriyā Yoga meditation practices awakening them. The practice of Hāṭha Yoga techniques balances the sympathetic and parasympathetic nervous systems, and influences the workings of the body organs. The Sanskrit word *Hāṭha* consists of two letters: *hā* stands for *iḍā* or lunar *nāḍī*, and *ṭha* stands for the *piṅgalā* or solar *nāḍī*.

When the flow of *prāṇa* in the *iḍā* is equal to the flow of *prāṇa* in the *piṅgalā*, the *kuṇḍalinī* automatically takes place. Hāṭha Yoga is concerned with balancing the flow of *prāṇa* in these two main *nāḍīs*, in order to activate the *kuṇḍalinī*.

The Hāṭha Yoga practices directly stimulate the *chakras*, which in turn influence the mind and body. Hāṭha Yoga practices such as the *shat kriyās* (six purification techniques) stimulate, purify, strengthen and improve the condition of the body organs, helping the *chakras* to awaken. For example, *kapālabhāti*, an invigorating breathing technique, physically purifies the frontal lobe of the brain at the *ājñā chakra*, awakening dormant centres which are responsible for subtle perception. Another technique called *neti* stimulates nerve connections in the olfactory bulb of the brain above the nostrils, which is considered to be a major stimulation point for the *ājñā chakra*. Similarly, the technique known as *nauli* massages and energizes the abdominal region of the body, influencing the *maṇipūra chakra*.

Authentic Representation of the Chakras

In the West the *chakras* have been misinterpreted by the so-called 'New Age' philosophies and thought that have sprung up since the 1970s. These philosophies have changed and adapted the meaning and purpose of the *chakras* to suit their own needs. The authentic yoga meaning and purpose of the *chakras* is to awaken the *kuṇḍalinī* and open the *chakras* to unfold the powers of the subtle and causal bodies to connect us with our true essential nature, and to unite the individual consciousness with Cosmic Consciousness. In other words the realization of the Self is the ultimate vision, the ultimate knowledge and the ultimate achievement. On realizing Truth, one recognizes that Self as *sat-chit-ānanda* (existence–consciousness–bliss).

The *chakras* do not become active and opened during ordinary consciousness. The *chakras* only become active when the mind and *prāṇa* have entered into the *suṣumnā* through yogic practices with deep concentration and meditation. It is a subtle experience and it is not on the physical level. When one gains the power to make the prāṇic energy flow by one's will through the *nāḍīs* and *chakras*, then, under the guidance of an experienced guru, one can attain Self-realization by the activation and awakening of the six *chakras* and the *sahasrāra*.

Opening each *chakra* gives us an understanding of the respective elements, sense organs, organs of action and *prāṇas* they rule according to their cosmic nature, which are all aspects of consciousness itself. The yogi experiences that consciousness directly and masters the energies of each *chakra*.

The activation of *sahasrāra* in *tantra* and the attainment of the superconscious state, *samādhi* in Rāja Yoga are both the same. The only difference is in the means of attainment. In *tantra*, Kuṇḍalinī Yoga practices are used, while in Rāja Yoga, *aṣṭāṅga* (eight limbs of yoga) practices are used.

New Age ideas about *chakras* are quite different from the original and authentic Tantric Yoga purpose of meditating on the *chakras* to realize the truth of one's own Self (which cannot be known by the power of the intellect), and to merge that individual consciousness into Pure Consciousness, in which there is no separation. There is no mention in the original Tantric Yoga texts of opening the *chakras* to heal a disease or to release blocked emotions, or of using crystals or flower remedies to balance the *chakras*. This has nothing to do with the purpose of yoga or the *chakras*.

Spiritual life is not for casual fun in New Age amusements that appeal to the mind, the senses, and the body. Many people are easily distracted by the New Age philosophies, with their toys and gadgets sold at Mind–Body–Spirit Festivals, that claim to bring us spiritual fulfilment, realization, and healing, but these distractions only make us more confused and restless. True spiritual life and yoga are founded on the self-discipline necessary for the one-pointed focus of the mind. The aim of that one-pointed focus is God, the Divine Self or the divine source of consciousness.

We need to discriminate between the true opening and awakening of the *chakras* and merely experiencing a fascinating but fleeting subtle state that leaves us in a realm of illusion. It is easy for the ego-self to fall into this trap.

In *tantra*, the whole body, with all its biological and psychological processes, becomes an instrument through which the cosmic power reveals itself. The object of Tantric, Kuṇḍalinī and Kriyā Yoga is to awaken this cosmic energy and cause it to unite with the Pure Consciousness (*Śiva*), pervading the whole universe. This is not easily achieved. It requires a balanced but strong, sustained and persistent spiritual effort in the yoga practices of Kuṇḍalinī Yoga, and Aṣṭāṅga Yoga. It requires self-discipline and strong willpower to overcome the delusions and the pull of the world. Spiritual effort appears unpleasant initially. Gross sensual pleasures are easily accessible, but the more subtle joys of the Self can only be attained after a complete redirection of our energies, a refocussing of our attention and a conquest of bad habits established over many lifetimes. When steady effort has resulted in the first glimpse of God's bliss, then our enthusiasm becomes aroused, and worldly amusements cease to attract us.

For activation of the *kuṇḍalinī*, it is necessary to purify the *nāḍīs*, *chakras*, and the *tattvas* by practising *āsanas*, *prāṇāyāma*, *neti*, *kapālabhāti*, *mudrās and bandhas*. Eating vegetarian sattvic (pure) food that is simple, light and nutritious is also helpful in preparation for activation of the *chakras*. An imbalanced diet, wrong action, wrong practice, disease, impurity, fear, doubts, ego, and misuse of divine powers (*siddhis*) are all obstacles on the path to awakening the *chakras*.

Purifying the Elements of the Chakras (Bhūta Śuddhi)

As human beings we are a complex of body, mind and consciousness. The physical body is gross matter, the mind is subtle matter, and consciousness is immaterial spirit. It is consciousness that manifests the operation of our mind and senses. Consciousness is ever present in us – in the waking, dream and sleep states. Waking consciousness and dream consciousness are reflections of the light of the One Pure Consciousness or Spirit in matter. Pure Consciousness, the Self, is the permanent and immutable and eternal witness. It can be realized when the ego is transcended.

Unlike Consciousness, the body and the mind are subject to change, and are non-permanent – they have a beginning and ending. Pure Consciousness is like the light of the sun which reveals itself to us directly and also reveals any object when its rays of sunlight illuminate it. Likewise, Pure Consciousness reveals its own existence to Itself, and also reveals a mind or a body with which It is in contact by illuminating it. Just as the sun does not need the help of a candle to illumine itself – its own light reveals it and reveals other things as well – so Consciousness is its own proof. It is self-existent and self-evident.

The Self or the soul in its true nature is ever perfect and pure; it does not need any purification. But it is a different story with the body and the mind. Due to the changeable nature of the body and mind, impurities arise in them. The physical body is subject to disease, injury and instability. The mind is subject to instability and subject to impurities in the forms of bad habits, negative emotions, negative attitudes, inner resisting influences, restlessness, inertia, desires and other psychological tendencies. All of these are obstacles to reaching the higher spiritual goal of life.

To reach the higher spiritual goal of life is the purpose of yoga, which is to unite the individual self with the universal Self, God. It is an ascent from matter into Spirit. The body and mind are instruments, vehicles for the expression of the soul. But if the mind is covered with impurities, the light of the soul or true Self cannot shine through. Both the body and the mind can become obstacles, they influence each other and can easily go out of control.

To control the mind, first the physical body and the nervous system has to be purified and strengthened. The practices of Hāṭha Yoga – *shat kriyās, āsana* and *prāṇāyāma* were designed for this purpose.

Then the subtle and causal levels of the mind need to be purified. These subtle levels of the mind are subjected to the influence of *saṁskāras. Vṛttis* create *saṁskāras,* impressions or prints of past actions in the mind, and the *saṁskāras* create *vṛttis*, vortices of desires and attachments formed by feelings that revolve around the ego and settle in the spine and lower three *chakras*; it is a continuing cycle, and it is difficult to break. Over time, the practice of Kriyā Yoga dissolves the *vṛttis*, enabling their energy to be directed upwards toward the Spiritual Eye of the sixth *chakra*.

It is only when the *vṛttis* have been neutralized or dissolved that we will find true lasting peace.

Part 2

PRACTICES

The following Yoga practices balance, purify and remove energy blockages in the *nāḍīs* and all the *chakras*, preparing the way for deep meditation. When the body is released from tension, the mind freed from restlessness, the *nāḍīs* purified and the *prāṇa* balanced, then the *chakras* will open, allowing the energy in the spine to rise to the higher *chakras*.

Guidelines before you Practise

- Always practise on an empty stomach – allow at least 3–4 hours after eating a meal before you begin.
- Practise in a clean, quiet and peaceful room or environment where you will not be disturbed.
- Wear loose comfortable clothing to do your practice.

Chapter 10

Chakra Awareness

Locating the Chakras

The following exercise is for locating the *chakras* in your spine.

Sit in a comfortable and relaxed meditation posture with your head, neck and spine aligned. If you are unable to sit with your legs crossed, then sit in an upright chair. It is important to keep your spine upright so that the energy can flow unimpeded to the higher brain centres.

First, become aware of your astral spine as a tube of light by placing your left hand at the base of your spine and your right hand at the base of your skull at the medulla oblongata. Close your eyes and calmly look into your Spiritual Eye. Inhale and feel your breath rising up from the base of your spine to the medulla oblongata. Exhale and feel the breath moving down through the astral spine. Practise 12 breaths.

Now place your left hand at the Spiritual Eye while keeping your right hand at the medulla oblongata. As you inhale, feel the breath flow through the psychic passage in the brain from the medulla oblongata (negative pole of *ājñā chakra*) to the Spiritual Eye (positive pole of *ājñā chakra*). Exhale and feel your breath and energy flow from your Spiritual Eye to the medulla.

In the second part of this exercise you will contract and relax certain parts of the physical body, and visualize each *chakra* as a lotus flower.

Mūlādhāra

Mūlādhāra is the direct switch for awakening *ājñā chakra.*

For men: Contract and relax the perineum muscles located midway between the anus and the scrotum.

For women: Contract the vaginal muscles inwards and upwards so that the walls of the upper vagina contract. Try to do this without contracting the anus or the front part of the perineum (clitoris and urinary opening).

During contraction visualize a lotus with its petals closed and pointing downwards. Then visualize this lotus turning through 180 degrees so that it is pointing upwards, opening its petals. Now mentally chant the *mantra 'oṁ'* three times. Relax the contraction and direct the energy (the lotus rays of energy from the petals) up to the next *chakra*.

Svādhiṣṭhāna

The trigger point for *svādhiṣṭhāna* is at the region of the pubis, at the level of the pubic bone.

For men: Bring your awareness to the urethra (urinary passage) inside the penis and try to draw it upwards. Contract the urethra like when you control the urge to urinate, then relax. This is called *vajroli mudrā.*

For women: Contract the urethra in the same way as when trying to control the urge to urinate.

Repeat as above, visualizing the lotus and mentally chanting *oṁ* three times. Direct the energy up to the next *chakra*.

Maṇipūra

Maṇipūra is located directly behind the navel on the inner wall of the spine. The trigger point is situated at the navel. Contract and draw the navel sharply in towards the spine and hold it there; feel the pulse beat at this point.

Repeat the visualization and mental chanting as above and move the energy to the next *chakra*.

Anāhata

Anāhata is located in the spine on the inner wall, directly behind the centre of the chest, at the level of the depression in the sternum. This is the *hridayakaśa* (the space within the heart where purity resides). Contract and pull the shoulders back, and place one hand on the centre of the chest, and concentrate on the sensation in the heart space of this *chakra*.

Repeat the lotus visualization and mental chanting as above and direct the energy up to the next *chakra*.

Viśuddha

Viśuddha is located in the cervical plexus directly behind the throat pit. The trigger point is in the front of the neck, at the throat pit. Place three fingers of one hand on the throat pit and three fingers of the other hand on the spine directly behind. Gently press both points and feel the sensation at this *chakra*.

Repeat the visualization and mental chanting as before and move the energy to the next *chakra*.

Ājñā

Ājñā corresponds to the pineal gland and is located inside the brain directly behind the eyebrow centre, in the midline of the brain directly above the spine. Concentrate deeply at the point between the eyebrows by gently turning the eyes upwards to this point. Try to feel a subtle pulsation within this *ājñā chakra* region and synchronize the *mantra oṁ* (mentally) with the pulsation, so it becomes *oṁ, oṁ, oṁ, oṁ, oṁ* . . .

Mūlādhāra is the direct switch for awakening *ājñā chakra*, so by practising *aśvinī mudrā* (contraction and relaxation of the anal sphincter muscles) at a medium speed, you should be able to feel the *ājñā chakra.*

Sahasrāra

Sahasrāra is the supreme seat of higher expanded awareness situated at the crown of the head. It is correlated to the pituitary gland in the brain. The power of the *chakras* resides in *sahasrāra.*

Transcendence and Self-realization begins at the sixth centre, *ājñā chakra,* in *savikalpa samādhi*. But final enlightenment and final liberation are attained in *nirvikalpa samādhi* or transcendental Cosmic Consciousness, which occurs in *sahasrāra,* the seventh centre at the crown. So we meditate at the *ājñā chakra* until realization or enlightenment is attained. Then, when the gateway opens, and the currents of energy flow together up to *sahasrāra,* the thousand-rayed cerebral light, human consciousness is united and expanded with Cosmic Consciousness.

Chapter 11

Sitting Postures for Prāṇāyāma and Meditation

Sitting for meditation or for *prāṇāyāma* requires a stable posture that is relaxed and comfortable, a posture in which you can maintain the natural curves of the spine, and which you can remain in for a significant amount of time without any movement. When the body posture is held without effort, the breath is steady, quiet and subtle, and the mind is perfectly calm, you will be able to enter a deep state of stillness.

When sitting for meditation or for practising *prāṇāyāma*, it is necessary and important to sit with the upper body straight. To sit steadily and comfortably for any length of time the head, neck, spine and pelvis must be in alignment directly over the base of the spine. The neck, shoulders, back muscles, hips, knees and legs need to be relaxed. To maintain the natural curve of the lumbar spine, you need to sit up on the front of your sitting bones, not slumping back or arching forward. To sit in a cross-legged posture on a cushion or folded blankets, you need to sit high enough so that your knees are lower than your hips. This creates space in the front of the groin, making it easier for the pelvis to tilt into proper alignment.

A balanced spine supports the relaxation of the whole nervous system. If there are any imbalances and misalignments of these body structures, they will create discomfort, tension and pain. These imbalances can also impede or block the natural flow of prāṇic energy in the *suṣumnā nāḍī.*

Regular practice of yoga postures will help enormously to improve alignment and comfort in the sitting poses by developing flexibility in the legs, hips, knees and spine. The yoga postures will also help in strengthening the lower back and opening the chest, and developing and maximizing your breathing.

Apart from *virāsana* and *vajrāsana,* all the other sitting poses listed below are cross-legged poses. These have the advantage of drawing the energy inwards toward the body and directing it upwards in the spine. It is also easier to apply *bandhas* (locks) in the cross-legged poses.

There are seven Classical Yoga sitting postures (*āsanas*) for meditation:

Sukhāsana – Comfortable or easy pose (cross-legged)
Siddhāsana – Adept pose
Svastikāsana – Auspicious pose
Virāsana – Hero pose
Vajrāsana – Diamond pose or Thunderbolt pose
Ardha Padmāsana – Half-Lotus pose
Padmāsana – Lotus pose

Sukhāsana

Those who have difficulty in sitting for long periods in *siddhāsana, vajrāsana, ardha padmāsana or padmāsana* can sit in *sukhāsana* (easy pose). This is simply sitting cross-legged.

Sit on a firm cushion at an appropriate height for you to make the posture comfortable. Sitting on a firm cushion helps in stimulating and directing subtle energies. To avoid straining the back muscles try to keep the knees lower than the level of the hips, or at least at the same level. This allows your thighs to relax downward, reducing tension in the hips, and frees the spine to lengthen upwards. If you have a knee injury then support both knees with firm cushions, bolsters, or rolled blankets under them.

Cross both legs and place the right foot under the left thigh and the left foot under, or in front of, the right calf on the floor. If it is more comfortable cross the legs in the opposite way. Sit upright with the weight of your body toward the forward edges of your sitting bones. Align the upper body and shoulders directly over the base of the spine. Lengthen the spine and open the chest, and draw your shoulders back. Place your hands relaxed on your knees or thighs.

Sitting on a chair

If you are unable to sit comfortably and painlessly in *sukhāsana* then sit on an upright chair that has no armrests. (If your feet do not touch the floor, then support them with folded blankets.) The most important points are that the body is straight and in alignment, with the natural curves of the spine supporting the actions of the body; that the body is comfortable and relaxed; and that the body can remain still throughout the duration of the meditation or *prāṇāyāma* practice.

When sitting on a chair for meditation, sit with your back away from the back of the chair. Sit on the forward edge of the chair, with the soles of your feet flat on the ground and your spine upright. Gently round and arch the lower back a few times, tilting the pelvis forward and back, until you have centred your spine and sitting bones. When you feel your head, neck, spine and pelvis are aligned, then slightly lower your chin and lift the back of the skull to create space at the base of the occiput, where the head meets the neck.

For your comfort, make sure the chair is padded, or place a small cushion or folded blanket on it. Place the feet hip-width apart on the floor, with the lower legs perpendicular to the floor. You may find it useful to have your hips slightly higher than the knees, so that the thighs slope slightly downward to minimize strain in the legs. A cushion can be used to raise the height of the seat if necessary. If you wish, you may place a woollen or silk cloth over your chair and extend it on to the floor, for your feet to rest on. According to the yogis, wool and silk insulate against the subtle magnetic currents in the earth, which tend to pull the energy down.

Place the hands relaxed, palm upwards, at the junction of the thighs and abdomen (palms turned down you feel more grounded; palms turned up you feel more energized). Lift your shoulders, roll them up and back, and then drop and relax them. Keep the chest up. Lift up through your spine to the top of the head, so that your head, neck and spine are aligned straight, so that there is no impediment to the flow of subtle energy ascending in the spine to the higher brain centres.

Sitting on a meditation stool

Another useful prop for sitting is to use a wooden meditation stool with a slanting seat that provides support and lift to the spinal column. A meditation stool usually stands approximately 20 cm (8 in.) high, and is padded for comfort, or a small cushion may be placed on it.

To sit on the meditation stool you need to go into a kneeling position with the buttocks on the stool and the shins resting on the floor. Keep the thighs parallel and straight out from the hips. Place the hands relaxed on the upper thighs, and keep the head, neck and spine aligned.

Sitting Postures for the Adept

Those of you who have more flexibility and suppleness in your body, and are are not suffering from knee injuries, may sit in any of the following postures: *Siddhāsana, Vajrāsana, Virāsana, Ardha Padmāsana* or *Padmāsana.* These postures presents a greater challenge to your hips, knees and ankles.

Virāsana

For this sitting pose you will need one or two brick-shaped rubber blocks or folded blankets for a sitting support. Kneel on the floor with your knees about 10 cm (4 in.) apart with your feet separated slightly wider than your hips. The tops of the feet rest on the floor pointing straight back. Position the support block(s) between your feet with the long side of the block placed horizontally between your ankles. Make sure that both of your sitting bones are balanced evenly on the block, and comfortably supported.

If you are comfortable sitting on your heels without the block, then lift up enough to allow you to use your hands to pull your outer calf muscles away from the thighs, before you sit down between your heels.

Place the hands, palms down, on your thighs close to the abdomen. To come out of the pose, lean forward onto your hands and slowly straighten the knees, walk back and stand up.

Caution: *Virāsana* puts a slight twist in the knees, so if you have a knee injury be careful, and practise with awareness and only under the guidance of a competent and experienced teacher.

Vajrāsana

This pose is also used by Muslims and Zen Buddhists as a position for prayer and meditation.

Come up on to the knees (knee stand). Place the legs together, tilt the upper body forward and sit back by lowering the buttocks onto the inside surface of the feet with the heels touching the sides of the hips. Cross the right big toe over the left or alternatively have the big toes touching each other.

Keep the trunk upright and place the hands palms down, relaxed, on the thighs. The head, neck and back should be kept straight and relaxed.

Siddhāsana

Siddhā means 'perfected', 'accomplished'. A *siddhā* yogi is one who is perfected, accomplished or adept in yoga.

Sit on the edge of a firm cushion or a folded blanket. Bend your right leg and place the sole of the foot flat against the inner left thigh with your heel pressing against the perineum (the area midway between the genitals and the anus), sitting on top of the right heel. Then bend your left leg and place the left ankle directly over the right ankle so that the ankle bones are touching and the heels are positioned one above the other. Press the pubis with your left heel directly above the genitals. Push the outer edge of the left foot and the toes between the right calf and thigh muscles. Grasp the right toes and pull them up in between the left calf and thigh.

In men the base of the penis rests against the bottom heel. Lift the penis, scrotum and testes up and out of the way, and then place the left heel close to the pubic bone.

Sit with the head, neck and spine in straight alignment, and with the knees touching the floor. Close the eyes, and place your hands on your knees or thighs with the palms either downward in *jñanā mudrā* (gesture of intuitive knowledge) or palms upward in *chin mudrā* (gesture of consciousness). In both *mudrās* the tip of the index finger and thumb touch. The other three fingers are extended and relaxed.

Chin mudrā represents the union of the cosmic with the individual consciousness. The index finger represents individual consciousness and the thumb, cosmic consciousness, The three remaining fingers symbolize the three *gunas* (*sattva, rajas* and *tamas*), the three fundamental qualities of Material Nature (*Prakṛti*). The goal of the yogi is to transcend the three *gunas* and to unite with the Cosmic Self.

Both *mudrās* help to activate the lower lungs and encourage diaphragmatic breathing, and stimulate the grounding effects of *apāna vāyu* (functions in the region of the navel to the feet). *Chin mudrā* also stimulates *prāṇā vāyu*.

In this pose, the pressure of the heel against the perineum stimulates *mūlabandha,* and the pressure against the pubic bone stimulates the *svādhiṣṭhāna,* directing the prāṇic flow of energy from the lower *chakras* upward through the spine, stimulating the brain and calming the entire nervous system.

Women, like men, should position the heel against the inner surface of the inferior pubic rami. But this means that the heel will have to be placed directly against the soft tissues of the genitals, well in front of the fourchette (the fold of skin which forms the union of the lower ends of the labia minora). The heel will be more intrusive in the female because the upside-down V formed by the pubic rami is shallower than in the male. If women sit directly on the floor without a cushion, the back of the lower heel will be in the exact place where both the urogenital and pelvic diaphragms are interrupted by the vaginal introitus. The posture used by women is called *siddha yoni āsana.*

Sit with the legs straight in front. Bend your right leg and place the sole of the foot flat against the inner left thigh. Place the heel of the right foot firmly against or inside the labia majora of the vagina. Bend the left leg and position the left heel directly on top of the right heel so it presses the clitoris, and tuck the left toes down between the calf and thigh. Hold the toes of the right foot and pull them up between the left calf and thigh. The knees should be firmly on the floor, and the head, neck and spine aligned straight. The hands are placed on the knees in either *jñanā mudrā* or *chin mudrā.*

Svastikāsana

The symbol of the *svastika* represents the different corners of the earth and universe in the spokes, and their meeting point is the centre of consciousness.

Sit on the edge of a firm cushion or two folded blankets with the legs stretched forward. Bend the left leg and place the sole of your left foot against the right inner thigh. Take your right foot by the ankle and place it on top of your left calf and position the outer edge of the foot and the toes in between the thigh and calf muscles. Place your hands relaxed on the knees with the thumb and index fingers touching, positioned in either *jñanā mudrā* or *chin mudrā.* Keep the head, neck and spine in straight alignment.

The difference between this pose and *siddhāsana* is that in *svastikāsana* the heels are not in line with each other. This makes it slightly easier as it requires less hip flexibility than *siddhāsana.* In *siddhāsana* and *svastikāsana,* both knees come close to the floor. This supports the lower back by creating a natural inward tilt to the sacrum, giving a slight arch to the lower back.

Svastikāsana activates and rejuvenates the entire nervous system.

Ardha Padmāsana

This posture is recommended for those unable to sit comfortably in the full lotus pose (*Padmāsana*).

Sit on the edge of a firm cushion or two folded blankets with the legs stretched forward. Bend the right leg and place the foot very close to the body on the floor. Then bend the left leg and bring the foot very close to the body on top of the right thigh. Keep the head, neck and spine in straight alignment, and both knees resting on the floor.

Ardha padmāsana can also be practised by bending the left leg first and bringing the right foot on top of the left thigh. To prevent imbalances in the hips and pelvis it is good to change the crossing of the legs regularly, so that both hips remain equally open. This principle also applies to the other crossed-leg postures.

Padmāsana

Padmāsana is the classic yoga sitting pose for meditation that has a balancing influence on all the *chakras*. In pictures we see the great yogi masters like Mahavatar Babaji, Lahiri Mahasaya, Swami Śrī Yukteswar and Paramhansa Yogananda in the superconsciousness state of *samādhi*, while sitting in the full lotus pose. But for most Westerners it is one of the most challenging poses to perform and so it is not practical as a meditation pose. It places stress on the knees and hip joints; it demands a very strong external rotation of the thigh bones in the hip sockets, and if the hip joints are tight, this pose can place enormous stress on the knees. The knee is a hinge joint with a limited capacity to rotate, and it is usually the intra-articular structures of the knee such as the cruciate ligaments and menisci (which act as pads for the knee joint) that get torn in an injury.

It is essential first to be able to perform a full range of motion of the ball and socket hip joint to protect the hinge knee joint. So, unless you have practised the pose in your childhood and youth, it is not likely to work satisfactorily. But for those adepts who have mastered this beautiful-looking pose, it is said to bring an incomparable feeling of repose and calmness to the mind.

If you are going to attempt *padmāsana* do not force yourself into it, but carefully learn progressively with appropriate warm-up stretches and modifications under the guidance of an experienced teacher, who is able to practise it competently and safely. Avoid this pose if you have knee problems or varicose veins.

To achieve the pose, sit with the legs extended straight in front of you. Then slowly and carefully bend your left leg, holding the left foot with your hands. Turn the foot around so that the sole is facing you. Place the instep up high on the thigh as you lower the knee to the floor. The heel should be close to the pubic bone.

Bend the right leg. Holding the right foot with your hands, place the instep up high on the left thigh.

In the final position, both knees should ideally touch the floor. The head, neck and spine must be aligned with the shoulders relaxed, and the hands relaxed on the knees in either *jñanā mudrā* or *chin mudrā*. Close the eyes and relax the whole body.

When you come out of *padmāsana*, straighten the leg, raise the kneecap, and pull the toes toward the body, so as to elongate the hamstring and relieve any cramps in the muscles.

If *padmāsana* or the 'lotus pose' can be practised properly and correctly, and one is able to sit in it comfortably, it gives great stability and strength to the lower back while locking the legs securely in place. It is difficult to fall over even if you fall asleep; this is why it is the chosen pose for yogīs going into the superconsciousness state of *samādhi*.

Warm-ups for Lotus Pose

It is good practice before any exercise where the knees are to be rotated into advanced sitting poses to take time to warm and relax them by rubbing the sides of both knees with the palms of your hands. Rub vigorously using a rotating motion. This allows the bursae around the joint (which function to cushion the knee) to lubricate, protecting the knees from sudden forcible flexion. The aim of lotus warm-ups is to increase movement in the hip and knee joints, and stretch the thigh muscles. Therefore, exercises where you perform both inward and outward rotation are helpful in augmenting the multidirectional range of motion in the hips.

First warm-up – Half Butterfly pose

Sit with your back and legs straight. Breathing normally, place the right foot with the sole of the foot facing upward, on top of the left thigh as close to the hip as possible. (If this leg position is difficult then place the foot on the floor alongside the inside of the thigh close to the body.) Hold the toes of the right foot with the left hand, and with slight pressure move your knee up and down ten times with the right hand. Return to the starting position and perform the exercise with the left leg.

This stretches the muscles of the inner hips and thighs and encourages blood circulation into the hips.

Second warm-up – Full Butterfly pose

Resting firmly on your sitting bones, sit on a cushion on the floor. Bring the soles of the feet together and draw the heels close into the groin. Clasp the feet with interlocked fingers and pull against the feet for leverage. Open the knees and press them toward the floor.

Inhale, lift the lower back and, extending the sternum, elongate the spine to the crown of the head. Exhale, creating a shoulder-blade squeeze, and slightly arch the lower spine, and work to lower the thighs toward the floor.

Third warm-up – Cradle pose

From the same sitting position as before, stretch out your right leg. Take hold of the left leg and, keeping the left foot up high, place it into the crook of the right arm at the elbow. Bring the left arm around and interlock the hands, creating your cradle (like holding a baby). Inhale, elongate and straighten the spine by extending the sternum upward. Exhale as you rock the cradled leg from right to left.

Inhale, elongating the spine again. Exhale, this time hugging the leg closer to your chest. Hold the position and feel the stretch in the thigh. Repeat the process with the other leg.

A Comfortable Alternative

This is an alternative – a comfortable, steady, supported version that strikes a balance between the stability of *padmāsana* and the ease and comfort of *sukhāsana* to create stability, comfort and ease.

To begin your practice you will need to sit against a wall on a carpeted floor to cushion your ankles (or you can fold a yoga mat). You will also need three or four folded blankets to sit on and another blanket rolled into a long roll to place over your feet. Place the three or four folded blankets parallel against the wall.

Sit on the folded blankets with your back upright against the support of the wall. Then cross your legs and bring the right leg in so that your shins contact each other, and each foot rests on the floor under the opposite thigh. Adjust the height of the knees until they are parallel to the floor. Place the long rolled blanket over the tops of both feet and adjust it to support the legs.

Tilt your pelvis forward by leaning your upper body forward, then sit upright with your back against the wall. Rest the backs of your hands on your thighs, so that the hands are relaxed.

Roll the tops of your shoulders back and lean your head gently against the wall. With the head, neck and spine in alignment keep the chest lifted and relax your abdomen and diaphragm muscle as you breathe slowly and rhythmically.

Chapter 12

The Four Purifications

In the tradition of Classical Yoga there are six purification techniques known as the *shatkarmas*. These are *dhauti* (cleansing of the digestive tract); *vasti* (colon cleansing); *neti* (nasal cleansing); *tratak* (steady gazing at a particular point, such as a candle flame); *nauli* (intestinal cleansing); and *kapālabhāti* (purification and vitalization of the frontal lobes of the brain. The *Hāṭha Yoga Pradīpikā* makes the point that those who wish to practise yoga who are of a flabby and phlegmatic constitution should first practise the *shatkarmas*. There are four purification techniques based on these which were devised by yogis to simplify and make safer the methods of purification. These four techniques can be practised instead of the *shatkarmas* for purifying the *nāḍīs*, and for awakening the *chakras* and the life energy in the body.

The four purifications are practised in the following order:

1. *Nāḍī śodhana*
2. *Kapālabhāti*
3. *Āgnisara kriyā*
4. *Aśvinī mudrā*

Practice time

To prepare the body and purify the *nāḍīs* for the practice of *prāṇāyāma* (breath control), the four purifications are practised over a period of two to three months. This is important for those who are beginners and have had no experience of practising *prāṇāyāma* before.

Method

Throughout the practice, sit in a comfortable meditation posture with the head, neck and spine aligned straight. With the eyes closed, concentrate on the midpoint between the eyebrows at the Spiritual Eye (*ājñā chakra*).

Nāḍī Śodhana (Subtle Channel Purification)

Śodhana (pronounced as 'shodana') in Sanskrit means 'to purify'. This is the alternate nostril breathing *prāṇāyāma*, that maintains an equilibrium in the catabolic and anabolic processes in the body. It purifies the blood and the brain cells. It brings consistency and regularity to our patterns of breathing, and it has a calming effect on the nervous system.

A smooth and unobstructed flow of *prāṇa* is needed for concentration and meditation. For the yogi it is usual to make the breath flow equally in each nostril. When the flow of air is equal in each nostril, then the flow in the *iḍā* and *piṅgalā nāḍīs* is also equalized – they become balanced. Under these balanced conditions, *prāṇā* begins to flow in the central *suṣumnā nāḍī*, influencing all the *chakras*, and the mind becomes centred and still for the purpose of entering into meditation – calm awareness of the inner Self.

Method

Sit in any comfortable meditation pose, with the head, neck and spine aligned straight. Close the eyes and relax the whole body. Keep the body still and bring your attention and awareness to the point between the eyebrows at the Spiritual Eye

Place your left hand, palm upwards and relaxed, on your left knee. Raise your right hand (in *viṣṇu mudrā*, an energy seal that helps to contain *prāṇā* within the body) with the palm in front of your face, and fold down your middle and index fingers into the palm, keeping the thumb and ring and little fingers extended. Exhale and close the right nostril with your thumb. Inhale slowly, smoothly and deeply through the left nostril. Pause. Close the left nostril with the ring finger and slowly exhale through the right nostril. Pause. Inhale through the right nostril. Pause. Close the right nostril with your thumb and exhale through the left nostril. This completes one round. Begin with 5–10 rounds and over a period of time gradually increase to 20 rounds.

Breathing ratios for beginners

It is advisable to start with a 1:2:2 breath ratio for a few months before taking up the advanced ratio 1:4:2. For beginners this means that the breath retention is twice that of the inhalation, and the duration of exhalation is the same as that of the retention. For advanced students it means that the breath retention is four times that of the inhalation, and the duration of exhalation is twice that of the inhalation.

The maximum starting count (in seconds) for a beginner is 4:8:8. After having practised this for one month, then increase the duration to 5:10:10. Then build up gradually until you reach 8:16:16. On no account should you increase this until you are able to practise it with comfort and ease. You must *never* force, strain or interrupt the overall rhythm of your breathing practice. To do so could cause injury to the physical body. If your next breath is gasping or hurried, then you have certainly held your breath for too long. Always seek advice from an experienced and qualified teacher who practises *prāṇāyāma.*

Breathing ratios for advanced students

As you progress with these ratios, you will be able to change to the advanced ratio of 1:4:2, gradually increasing the count to 8:32:16. It could take up to two years to reach this level.

Note that when the breath retention (*kumbhaka*) is longer than ten seconds, then it is important to hold *jālandhara bandha* (chin lock).

Kapālabhāti

In Sanskrit, *kapāla* means 'cranium' and *bhāti* means 'light,' 'splendour,' or 'to shine', by means of cleansing or purifying. *Kapālabhāti* is one of the six Hāṭha Yoga *shatkarmas*, a powerful frontal brain cleansing, clearing and energizing technique that invigorates the brain and its entire circulation, including the pineal and pituitary glands, and awakens the dormant centres which are responsible for subtle perception. It is an excellent technique in preparation for meditation. The *ājñā* and *maṇipūra chakras* are particularly awakened with prāṇic energy by *kapālabhāti.*

Method

Sit in any comfortable meditation pose, with the head, neck and spine aligned straight. Close the eyes and relax the whole body. Keep the body still and bring your attention and awareness to the point between the eyebrows at the Spiritual Eye.

Now bring your awareness to your navel. Note that the chest is not activated; only the abdominal muscles are activated in *kapālabhāti.* The strong contraction of the abdominal muscles causes the short, quick and rhythmic expulsions of breath. In *kapālabhāti* there is no resistance to breathing. Both the nostrils and the glottis are wide open. The muscles of the neck and the face are kept relaxed so that the air escapes smoothly.

Exhale fully, and then inhale deeply through the nose to expand your chest fully. Keep the chest expanded and passive throughout the active round of breathing. Also keep your shoulders steady and passive, and your face, jaw and neck relaxed. As you exhale and inhale (about every 1–2 seconds or the speed of an eye-blink) rapidly and lightly with a series of short, light breaths through both nostrils, emphasize the exhalation with a short, forceful contraction of the abdominal muscles (moving the navel towards the spine). The abdomen contracts, and presses upwards against the diaphragm, pushing the breath out through the nose. The inhalation comes as a natural reflex, with the release downward of the diaphragm as the abdominal muscles are relaxed after contracting them to exhale.

Beginners' level

Beginners can practise three to five rounds of ten *kapālabhāti* breaths. After each round, inhale and exhale deeply twice, using the complete yogic breath. Then, after completing three to five rounds, return to normal breathing and sit still for meditation. Maintain your awareness at the Spiritual Eye.

If this is your first time in practising *kapālabhāti*, you may feel dizzy, caused by hyperventilation. If this happens then stop and lie down on your back and relax. So you don't experience dizziness again, make sure that only your abdomen is moving when you practise *kapālabhāti*, not the chest. The abdomen should contract and move inward every time you exhale. Also, do not pump too fast, as this may also cause dizziness.

Intermediate level

In the intermediate practice of *kapālabhāti*, perform ten breaths. On the tenth breath exhale slowly and fully, emptying the lungs of carbon dioxide. Then inhale and exhale with a full yogic breath, and return to normal breathing. Sit for meditation, maintaining your awareness at the Spiritual Eye.

Practice five rounds of ten *kapālabhāti* breaths. Over a period of time you can gradually increase the number of breaths and rounds.

Advanced level

In the advanced practice breath retention can be added. After completing your last round of *kapālabhāti* exhale fully, allow a natural pause to take place, then inhale with a full yogic breath (use *ujjayi* breath, with slight contraction of the glottis in the throat). Lower your head and apply the chin lock with your chest and shoulders fully open. Without any unnecessary tightening in the throat, neck and shoulders, hold the breath in for as long as comfortable. Do not force or strain.

To exhale, first, release the *jālandhara bandha,* by lowering the shoulders and raising the head, and slowly and smoothly exhale with *ujjayi* breath. Then inhale and exhale with a full yogic breath, and continue with the next round. You can gradually increase the speed and number of breaths up to a total of 120 exhalations per round.

After completing a number of rounds of *kapālabhāti,* sit still and calm in the inner silence of meditation. With your eyes closed, fix your whole attention with your relaxed inward gaze at the point between the eyebrows, at the Spiritual Eye. Expand your consciousness into infinity and experience that ineffable peace that is God within you.

Benefits: *Kapālabhāti* stimulates the nerves and in turn they activate the *nāḍīs,* which activate the *prāṇās*. The *prāṇās* then gravitate towards the area where the action is taking place in the frontal lobes of the brain. This brings an awakening to the Spiritual Eye (*ājñā chakra*).

Kapālabhāti purifies the *iḍā* and *piṅgalā nāḍīs* and stimulates every tissue in the body by eliminating large quantities of carbon dioxide, making the blood rich with oxygen. It helps in awakening the *kuṇḍalinī* power and induces alertness and inner awareness, preparing the mind for concentration and meditation. The fast abdominal breathing in *kapālabhāti* has a soothing and calming effect on the central nervous system and the autonomic nervous system.

Kapālabhāti cleanses and drains the sinuses, and opens the lungs and the breathing passages. The overall breathing efficiency is increased by the strengthening and toning of the diaphragm. The heart is given a gentle massage.

Contraindications: There should be no undue strain on the breathing mechanism at any stage of the practice of *kapālabhāti*. In the beginning, practise carefully under the expert guidance of a qualified teacher. *Kapālabhāti* is best done in the morning before meditation. Do not practise at night, since it activates the brain and nervous system and may prevent you from sleeping when you go to bed. Do not practise if you have high blood pressure, epilepsy, lung disease or heart disease. Do not retain the breath longer than is comfortable. If you feel dizzy or feel that you are going to faint, stop and calmly return to normal breathing.

Agnisāra Kriyā (Fire Purification)

In Sanskrit, *agni* means 'fire', the elemental quality for digestion, and transformation. *Sāra* means 'essence'. *Kriyā* means 'action'. *Agnisāra kriyā* means 'cleansing with the essence of fire'. *Agni* is the presiding element of the *maṇipūra chakra* at the navel centre. The subdivisions of *prāṇā* function with the *maṇipūra chakra* to nourish and sustain the body.

Method

The best time to perform *agnisāra kriyā* is in the early morning after emptying the bowels. It is easier and safer with an empty stomach, so you can practise before meals and during your *āsana* practice. Allow at least three hours after a meal before you atempt *agnisāra kriyā*.

First stage – uddiyana bandha (abdominal lock)

Stand comfortably with the feet slightly wider than hip-width apart. Bend your knees and rest your hands on the thighs. Lean forward slightly to bring the weight of the torso over the straight arms so you can relax the deep muscles of the abdomen that support the lumbar spine. Lengthen the spine and the back of your neck, tuck the chin in, and look down at your navel.

Inhale, then exhale deeply, emptying the lungs as much as possible. Hold the breath out and contract the lower abdomen, forming a hollow. As you contract your abdomen pull it inward and upward. Contract the sphincter muscles and the pelvic floor, drawing inwards and upwards. While contracting the lower abdomen and the pelvic floor, hold the breath out for as long as comfortable. Then inhale, release the muscle contractions, and completely relax. Repeat the practice five to ten times.

Benefits: Massages the internal organs, improves digestion and elimination, increases and improves the circulation of lymph and blood in the abdominal area, gently massages the heart and lungs, tones and improves the abdominal muscles. It encourages the prāṇic energy to flow upwards.

Second stage – abdominal pumping

From the same standing position as before, inhale, then exhale deeply, emptying the lungs as much as possible. Hold the breath out and contract the pelvic floor and the lowest part of the abdomen just above the pubic bone. Then contract and pull the lower abdomen firmly inwards and upwards, draw the diaphragm up under the ribs. Immediately release the diaphragm, abdomen and pelvic floor and begin to inhale. In quick succession repeat this rapid in-and-out movement of the abdomen while the breath is held out without strain.

Begin with three to five repetitions and increase gradually to ten, beginning with 20 pulls and increasing to 60 in each breath. Practise daily.

Third stage – nauli (abdominal massage)

The Sanskrit word *nauli* comes from the root *nala* or *nali*, which means a 'tubular vessel' or 'pipe', referring to the pipelike appearance of the rectus abdominus muscles as they are contracted. *Nala* is the term for the rectus abdominus. *Nauli* is also known in Sanskrit as *lauliki karma*. *Lauliki* comes from the Sanskrit root *lola*, which means 'rolling and agitation'. *Nauli* is a Hāṭha Yoga technique and rolls, rotates and agitates the whole abdomen with all its associated nerves and muscles.

In this technique the abdominal muscles are isolated by contraction, and are rotated.

Before attempting *nauli*, *agnisāra kriyā* and *uḍḍīyāna bandha* should be perfected. *Nauli* should be performed only when the stomach is completely empty. Allow at least five hours after meals. The best time to practise *nauli* is therefore in the morning after emptying the bowels and before breakfast.

Madhyāma nauli (middle isolation)

Stand as you did in the previous two stages, with the feet slightly wider than hip-width apart. Bend the knees slightly, lean forward and place your hands on the thighs with the arms straight and the fingers pointing toward each other. Exhale fully and perform the two locks – *uḍḍīyāna bandha* and *jālandhara bandha* – while maintaining external breath retention (*bahir kumbhaka*). Then contract the rectus abdominus muscles so that they form a vertical tubular shape along the centre of the abdomen. This is called *madhyāma nauli* (the middle isolation). Maintain the contraction with the breath held out for only as long as comfortable. Do not strain.

Release the contraction and *bandhas*, raise your head and return to the upright standing position. Inhale slowly and deeply, and relax the whole body. Allow the breath and the heartbeat to return to normal.

Start with five rounds of *madhyāma nauli* and gradually work up to ten. When *madhyāma nauli* has been mastered, then you can proceed to try *vama nauli*.

Vama nauli (left isolation)

Follow the same instructions as for *madhyāma nauli*, to contract and isolate the rectus abdominus muscles so that they form a vertical tubular shape along the centre of the abdomen. Then isolate the rectus abdominus muscles to the left side by pushing down on the left thigh, so that the rectus abdominus muscles form the vertical tubular shape only on the left side of the abdomen. Hold for as long as comfortable without strain, and return to *madhyāma nauli*. Release the abdominal contraction, raise your head and return to the upright position. Inhale slowly and deeply. Completely relax, allowing the breath and heartbeat to return to normal.

Dakśina nauli (right isolation)

Now repeat the exercise in the same way, by isolating the rectus abdominus muscles on the right side of the abdomen.

Once you have mastered isolating the middle, left and right rectus abdominus, then you can proceed to abdominal rotation.

Abdominal rotation or churning

Practise rotating the rectus abdominus first to the left, then to the right, and back to the left in a continuous rolling or churning movement several times. To begin with perform three continuous rotations. Release the abdominal contraction, raise your head and return to the upright position. Inhale slowly and deeply and relax, allowing the breath and heartbeat to return to normal.

Start with five to ten rotations, gradually increasing to 25 rotations over a period of months.

Benefits: *Agnisāra kriyā* is an invigorating practice that works on the deep muscles of the lower abdomen, and has a beneficial effect on all the physiological functions of the abdomen. It strengthens the muscles of the pelvic floor and abdominal wall. Internally, *agnisāra kriyā* tones, activates, and cleanses the digestive and eliminative systems in the body.

According to the life science of Ayurveda, many diseases start from stagnation and toxins (*āma*) that build up in the digestive tract, so *agnisāra kriyā* can help to a great extent in keeping the digestive tract and the other organ systems in the body functioning healthily. Contractions of the lower abdominal muscles massage the bladder. The lymphatic vessels in the lower abdomen and pelvic area are massaged and flushed, stimulating healthy functioning of the immune system. *Agnisāra kriyā* improves the circulation to the reproductive organs in the pelvic area, and other organs in the abdomen.

On more subtle levels, *agnisāra kriyā* creates a strong upward movement of energy, increasing one's vitality. It strengthens *uḍḍīyāna bandha,* and creates heat at the navel centre (*maṇipūra chakra*), which purifies the *nāḍīs* and stimulates the digestive system. *Agnisāra kriyā* stimulates the five *prāṇās (prāṇā, apāna, samāna, udāna* and *vyāna*), especially *samāna prāṇā,* which connects two main *chakras* – *anāhata* and *maṇipūra chakras. Samāna prāṇā* is strengthened through the practice of *agnisāra kriyā* and *nauli.* The most effective technique for awakening *samāna prāṇā* is Kriyā Yoga. The practice of Kriyā Yoga warms the entire body. This is due to the rising of *samāna prāṇā.*

Nauli stimulates and purifies the *maṇipūra chakra,* the storehouse of *prāṇā.*

Contraindications: Do not practise *agnisāra kriyā* if you have high blood pressure, cardiovascular disease, hiatus hernia, acute duodenal or peptic ulcers, kidney or gallstones, chronic diarrhoea, and during menstruation (*agnisāra kriyā* stimulates an upward flow of prāṇic energy that is counter to the cleansing downward flow during menstruation) or pregnancy.

Aśvinī Mudrā (Horse Gesture)

Aśvinī is the Sanskrit word for 'horse' and *mudrā* means 'seal' or 'lock'. *Mudrās* are practised to awaken and direct the flow of *kuṇḍalinī,* to induce stillness and strength, and to 'lock in' the benefits resulting from the other practices.

Aśvinī mudrā is so called because, after a horse has evacuated its faeces, it then dilates and contracts the anus several times. During defecation, peristaltic waves in the colon push faeces into the rectum, which triggers the defecation reflex. Contractions push the waste along, and the anal sphincters relax to allow it out of the body through the anus.

The practice of *aśvinī mudrā* is a preparation for *mūla bandha.*

Note: *Mūla bandha* (root lock or perineum lock) differs from *aśvinī mudrā* (horse gesture) in that there is no alternating contraction and dilation of the anal sphincter. In *mūla bandha* the actual point of contraction is the centre point of the perineum, a diamond-shaped region of muscles between the anus and the genitals. *Mūla bandha* is a gentle contraction of the pelvic diaphragm and the muscles of the urogenital triangle. It does not counter intra-abdominal pressure so much as it seals urogenital energy within the body, controlling and restraining it during *prāṇāyāma* and meditation. In *aśvinī mudrā* the pelvic diaphragm, the anus and the gluteals are strongly activated.

Method

Stage 1: Sit in a comfortable meditative pose with the head, neck and spine aligned. Close the eyes and relax the whole body.

Become aware of your natural breath, then after a few minutes, breathing normally, focus your attention on the anus, and practise contracting the anal sphincter muscles, slowly and smoothly with maximum contraction, for a few seconds. Then, without straining the muscles, totally relax them for a few seconds. Then repeat the whole process evenly and rhythmically a few more times, gradually increasing the speed with which you contract and relax the sphincter muscles.

Stage 2: Sit in a comfortable meditative pose with the head, neck and spine aligned. Close the eyes and relax the whole body.

Inhale deeply and hold the breath in. Contract and release the anal sphincter muscles rapidly and repeatedly for as many times as you can comfortably hold your breath. Then relax the contraction and exhale.

Start with three rounds of 30 contractions each, gradually increasing this number to 10 rounds of 60 contractions each. End the practice by allowing the breath to return to normal. Sit calmly with the eyes closed in meditation.

Benefits: *Aśvinī mudrā* strengthens the anal muscles and pelvic floor, preventing prolapse of the rectum and uterus. It prevents constipation by stimulating the intestinal peristalsis, and tones up the seminal glands and nerves in the pelvic area. It strengthens *mūla bandha* and redirects the *prāṇa* upwards.

Contraindications: High blood pressure, heart conditions, fistula.

Chapter 13

Purification Practices for Awakening the Chakras

Śākti Bandha Sequence

The Sanskrit word *śākti* refers to the body's energy or power. *Bandha* means to lock, contract or bind. Here it means to release the energy blocks that impede the flow of energy and *prāṇa* in the body, *nāḍīs* and *chakras*. *Śākti* is also the *kuṇḍalinī* power, the primal female energy that resides at the base of the spine in the *mūlādhāra chakra*. When awakened *kuṇḍalinī śākti* rises through the subtle *suṣumnā* channel in the spinal cord to unite with *Śiva* (Pure Consciousness), her masculine opposite pole, residing in the *sahasrāra*, the thousand-rayed lotus just above the crown of the head.

The *śākti bandha* sequence of postures is mainly practised in the kneeling pose of *vajrāsana* (thunderbolt pose). This pose is good for relaxation, concentration and absorption; it holds the body upright without effort, and will only be a problem to sit in if you have a knee injury. It is the best meditation *āsana* for those suffering from sciatica. *Vajrāsana* stimulates the *vajrā nāḍī*, activates *prāṇa* in the *suṣumnā*, and redirects sexual energy to the brain for spiritual meditation.

When practising the *śākti bandha* sequence it is important to remain in *vajrāsana* all the time, as you move from one exercise to the next. If you are uncomfortable, then you may stretch your legs slowly with awareness between each exercise, but do not lose your concentration.

1 – Vajrāsana (thunderbolt pose)

Practise five to ten minutes. As the starting position for the *śākti bandha* sequence, this pose prepares the mind and body for relaxation and concentration.

Kneel down with the knees together, the heels apart and the big toes touching. Sit with the buttocks resting in the 'bowl shape' formed by the feet. Rest the palms of your hands on your knees. Without tension, keep the head, neck and spine upright.

Now clasp your hands together with the fingers interlocked but relaxed on the chest, and close your eyes. With awareness, experience your physical body. First become aware of the sensation of the crown of the head . . . forehead . . . ears . . . eyes . . . nose . . . cheeks . . . mouth . . . jaws. Now become aware of the back of the head . . . neck . . . throat . . . Be aware of your whole head . . . Now experience your shoulders . . . arms . . . chest . . . back . . . abdomen . . . navel . . . lower back . . . buttocks . . . thighs . . . knees . . . lower legs . . . ankles . . . feet . . . soles of feet . . . heels . . . toes. Now become aware of your whole body, feel its form and shape, size and density from without and from within . . . Now, with the attitude of absorption, go inward and just experience the sensation, and the feeling of your hands.

After some time of being aware of your hands, turn your attention again to awareness of the whole body . . . Now, become aware of the natural rhythm of your breathing, keep your attention on the flow of air in and out of the nostrils. You may continue to sit in this attitude of absorption for as long as comfortable.

2 – Padadhirāsana (breath-balancing pose)

Practise five to ten minutes. Still sitting in *vajrāsana,* cross your arms over your chest and tuck your hands under the arms in the armpits, with your thumbs in front pointing upwards. Press the thumbs and forefingers firmly against the armpits.

This position will help to equalize the flow of the breath in each nostril.

Now close your eyes and free your mind from all distractions. With the attention fixed at the point between the eyebrows, the centre of calmness, at the Spiritual Eye, become aware of your breath in this moment . . . Don't try to change the natural rhythm of the breath, just remain aware of it . . . Feel the breath moving in and out of your body . . . Feel the abdomen rise as you inhale and fall as you exhale.

Feel the calmness and stillness within . . . Remain here and now in the present moment, and become aware of the breath where it enters the body, in the nostrils . . . Feel the sensation of the breath in the nostrils as it flows in and flows out . . . Now feel the breath higher in the nostrils . . . then feel the breath at the point between the eyebrows, and as the breath naturally flows in of its own accord, mentally follow the breath with the *bīja mantra 'hong'*. Then as the breath naturally flows out, mentally follow it with the *bīja mantra 'sau'* (pronounced as 'saw') . . . Make no attempt to control the breath, you are simply watching the breath while listening inwardly to the *hong-sau bīja mantra.* Throughout this process, the concentration is focused on the breath and *mantra,* while simultaneously looking into the Spiritual Eye, midway between the eyebrows. This *mantra* coordinated with the breathing frees the mind from restlessness, and brings about deep concentration and inner calmness. The *bīja mantra hong-sau* means 'I, the manifested Self, am He, the Unmanifested Spirit.'

3 – Simhāgarjanāsana (roaring lion pose)

Sit in *vajrāsana* with your knees 45 cm (18 in.) apart, and with the toes of both feet touching each other. Place your hands on the floor between the knees with the fingers pointing in towards the body, and the thumbs out to each side. Keeping the arms straight, lean forward, arching the back, and rest part of your body-weight on the arms. Without straining the neck, tilt the head backwards, and open the mouth and extend the tongue out as far as comfortable towards the chin. Open your eyes wide and direct your vision upwards to the midpoint between the eyebrows. As you assume this position exhale loudly through the mouth. Let a long, steady 'aaah' sound come from the throat – like the great roar of a lion. Hold the breath out for a short while in this position, then inhale through your nose and relax back onto your heels.

Repeat this process seven times. Each time, bring your whole attention to the eyebrow centre. In between each round relax the eyes, tongue and mouth.

Simhāsana relieves tension from the throat, chest and diaphragm, and has a very calming affect on the mind and is a good preparation for meditation.

4 – Śaśāṅkāsana (moon pose)

Sit in *vajrāsana* with the head, neck and spine straight, and rest the palms of the hands just behind the knees. Close your eyes and relax any physical and mental tensions. As you inhale, very slowly raise the arms above your head. As you exhale, slowly bend the trunk forwards (synchronize your breathing with the movement) from the hips while keeping the arms in line above the head, until the forehead and the outstretched arms and hands simultaneously touch the floor. Relax in this position, with the arms in front of the knees, while holding the breath out for as long as comfortable. Then, inhale slowly while raising the arms and trunk up from the floor, and return to the upright position of *vajrāsana.*

Repeat the whole process seven times with pauses in between. Breathe in *ujjayi* breath throughout the practice. *Ujjayi prāṇāyāma* is practised by gently contracting the glottis at the back of the throat to produce a soft snoring sound that is very quietly audible. Both the inhalation and exhalation are long, deep and controlled. *Ujjayi prāṇāyāma* has a calming effect on the nervous system and brain, and it slows down the heart rate.

Benefits: *Śaśāṅkāsana* stretches the back muscles and tones the pelvic muscles and reproductive organs. Rejuvenates the digestive system. It relaxes the sciatic nerves and regulates the functioning of the adrenal glands, and has a very calming effect on the whole nervous system.

Contraindications: It should not be practised if you have a slipped disc or very high blood pressure.

5 – Śākti Bandha

Sit in *vajrāsana* with the head, neck and spine straight. Clasp your hands behind your back, inhale, and bend your trunk forward to rest the forehead on the floor. Then, holding the breath, raise your arms as far above your back as possible, so that your clasped hands are directly above your shoulders with the arms straight. Now, still holding the breath, swing your arms with the hands clasped from side to side. As you swing the arms one shoulder will touch the knee and the other shoulder will raise up.

Then return to the sitting position of *vajrāsana.* Lower the arms and exhale. With your eyes closed, rest for a few breaths, then inhale and repeat the exercise six more times.

Note: The swinging of the arms may be fast or slow. Fast is more energizing. It may also be more comfortable for some people if the knees are separated slightly.

Śākti bandha releases tensions in the shoulders and spine, enabling the energy to flow into and up the spine.

6 – Uṣṭrāsana (camel pose)

Sit in *vajrāsana* and come up into the kneeling position with both the knees and the feet 45 cm (18 in.) apart. Place your hands on your waist with your thumbs forward and your fingers pointing back and down. Press your shins against the floor as you draw your tailbone down and lift the top of your ribcage. Begin to arch up and back without letting your thighs tilt backward. Maintain the lift of the chest and continue to draw your tailbone down as you deepen the back arch.

If you can, try to bring your hands to your heels. Begin by curling your toes under to raise your heels. Inhale, and slowly bend the torso backward, sliding your hands down the buttocks and the backs of your legs onto your raised heels. Inhale, then exhale as you press down through your hands on to the heels to raise the chest. With the head back, push your hips and thighs forwards and bend the trunk further. Feel your spine lengthen as you stretch back.

Hold the pose for 5–30 seconds while breathing smoothly and slowly with your concentration on the navel area and the corresponding point on the spine behind the navel.

To come out of the pose, press your shins against the floor, release one hand at a time from your heels and, as you inhale, lift your chest, bend your knees and relax back into *vajrāsana.*

Counterpose: From *vajrāsana*, relax in the forward bend of *Śaśāṅkāsana* to release any tension in the back.

Note: Be very careful not to strain the neck (cervical spine). Before you can safely tilt the head back, you will need to extend each thoracic vertebra. To achieve this, stretch the intercostal muscles that connect the ribs as well as the abdominal muscles that link the ribs to the front of the pelvis to extend the thoracic spine for this backbend.

Contraindications: Persons with any spinal problems should practise this *āsana* only under an experienced teacher's guidance.

Benefits: Tones and stretches the back muscles, stimulates the spinal nerves. Beneficial for the digestive, excretory and reproductive systems.

7 – Śāvāsana (corpse pose)

Practise for five to ten minutes. Lie flat and comfortably on your back with your arms slightly away from the body relaxed at your sides, with the palms facing upwards. Have your legs and feet slightly apart and allow the feet to fall relaxed to the sides. Ensure that your head and neck are straight and in line with the spine. If necessary place a small cushion or folded blanket under the head or the knees to ensure the neck and lower back are comfortable.

Close your eyes and keep the body completely still . . . Take a long, slow, deep breath in, and as you exhale feel your whole body relaxing and settling into the posture . . . Again, inhale deeply, and as you exhale, let go of all physical and mental tensions. Let go of the past and the future and relax your whole body into the present moment . . . Bring your awareness to each part of the body, and gradually and consciously relax each part, until the whole body feels relaxed. Then become aware of your breathing . . . without changing the natural rhythm of the breath, be totally aware of each inhalation and exhalation.

8 – Bhrāmarī Prāṇāyāma (humming bee breath)

Basic practice: seven rounds. Sit in any comfortable meditation pose, with the head, neck and spine straight. Close the eyes and relax the whole body. Bring your attention and awareness to the point between your eyebrows at the Spiritual Eye.

Raise your arms sideways to shoulder level and close the ears using your index fingers. You can press the *tragi* (ear) flaps to close out any sounds. Inhale deeply through both nostrils, then exhale slowly through the nose while making a smooth, continuous, deep, and steady humming sound like a bee. This humming sound is made with the mouth and jaw relaxed, and with the lips gently closed and the teeth slightly separated. Concentrate on the sound vibration reverberating in the brain. Let the sound vibration fill your consciousness. As you gaze into the Spiritual Eye, be aware of the effect of the vibrating resonance in the frontal brain area.

Begin with seven cycles of *bhrāmarī prāṇāyāma,* then gradually increase to as many as you can comfortably perform.

Advanced practice: up to 15 minutes. After you have mastered the basic practice, you can introduce the chin lock (*jālandhara bandha*) and the anal lock (*mūla bandha*). *Bandhas* have an effect on the prāṇic body by redirecting the flow of *prāṇa* into the *suṣumnā*. These two *bandhas* are applied after you have inhaled and are holding the breath.

First apply the *jālandhara bandha*. Inhale deeply and hold the breath. Place the two hands on the knees, lift the shoulders and tilt the body forward slightly, keeping the spine straight. Press the chin firmly between the collarbones to close the windpipe and oesophagus. Then, while still holding the breath retention with the *jālandhara bandha,* apply the *mūla bandha* by firmly contracting the perineum and anal muscles. Hold the two *bandhas* for five seconds, then release the *jālandhara bandha,* followed by the *mūla bandha,* and exhale slowly and continuously with the humming sound.

As you become more advanced with this practice you will be able to hold the breath (*kumbhaka*) with the two *bandhas* for a longer duration, but do not strain – it needs to be carefully and gradually increased over a period of time.

Benefits: Releases tensions in the brain caused by mental irritation, anger, worry and anxiety. Lowers high blood pressure, and purifies the blood. Calms the mind and nervous system for relaxation and meditation. It makes the prāṇic energy stronger and subtler, and awakens the inner sound (*nāda*) which dissolves the mind and helps one to enter into *samādhi*.

Contraindications: Do not practise while lying down. Those with heart disease may practise the basic technique but should not attempt the breath retention.

General Benefits of the Bandhas

The *bandhas* are beneficial for the brain centres, *chakras* and *nāḍīs*. When a *bandha* is practised, the energy flow to a particular area of the body is temporarily blocked. When the *bandha* is released, the energy flows more strongly through the body with increased pressure.

Jālandhara bandha awakens the *viśuddha chakra,* and improves the ability to retain the breath for a longer period; it also develops the concentration.

Mūla bandha activates and purifies the *mūlādhāra chakra.* It awakens dormant consciousness and the *kuṇḍalinī śākti. Mūla bandha* acts like a seal to contain the downward flow of *apāna vāyu* (associated with the exhalation and *mūlādhāra chakra*), and merges it with the upward motion of *prāṇā vāyu* (associated with the inhalation and *anāhata chakra*) in the lower abdomen/pelvic area. As it merges, the *prāṇā* enters the *suṣumnā nāḍī* and rises powerfully upward in the subtle spine.

9 – Meditation

To end the *śākti bandha* sequence prepare yourself for meditation. You may sit for meditation for as long as you want to.

Now with the mental and physical tensions released and the body relaxed, sit in any comfortable meditation pose, with the head, neck and spine aligned straight. Close the eyes and relax the whole body. Keep the body still and bring your attention and awareness to the point between the eyebrows at the Spiritual Eye, the seat of spiritual consciousness. Continue to feel the sound resonance in the brain from the humming breath . . . feel it permeating your consciousness, bringing you inward toward the centre of consciousness, to that still point within . . . Be aware of the energy activated in the spine, the *chakras,* and the brain . . . Breathe in, imagine you are drawing light into the crown of your head, and as you breathe out, a soothing, peaceful, healing light gently cascades down, penetrating and permeating every tissue, bone, muscle, organ, cell and atom throughout your whole body . . . cleansing and purifying all impurities.

Remain in the state of the present-moment stillness and deep inner calmness. Dissolve all sense of individuality and separateness . . .

Expand your consciousness into the Infinite and feel that Oneness with all that is God . . . mentally affirm that the infinite presence of the Divine is ever within you: 'I am resting in the calm stillness of eternal peace and eternal love, that is God.'

Chapter 14

Mudrā

In yoga *mudrā* means 'gesture' and is a powerful way of tuning oneself to higher states of consciousness. By practising *mudrā*, our intention is to align our own individual prāṇic flow of energy with the source of Cosmic *prāṇa* that surrounds and suffuses us with life. Another meaning of the word *mudrā* is that it expresses the inner state of the practitioner performing the *mudrā*.

Through the practice of *mudrās*, the unwanted physical responses are controlled and the prāṇic energy in the subtle body is voluntarily activated and made to flow for spiritual benefits, bringing about a deeper awareness and concentration.

Prāṇa Mudrā

Prāṇa mudrā (invocation of prāṇic energy) awakens and distributes prāṇic energy throughout the body, increasing health, strength, and vital energy. The practice of *prāṇa mudrā* also develops the awareness of the flow of prāṇic energy through the *nāḍīs* and *chakras*. This practice is both an expression of offering of oneself and of receiving from the Divine. From the practice arises a sense of uniting the individual self (*jīvātma*) with the Supreme Self (*Paramātma*), a peaceful feeling of oneness.

Sit relaxed in a comfortable meditation posture with the head, neck and spine aligned, and with your hands in *bhairava mudrā* (gesture of Śiva: place the right hand on top of the left, so that the palms of both hands face upward) resting in your lap. Close the eyes.

Stage 1

Take a few deep yogic breaths, then exhale deeply and contract the abdominal muscles. Retain the breath out (*antar kumbhaka*) for as long as comfortable, and perform *mūla bandha.* Concentrate on *mūlādhāra chakra* at the base of the spine.

Stage 2

Release the *mūla bandha* lock. Inhale slowly and deeply in *ujjayi* breath, drawing the breath deep into the lower abdomen and pelvis, feeling an expansion with the breath. Coordinating the breath with the movement of the hands, simultaneously raise your hands up in front of your navel with your hands relaxed and open, palms facing your abdomen, with your fingertips pointing toward each other without touching. As you do this visualize and feel the prāṇic energy rising from the *mūlādhāra chakra,* up through the *svādhiṣṭhāna chakra* to the *maṇipūra chakra.*

Stage 3

Continue inhaling, expanding the breath into the chest from the navel and solar plexus, while slowly raising your hands up until they are aligned with your chest in front of the heart centre (the palms and fingers should be positioned as before). As you do this, feel and visualize the prāṇic energy rising from the *maṇipūra chakra* to *anāhata chakra.*

Stage 4

Now expand the breath into the higher lobes of the lungs in the upper chest, while raising the hands in front of the throat. As you do this feel and visualize the prāṇic energy rising from the *anāhata chakra* to *viśuddha chakra.*

Stage 5

Retain the breath, and stretch out your arms to the sides with your elbows slightly bent. Keep your hands in line with your ears and turn the palms upward. Feel and visualize the prāṇic energy rising upward from the *anāhata chakra* to *ājñā chakra*. Feel the energy as it expands as waves of pure light rising from the space between the eyebrow centre to the crown centre at the top of the head. Now, while retaining the breath for as long as comfortable, concentrate on the *sahasrāra* and visualize it as a source of pure divine light. Feel that peaceful vibrations are emanating from you and are spreading out in all directions in waves of vital prāṇic energy. Feel that the life force and divine consciousness are merging together as one. Bathe your consciousness in this divine light.

Now exhaling, perform the five steps in reverse order down through the *chakras*, returning to *mūlādhāra chakra*. Perform *mūla bandha* while concentrating on *mūlādhāra chakra*. Release the *bandha* and relax. Return to normal breathing and, feeling that your body is filled with light, gaze deeply into the Spiritual Eye and meditate in the stillness.

Meditation

Continue to sit and meditate in the stillness with your eyes closed and your inner gaze at the Spiritual Eye, midpoint between the eyebrows. Feel your little wave of consciousness expanding into the Infinite ocean, dissolving all sense of ego.

Mentally affirm: 'I am awake in God's infinite ocean of radiant joy.'

Mahāmudrā

Out of the many Mudrās, the following ten are the best: (1) Mahāmudrā, (2) Mahābandha, (3) Mahāveda, (4) Khecarī, (5) Jālandhara, (6) Mūlabandha, (7) Viparītkaraṇī, (8) Uḍḍīyāna, (9) Vajroli, (10) Śākticālana.

Siva Saṁhitā, 4: 15

Mahāmudrā ('Great Gesture') and other Classical Yoga *mudrās* are listed and explained in the ancient Hāṭha Yoga treatises: *Śiva Saṁhitā, Gheraṇḍa Saṁhitā* and *Hāṭha Yoga Pradīpikā*. The path of Hāṭha Yoga was formulated and laid out by the great *siddha* yogis Matsyendranath, his disciple Gorakshanath and others, fourteen altogether.

The Sanskrit word *mahā* means 'great' and *mudrā* means 'gesture' or 'attitude', as noted above. *Mahāmudrā,* is a good preparation for the practice of meditation. It is a powerful technique, and, when performed properly, provides not only various kinds of physical benefits, but it also balances and opens the *iḍā* and *piṅgalā nāḍīs*. In the Kriyā Yoga tradition *mahāmudrā* is used to great effect in opening the spinal passage, allowing the life-force (*prāṇa śākti*) to flow upward in the *suṣumnā*. Unless this passage is opened the *prāṇa śākti* cannot rise to *ājñā chakra.*

This *mudrā* only becomes really effective when its subtle aspect is mastered.

Practice of Mahāmudrā

Before practising *mahāmudrā,* practise head-to-knee pose (*jānuśirṣāsana*) to improve your understanding of the stretching movements needed.

Props needed: one or two folded blankets and a belt.

Jānuśirṣāsana (head-to-knee pose)

Begin by sitting, with the spine upright, on one or two folded blankets in *dandāsana* (staff pose), with the legs together and stretched straight out in front. Press the palms of the hands flat on the floor (to lift the back further) on either side of the hips with the fingers facing forward. Draw the shoulder blades towards the spine and downward, opening the chest. Bend the right leg and bring the right heel into the right groin. Keep the left leg straight and the foot upright. Loop a belt around the left foot and hold the ends in your hands. Inhale, straighten your arms, and stretch your trunk upward. Concave the lower back and lengthen the front of the body. Gaze upward and breathe smoothly and evenly.

Exhale, bend your elbows outwards and extend forward from the lower back, and lower your trunk down over the leg. Stay and relax in the pose for ten slow, even breaths, or half a minute. Release your hands and come up slowly as you inhale.

Repeat on the other side.

Mahāmudrā in the Classical Tantric Treatises

Pressing carefully the anus by the left heel, stretch the right leg, and take hold of the great toe by the hand; contract the throat (not expelling the breath), and fix the gaze between the eyebrows. This is called Mahāmudrā by the wise.

Gheraṇḍa Saṁhitā, 3: 6–7

In accordance with the instructions of the Guru, press gently the perineum with the heel of the left foot. Stretching the right foot out, hold it firmly by the two hands. Having closed the nine gates of the body, place the chin on the chest. Then concentrate the vibrations of the mind and inhale and retain it by kumbhaka. This is the Mahāmudrā, held secret in all Tantras. The steady-minded Yogi, having practised it on the left, should then practise it on the right side; and in all cases must be firm in prāṇāyāma – regulation of the breath.

Śiva Saṁhitā, 4: 17

Pressing the anus with the left heel and stretching out the right leg, take hold of the toes with your hands. Then practise jalandhāra bandha and draw the breath through the suṣumnā. Then the Kuṇḍalinī becomes straight, just as a coiled snake when struck by a rod suddenly straightens itself like the stick. Then the two other nāḍīs become dead, because the breath goes out of them. Then one should breathe out very slowly and never quickly. This has been declared to be Mahāmudrā by the great siddhas.

Hāṭha Yoga Pradīpikā, 3: 10–13

Mahāmudrā – Version 1

Begin by sitting, with the spine upright, on one or two folded blankets in *dandāsana*, with the legs together and stretched straight out in front. Bend the right leg with the knee opened out to the side and the thigh relaxing down to the floor, and position the right heel under the anus. (If you have tight hips and you are unable to bring the knee down to the floor, place a rolled blanket under the thigh to support the knee.)

As you exhale, bend your trunk forward and with both hands clasp the big toe of the left foot. (If your back is stiff and you are unable to bend low, then loop a belt round the foot to hold as in the previous posture, *jānuśirṣāsana*.) Allow the whole body to relax.

Inhale deeply, tilt your head slightly backwards and hold the breath in. Bring your inner gaze to the Spiritual Eye and perform *mūla bandha*, by contracting the perineum and anal muscles. In a cycle, concentrate on *mūlādhāra, viśuddha* and *ājñā chakras* in sequence for one or two seconds each. After holding the breath in for as long as you comfortably can, then straighten your head, relax *mūla bandha* and slowly exhale.

Repeat the entire practice on the other leg, and then repeat with both legs together, this completes one round. Practise three to 12 rounds.

Mahāmudrā – Version 2

The initial position is identical to Version 1 above.

Exhale deeply, and in succession apply the three *bandhas*. Holding the breath out, apply *mūla bandha* by contracting the perineum and anal muscles; then contract the lower abdominal muscles in and upward in *uḍḍīyāna bandha*, drawing from the lift of *mūla bandha*; then, with the chest open, apply *jālandhara bandha*. Applying these locks draws the prāṇic energy upward in the spine toward the crown of the head.

Now, holding the three *bandhas*, bend your trunk forward and with both hands clasp the big toe of the left foot. (If your back is stiff and you are unable to bend low, then loop a belt round the foot to hold as in *jānuśirṣāsana*.) Pull on the big toe and stretch the spine, concentrating on energizing it by the resistance to the pull. Bring your inner gaze and attention to the Spiritual Eye and mentally chant *Oṁ* at that point six times. Feel a sensation of energy rising through the spine to the Spiritual Eye at the eyebrow centre.

After holding the breath out with the three *bandhas* for as long as comfortable, slowly release the three *bandhas* in succession: first release *mūla bandha*, then release *uḍḍīyāna bandha* by releasing your diaphragm downwards, followed by releasing the chin lock, then inhale smoothly. Return to normal breathing and relax the body.

Repeat the entire practice on the other leg, and then repeat with both legs together; this completes one round. Practise three to 12 rounds.

Mahāmudrā – Kriyā Yoga version

This Kriyā Yoga version of *mahāmudrā* is modified, with a different knee position. If you have problems with your knee, like a tear in the meniscus, or other knee injuries, then you may find this posture easier, as it does not require a rotation of the knee.

In this practice the purpose of sitting on the heel pressed against the anus, and keeping the fingers interlocked while pulling on the big toes, is to stimulate subtle energies in the body, and particularly in the spine.

Note: The full Kriyā Yoga version of *mahāmudrā* is taught with a different breathing technique to the one described here. You would need to be initiated into the practice of *kriyā prāṇāyāma,* as taught by Paramhansa Yogananda on the spiritual Kriyā Yoga path, to receive this technique.

Stage one: Sit upright with the head, neck and spine aligned, on a firm carpeted surface or a yoga mat to protect your ankles. Sit on your left foot, with the heel pressing against the anal region, or with the sole of your left foot resting under your left hip. Bend your right leg and place the foot flat on the floor. Then, interlocking the fingers of both hands, clasp your hands around the right knee and draw the thigh in against your torso, or as close as possible. Keep your spine straight and, while pulling on the right knee, inhale (breathing in *ujjayi* breath) slowly to a count of ten. Keeping your concentration and awareness in the spine, feel that you are drawing a cool current of prāṇic energy up the spine.

Then, hold the breath in and stretch the right leg out in front of you. Bend forward, and with the fingers of each hand interlocked, grasp your big toe and pull, so that you extend your trunk forward with your forehead toward the knee as close as is comfortable. (If you are not supple enough, then bend the knee slightly. The most important thing is to feel the spine stretching and a sensation of energy rising through it.) As you hold the breath in, apply the chin lock (*jālandhara bandha*), and with your focused attention at the Spiritual Eye, mentally chant *Oṁ* six times. Feel a sensation of energy rising up through the spine and then pulsating at the Spiritual Eye, radiating waves of bliss throughout the brain.

Release the chin lock, and with the clasped hands around the right knee draw the knee back up against your torso, while slowly exhaling to a slow count of ten. Keeping your concentration and awareness in the spine, feel a warm current of energy flowing down through the spine.

Stage two: Now change sides and repeat the previous instructions.

Stage three: Sit upright with your knees bent, and with your clasped hands (fingers interlocked) around the knees, pull in your thighs against your torso. Inhale (breathing in *ujjayi* breath) for a slow count of ten. Feel that you are drawing a cool current of prāṇic energy up the spine.

Now stretch both legs out together in front of you and, grasping the big toes with the interlocked hands, pull on the big toes and stretch your torso forward, feeling the stretch in the spine. Apply the chin lock and bring your forehead toward the knees. Hold the breath in, and with your focused attention at the Spiritual Eye, mentally chant *Oṁ* six times. Feel a sensation of energy rising up through the spine and then pulsating at the Spiritual Eye, radiating waves of bliss throughout the brain.

Release the chin lock, and slowly exhale to a count of ten. Keeping your concentration and awareness in the spine, feel a warm current of prāṇic energy flowing down the spine.

Then bring your knees and thighs back up against your torso, by pulling on the knees with clasped hands. Relax and return to normal breathing.

This completes one round of *mahāmudrā.* Practise three complete rounds. As you progress with this practice, you may increase the number to six or 12 complete rounds.

Meditation

After your practice of *mahāmudrā,* focus your attention within, in the stillness of your inner Self. As you meditate, keep your inner vision at the Spiritual Eye. Continue to feel the energy vibrating in the spine. Feel and visualize it radiating out into every cell and atom in your body, until your body is permeated with divine bliss. Then expand that blissful consciousness into the Infinite.

Mentally affirm: 'I am the ocean of Spirit that has become the wave of human life.'

To be Self-realized is to know your Self as the great ocean of Spirit by dissolving the delusion that you are a little ego, body, or personality.

Paramhansa Yogananda

Your Spine is the Pathway to God

The practice of *mahāmudrā* awakens and enlivens the subtle energy in the seven-centred astral *suṣumnā* passage in the cerebrospinal axis (the Pathway to God), through which all aspirants seeking liberation must pass to reach God consciously. It is a specific process by means of which one is able to awaken dormant forces in the lower three *chakras* and cause them to flow upward to the *ājñā chakra* and the thousand-rayed lotus at *sahasrāra,* at the crown of the head.

The spinal cord can be likened to an electrical wire. In the astral wire are located seven subtle centres of light (*chakras*) which are the sub-centres for the conduction and distribution of prāṇic life currents throughout the body. From the medulla oblongata energy flows into the cerebrospinal axis through the physical body. Just as electricity flows into a bulb through a wire, so the Cosmic Energy enters the medulla and flows through the brain (where it is stored) into the cerebrospinal axis and its seven subtle *chakras,* and is distributed throughout the network of subtle *nāḍīs* to the whole body.

The kriyā Yogi mentally directs his life energy to revolve, upward and downward, around the six spinal centres (medullary, cervical, dorsal, lumbar, sacral, and coccygeal plexuses) which correspond to the twelve astral signs of the zodiac, the symbolic Cosmic Man. One-half minute of revolution of energy around the sensitive spinal cord of man effects subtle progress in his evolution; that half-minute of Kriyā equals one year of natural spiritual unfoldment.

Paramhansa Yogananda, *Autobiography of a Yogi*

Jyoti Mudrā – Awakening the Inner Light

Jyoti mudrā ('Gesture of Light', 'Inner Light') is the gesture by which light is created. In yogic texts this *mudrā* is also referred to as *yoni mudrā.* The Sanskrit word *yoni* denotes the womb of creation, the source of origin because, like the baby in the womb, the yogi practising *yoni mudrā* has no contact with the external world, and therefore no externalization of consciousness. *Yoni* is also used to name the female sexual organs. The word *mudrā* in this case denotes a physical practice which has an effect on the mind.

In India there are specially carved stones in the form of a *yoni* in which the *Śivalingam* rests, representing the source which supports and sustains spiritual consciousness. When *yoni* unites with *linga,* it becomes a symbol of divine procreative energy. *Linga* is the mind, *yoni* is the *kūtastha,* the point between the eyebrows, where the spiritual light manifests. *Ājñā chakra* is the root of *kūtastha.* Everything evolves from *kūtastha-yoni.* When the *linga*-mind settles in *kūtastha-yoni* the yogi experiences a state of infinite bliss.

Yoni mudrā is also known as *śanmukhi mudrā. Śan* means 'seven' and *mukhi* means 'gates'. *Śanmukhi* means 'closing of the seven gates or doors of sense-perception' (the seven are the two eyes, two ears, two nostrils, and the mouth). *Jyoti mudrā* and *śanmukhi mudrā* are both Hāṭha Yoga practices mentioned in the *Hāṭha Yoga Pradīpikā* by Yogi Swatmarama. *Pradīpikā* actually means 'self-illuminating' or 'that which illumines'.

In the practice of *jyoti mudrā* the mind is brought to a point of relaxed absorption within itself. By closing the outer doors or gates of the senses, *jyoti mudrā* redirects the energy of the senses inward, which induces *pratyāhāra* (sense-withdrawal).

The purpose of *jyoti mudrā* is to take the energy awakened by the *kriyā prāṇāyāma* meditation in the spine, and draw it upward to focus it at the Spiritual Eye. *Jyoti mudrā* calms the breath in the region from the throat to the point between the eyebrows, enabling you to see the radiant light of the Spiritual Eye within the radiance of stirring light in the form of absolute stillness and absolute peace.

During the practise of *jyoti mudrā,* certain nerves in the body are affected and rejuvenated. This is similar to an acupressure rejuvenation treatment (though this is not the main purpose of *jyoti mudrā*). Around the head and eyes there are many acupuncture points which can be targeted to direct energy. The nerves that are affected when the fingers and thumbs are in position on the face in *jyoti mudrā* are as follows.

- The **thumbs** indirectly inhibit sensory stimulation of the eighth cranial nerve.
- The **index fingers** touch over the infratrochlear branch of the ophthalmic and the infraorbital branch of the maxillary.
- The **middle fingers** depress the nasal branches of the infraorbital nerve.
- The **little fingers** affect the inferior labial branch of the mandibular nerve (sensory branch).

Jyoti Mudrā Technique

1. To practise *jyoti mudrā,* sit upright with the head, neck and spine aligned in a comfortable meditation pose. Relax your whole body and with your eyes closed, bring your focused attention to the Spiritual Eye.
2. As you inhale slowly to a mental count of 10–12, drawing a current of prāṇic energy up in the spine, raise your arms in front of your face with the elbows parallel to the floor and pointing sideways, so that you are ready to assume

the finger positions of the *jyoti mudrā* at the end of the inhalation.

3. Hold the breath, and the prāṇic energy you have drawn up the spine, at the Spiritual Eye. While holding the breath, close off all the sense openings in your head with the fingers and thumbs of both hands, so that all the energy lights up the region between your eyebrows. Close the ears by pressing the ear flaps in with your thumbs. Place the index fingers on the corners of the eyelids, resting on the lower bony eye sockets and gently press the eyes shut (do *not* put pressure on the eyes). Use the middle fingers to close the two nostrils by pressing the soft nares of the nose just below the nasal bones. Place the ring fingers above the lips and the little fingers below the lips, squeezing the mouth shut, with the fingertips touching each other.
4. Now, while holding *jyoti mudrā*, feel that your fingers are directing the *prāṇic* energy to the Spiritual Eye and, with deep focused awareness, turn your gaze inward toward the inner light of the Spiritual Eye. If you perceive light at the Spiritual Eye, experience it and merge into it, and feel that you are one with the light.

   Hold your breath in for as long as comfortable without strain, and while gazing into the Spiritual Eye, mentally chant *Oṁ* continuously at the mid-point between your eyebrows. Observe the light of the Spiritual Eye that is gathering and intensifying at that point. You may see that the light condenses into a golden ring around a sphere of dark blue, with a scintillating silvery-white five-pointed star at its centre. This is the Spiritual Eye.
5. Then, release *jyoti mudrā* by removing your fingers from the sense openings. Keep the fingers and thumbs resting gently on the face, so that you are ready to practise another round of *jyoti mudrā.*
6. Exhale slowly to a mental count of 10–12, feeling the current of prāṇic energy descend to the *mūlādhāra chakra* at the base of the spine.

This completes one round of *jyoti mudrā*. Practise three rounds, then sit in stillness in meditation. *Jyoti mudrā* can be practised at any time, but the best time is in the deep calmness at night. After calming your mind and relaxing your body with deep breathing in *ujjayi prāṇayama*, practise *hong-sau*, followed by *jyoti mudrā*, then the Aum Technique of listening to the inner vibratory sound of Aum.

Meditation

After your practice of *jyoti mudrā*, focus your attention within, in the stillness of your inner Self. As you meditate, visualize yourself surrounded by God's all-pervading light. Feel yourself bathing in that radiant light.

Gaze deeply into the inner light of the Spiritual Eye, the seat of spiritual perception. Dive deep into the light, immerse and absorb your whole being in that light, until you feel at one with it. Feel God's Presence in the light as joy (bliss).

Mentally affirm: 'God's omnipresent light permeates every particle of my being. I am filled and sustained with that Divine light and joy.'

Chapter 15

Sūrya Namaskāra

Sūrya namaskāra literally means 'salute to the sun'. It is a sequence of 12 poses that join harmoniously together in a *vinyāsa* (a continuous dynamic flow), creating a dynamic balance in the mind, body, breath and *chakras*. The sun symbolizes spiritual consciousness, light, purity, vitality and clarity. Regular daily practice of *sūrya namaskāra* imparts the power and radiance of the sun. *Sūrya namaskāra* pays homage to the 12 houses of Vedic astrology. Each morning the *yogi* would perform the 12 *āsanas* of the *sūrya namaskāra vinyāsa* as a homage to the 12 houses in his or her birth chart, while concentrating on each *chakra*, with the corresponding *sūrya namaskāra mantra* repeated mentally before the change of each *āsana* position. This enabled the *yogis* to align their energies with the stars of their personal birth chart and align and integrate the *tattvas* of the body with the *tattvas* as they appear in the universe. When *sūrya namaskāra vinyāsa* is performed in a steady, meditative and rhythmic manner, it reflects the rhythms of the universe and the 12 zodiac phases of the year.

Sūrya namaskāra has a direct vitalizing effect on the solar energy which flows through the *piṅgalā nāḍī*, the solar *prānic* channel associated with the right nostril. Daily performance of *sūrya namaskāra* regulates the *piṅgalā nāḍī*, balancing both the mental and physical energy systems.

Sūrya namaskāra is an integrated spiritual yoga practice that combines the benefits of *āsana*, yogic breathing, concentration and meditation. There are no limitations due to age or gender; it can be practised safely by anyone fit and healthy enough to perform the movements, and very little is required to derive immediate and tangible benefit.

Sūrya namaskāra is traditionally performed at the beginning of *āsana* practice, because it warms the body and increases the circulation.

Benefits: It stretches and strengthens all the major muscle groups of the body, flexes the spine forward and backward, opening the front and back of the spine. Stretches the long muscles of the back and the backs of the legs in the forward bends. Stimulates and balances the circulatory, respiratory, digestive and endocrine systems. It warms the body by increasing the blood circulation, and oxygenates the blood to the brain. It coordinates breath, mind and body, and influences the pineal gland and hypothalamus. Balances the *chakras*.

Contraindications: Do not practise if you suffer from high blood pressure, coronary artery disease, or if you have had a stroke. Avoid practising if you have a slipped disc or sciatica. Women should not practise at the onset of menstruation.

The following 12 *āsanas* in the sequence of *sūrya namaskāra* bring the body and mind into balance, directing the life-force into stability and equilibrium, and into the realm of stillness in preparation for meditation, which is the path of Rāja Yoga.

I bow to that Primordial Supreme Being who has taught this science of Hāṭha Yoga, which is the best means for attaining Rāja Yoga for all those who desire to do so.

Benediction from the *Gheraṇḍa Saṁhitā*

Salutations to Adinātha [Śiva] who expounded the knowledge of Hāṭha Yoga, which like a staircase leads the aspirant to the higher pinnacled Rāja Yoga.'

Hāṭha Yoga Pradīpikā, 1: 1

Position 1 – Prāṇamāsana (Standing Prayer Pose)

Stand with the feet slightly apart. Bring the palms of the hands together in front of the chest, over the centre of your being, the heart centre, in the gesture of respect and devotion. Close your eyes and become aware of your whole body. Remain still and become centred within and become aware of your natural breath. Feel gratitude for the life-giving energy of the sun, and for the vitalizing *prāṇa* that flows through you.

Mantra: *oṁ mitrāya namaḥ* (Salutations to the Friend of all)
Bīja mantra: *hrāṁ*
Chakra: *anāhata*

Position 2 – Hasta Uttanāsana (Raised Arm Pose)

Inhale as you sweep your arms out to the side and raise them parallel above your head, with the upper arms aligned with the ears, with the palms facing the front. Feel the front of your spine lengthening and your chest and heart opening as you gently stretch backward. Look upwards. Feel that you are opening your being to vitality and life.

As a variation, instead of stretching the arms and torso upwards, you can stretch slightly backwards.

Mantra: *oṁ ravaya namaḥ* (Salutations to the Shining One)
Bīja mantra: *hrīṁ*
Chakra: *viśuddha*

Position 3 – Pādahastāsana (Hand to Foot Pose)

Exhale with the arms extended above the head and fold the torso forward from the hip joints and lumbar spine, keeping the spine long and straight. Let the forward bend be an offering of gratitude. Place your hands facing forward, flat on the floor, on either side of the feet with the fingers in line with the toes. Release your head so that its weight can stretch the long muscles of the back. Keep the knees straight and draw the thigh muscles up. At the end of the exhalation, draw your chin in and try to touch the knees with the forehead. Lift the sitting bones by contracting the abdominal muscles.

If your legs and back muscles are tight and you are unable to keep the knees straight in the forward bend, then bend the knees a little.

Mantra: *oṁ sūryāya namaḥ* (Salutations to the Lord of the Sun, initiator of activity)
Bīja mantra: *hrūṁ*
Chakra: *svādhiṣṭhāna*.

Position 4 – Aśva Sañcālanāsana (Horse Pose)

Inhale and step the right foot back as far as you can, lowering the top of the foot and the leg to the floor. The toes of the left foot are tucked under. Bend the left knee so that it is directly over the left foot with the shin perpendicular to the floor (the position of least strain for the knee ligaments). Press the pelvis forward. The hands remain parallel on the floor in line with the left foot. At the same time, lift the chest and raise your head and extend the front of your throat and neck without strain, looking upwards at the midpoint between the eyebrows.

Mantra: *oṁ bhānave namaḥ* (Salutations to the One who illumines)
Bīja mantra: *hraīṁ*
Chakra: *ājñā*

Position 5 – Adho Mukha Svanāsana (Downward-facing Dog Pose)

While exhaling, extend the left foot back beside your right foot. Form an inverted V with your body by raising the hips, buttocks and pelvis, and straighten the arms and legs. Push your heels down to the floor. The feet are facing forward, spaced 25 cm (12 in.) apart. Slightly roll your arms inwards, as you press the thumbs and index fingers to the floor. Move your shoulder blades toward your hands and your spine toward your pelvis. Look towards your navel, and draw your belly toward your spine, so that you concave the abdomen. Pull up on the knees and thighs. Stretch evenly from shoulders to hips, and down through the backs of the legs. Relax the head and back of the neck. Hold the pose for five breaths, feeling the flow of the breath.

Mantra: *oṁ khagāya namaḥ* (Salutations to He who moves quickly in the sky)
Bīja mantra: *hraūṁ*
Chakra: *viśuddha*

Position 6 – Aṣṭāṅga Namaskāra (Eight-limbed Salutation)

Without moving the hands and feet from the previous pose, bend your elbows and knees as you lower your body to the floor. Lower your chest, raise the hips and buttocks, and align the shoulders with the fingers. Only the knees, chest, chin and hands are in contact with the floor. Hold the breath out.

Mantra: *oṁ pūsṇe namaḥ* (Salutations to the One who cherishes and nourishes the world)
Bīja mantra: *hraḥ*
Chakra: *maṇipūra*

Position 7 – Bhujaṅgāsana (Cobra Pose)

Place your legs slightly more than hip-width apart, and your palms under the shoulders with the fingertips resting directly beneath the shoulders. Press your elbows against the body, inhale, and push up using your back muscles with some support from your arms. Slowly raise your torso, but keep the navel on the floor, while gently pressing the legs down. Try to create the back arch from the mid-back, rather than the neck and the lower back. Keep the chest open. Lift the head and extend the neck without straining it, and gaze straight ahead.

Mantra: *oṁ hiraṇyagarbhāya namaḥ* (Salutations to the Golden Embryo from which the creation emanates)
Bīja Mantra: *hrāṁ*
Chakra: *svādhiṣṭhāna*

Position 8 – Return to Position 5

Exhaling, make a smooth transition from the cobra pose into downward facing dog pose by coming up on to the knees first and then pushing back, lifting the hips high, with the head and trunk down. With the hands shoulder-width apart, press the heels of the hands into the floor, stretch the fingers and extend the arms up. As you press with your hands, try to lift your forearms away from the floor; this will help to stabilize your shoulders. Pull up on the knees and thighs, and stretch down through the backs of the legs. Press your hips back and up. Relax the head and back of the neck. Hold the pose for five breaths, feeling the flow of the breath.

Mantra: *Oṁ marīcaye namaḥ* (Salutations to the Lord of the dawn)
Bīja mantra: *hrīṁ*
Chakra: *viśuddha*

Position 9 – Return to Position 4

Start to inhale as you step forwards. Bend the left leg and step the left foot between the hands. The left knee should be directly over the left foot with the shin perpendicular to the floor. The hands should remain parallel on the floor in line with the left foot. Push the pelvis forward. At the same time, lift the chest and raise your head and extend the front of your throat and neck without strain, looking upwards at the midpoint between the eyebrows.

Mantra: *oṁ āditāya namaḥ* (Salutations to Āditi, the Celestial Divine Mother of every existing form and being)
Bīja Mantra: *hrūṁ*
Chakra: *ājñā*

Position 10 – Return to Position 3

Exhale with the arms extended above the head and fold the torso forward from the hip joints and lumbar spine, keeping the spine long and straight. Place your hands facing forward, flat on the floor, on either side of the feet with the fingers in line with the toes. Release your head so that its weight can stretch the long muscles of the back. Keep the knees straight and draw the thigh muscles up. Try to touch the knees with the forehead. Lift the sitting bones by contracting the abdominal muscles.

Mantra: *oṁ sāvitre namaḥ* (Salutations to Sāvitre, the power of consciousness)
Bīja mantra: *hraīṁ*
Chakra: *svādhiṣṭhāna*

Position 11 – Return to Position 2

Inhale, stretch fully and radiantly with a straight spine as you sweep your arms out to the side and raise them parallel above your head, aligning the upper arms with your ears, with the palms facing the front. Feel the front of your spine lengthening and your chest and heart opening. Look upwards.

Mantra: *oṁ arkāya namaḥ* (Salutations to the One whose radiance arcs across the sky)
Bīja mantra: *hraūṁ*
Chakra: *viśuddha*

Position 12 – Return to Position 1

Stand with the feet slightly apart. Bring the palms of the hands together in front of the chest, over the centre of your being, the heart centre, in the gesture of respect and devotion. Close your eyes and become aware of your whole body. Remain still and centred within and become aware of your natural breath as you feel the energy radiating through your body, and the heart-opening effects of this sequence.

Mantra: *oṁ bhāskarāya namaḥ* (Salutations to the luminous One, the source of enlightenment and wisdom)
Bīja mantra: *hraḥ*
Chakra: *anāhata*

This completes one round of *sūrya namaskāra.* As you perform the second round repeat all 12 positions, but this time in positions 4 and 9 – *aśva sañcālanāsana* – step the *left* foot back as far as you can, lowering the top of the foot and the leg to the floor. Bend the *right* knee so that it is directly over the left foot with the shin perpendicular to the floor.

Time of Practice

Although *sūrya namaskāra* can be practised at any time of the day, the early morning hours according to the yogis are particularly auspicious for practising *yogāsanas, prāṇāyāma* and meditation. The hour just before sunrise is called *Brahma muhūrta* ('time of God'); at this time there is a preponderance of sattvic or spiritual vibrations in the atmosphere, giving calmness and clarity to the mind. These early hours of the morning, from 3.45 a.m. to 5.30 a.m., and when the day breaks into night, between 6.30 p.m. and 8.00 p.m., are good times to practise *sūrya namaskāra, prāṇāyāma* and meditation. You will gain the maximum spiritual benefit during these times. Getting up early will allow you to experience inner stillness as you tune in to the Great Silence and offer your energy to a greater intention to start your day. You will be able to balance and awaken the energy in your *chakras*.

Different Ways of Practising Sūrya Namaskāra

You can open and close your *sūrya namaskāra* practice by reciting the *Gāyatrī mantra,* a prayer to the Divine Light. The *Gāyatrī* is a cosmic rhythm consisting of 24 syllables arranged as a triplet of eight syllables each. The individual syllables contain an energy seed for each of the seven celestial planes of light. The *chakras* become tuned to the energy of each of the seven planes of light by chanting the *Gāyatrī mantra* for many repetitions over a period of time.

The *Gāyatrī mantra* first appears in the ancient *Ṛg Veda* (III, 62: 10) and later in the *Yajur Veda* and *Sāma Veda,* and in the *Upaniṣads*.

Oṁ bhūr bhuvaḥ svaḥ
tat savitur vareṇyaṁ
bhargo devasya dhīmahi
dhiyo yo naḥ pracodayāt

We meditate upon the splendour of the Divinity, the Spiritual Effulgence of that Adorable Supreme Divine Reality, the Source of the Physical, the Astral and the Heavenly Spheres of Existence. May that Supreme Divine Being enlighten our intellect so that we may realize the Supreme Truth.

Slow meditative practice

Practise three to 12 rounds slowly with awareness on the movements of the body synchronized with the breathing.

Faster practice for physical benefits

Practise three to 12 rounds, moving more quickly, but still synchronizing the breathing with the movements of the body. Advanced students may increase the number of rounds, but strain and fatigue should be avoided.

Slow meditative practice using the long mantras

Practise three to 12 rounds slowly with your concentration on the *chakra* related to the yoga pose, while mentally reciting the full *mantra* for that particular pose. For example, in the first position – *prāṇamāsana* – concentrate on the heart *chakra*, and mentally chant *oṁ mitrāya namaḥ*.

Slow meditative practice using the short bīja mantras

Alternatively, you can practise reciting the *bīja mantras*, the seed syllables that set up powerful energy vibrations within the mind and body. For example, in the first position, concentrate on the heart *chakra*, and mentally chant the short *bīja mantra 'hrāṁ'*.

Chapter 16

Chanting in the Chakras

Begin with a prayer.

Heavenly Father, transfer my consciousness from the physical body to the astral spine and from it through the seven *chakras* to Cosmic Consciousness, where Thy glory and Light reign in the fullness of Thy manifestation; where the Life Force reigns in all Thy power. *Oṁ* Peace, Amen.

Chanting the Chakra Bīja Mantras

Chanting is an effective way to activate energy throughout the body. This practice activates and tunes the *chakras* using the sound vibration of the *bīja* (seed-syllable) *mantras.* Each seed *mantra* has a unique power, which clears the *chakras* of blockages so that they can function efficiently. This prepares the way to meditation.

Sit comfortably and relaxed in a meditative posture with the head, neck and spine aligned. Close the eyes.

Bring your awareness to *mūlādhāra chakra.* Inhale deeply and as you exhale, chant continuously aloud the *bīja mantra* '*laṁ*'. Feel the *bīja mantra* vibrating at *mūlādhāra chakra – laṁ, laṁ, laṁ, laṁ . . .*

It will depend on the length of your inhalation and exhalation on how many times you repeat the *bīja mantra.* If you have quite a good lung capacity you may be able to chant it 20 times in one exhalation.

Start at *mūlādhāra chakra* and ascend through the *chakras* to *ājñā chakra* chanting the following *bīja mantras* in a focused meditative way, feeling the vibration at the six *chakras*:

Chakras and bīja mantras

Chakra		*Bīja mantra*
First *chakra*	*Mūlādhāra*	*Laṁ*
Second *chakra*	*Svādhiṣṭhāna*	*Vaṁ*
Third *chakra*	*Maṇipūra*	*Rāṁ*
Fourth *chakra*	*Anāhata*	*Yaṁ*
Fifth *chakra*	*Viśuddha*	*Haṁ*
Sixth *chakra*	*Ājñā*	*Oṁ*

Mentally Chanting the Chakra Bīja Mantras

Sit comfortably and deeply relax in a meditative posture with the head, neck and spine aligned. Close the eyes, and bring your awareness to your breath, and as you breathe in feel the spaciousness expanding in the spine. Change the centre of your consciousness from the body and senses to the spine . . . Feel the subtle astral spine by slightly and gently swaying the upper body from left to right . . . Then, feel your consciousness with the breath move up and down the spine several times, from the *mūlādhāra chakra* at the base of the spine to the point between the eyebrows . . . Now bring your attentive awareness to the first *chakra, mūlādhāra,* breathe into this area and mentally repeat the seed *mantra 'laṁ'* once, feel it vibrating and resonating in the *chakra* . . . At the end of the exhalation remain in the stillness for short while. Then, feeling the energy pulsating like a magnetic current in *mūlādhāra,* expand it upwards to the second *chakra, svādhiṣṭhāna,* and mentally repeat the seed *mantra 'vaṁ'*, feeling it vibrating and resonating in the *chakra* . . . Then again, pause in the stillness, and feel the intensity of energy resonating in the *chakra*.

In the same way, continue ascending through the other four *chakras* mentally repeating the seed *mantra* for each and pausing in stillness after chanting in each *chakra*.

Then descend through the spinal passage to each *chakra* in the reverse order, mentally repeating the seed *mantras* for each and pausing in stillness after chanting in each *chakra*.

Perform 9–12 rounds.

Mentally Chanting the Oṁ Mantra in the Chakras

Sit comfortably and deeply relax in a meditative posture with the head, neck and spine aligned. Close the eyes, and bring your awareness to your breath, and as you breathe in feel the spaciousness expanding in the spine. Change the centre of your consciousness from the body and senses to the spine . . . Feel the subtle astral spine by slightly and gently swaying the upper body from left to right . . . Then, feel your consciousness with the breath move slowly up and down the spine several times, from the *mūlādhāra chakra* at the base of the spine to the point between the eyebrows at the Spiritual Eye . . . Your attention should be internalized on the *chakras* and the breath . . . Now exhale and take your awareness to the root of the spine in *mūlādhāra chakra*, and mentally chant *Oṁ* there. As you do this, visualize a lotus blossom with its petals turned downward . . . Feel the *mantra* vibrating with resonance awakening this *chakra*. As it awakens the lotus petals turn upward, sending rays of light up to the next *chakra* . . . Inhale and raise the energy in the spine to the second *chakra, svādhiṣṭhāna* . . . Exhale and mentally chant *Oṁ*, and again feel the *mantra* resonating and awakening this *chakra*, and sending rays of light upward to the next *chakra*.

Continue in this way mentally chanting *Oṁ* as you ascend through the other four *chakras*. Then reverse the process, descend through the spinal passage and *chakras* mentally chanting *Oṁ* at each *chakra* from *ājñā* to *mūlādhāra*.

Perform 9–12 rounds or continue the practice until you feel that your consciousness is transferred from the body into the astral spine.

Then meditate in the stillness, feeling your consciousness expanding into the Infinite. Feel the *Oṁ* vibration expanding up to the crown *chakra* into silence, stillness and space.

Chanting Oṁ with the Musical Notes

Another way of chanting *Oṁ* through the *chakras* is to use an Indian harmonium keyboard that is pumped by a bellows. With your focused attention internalized on the *chakra* and *Oṁ mantra*, chant *Oṁ* aloud three times in each *chakra* as you ascend the spinal passage, and once in each *chakra* as you descend. Practise several times until you feel that your consciousness is transferred from the body into the astral spine. End with with your attention focused at the Spiritual Eye in the sixth *chakra*. Then meditate in the stillness feeling your consciousness expanding into the Infinite. Feel the *Oṁ* vibration expanding up to the crown *chakra* (*sahasrāra*) into silence, stillness and space.

Chakras and musical notes

Chakra		Western musical note
First *chakra*	*Mūlādhāra*	G (below middle C)
Second *chakra*	*Svādhiṣṭhāna*	A
Third *chakra*	*Maṇipūra*	B♭
Fourth *chakra*	*Anāhata*	D
Fifth *chakra*	*Viśuddha*	E♭
Sixth *chakra*	*Ājñā*	
Medulla – negative pole		F
Spiritual Eye – positive pole		G (above middle C)

Chanting the Gāyatrī Mantra in the Chakras

The *Gāyatrī mantra* first appears in the ancient *Ṛg Veda* (III, 62: 10), and later in the *Yajur Veda* and *Sāma Veda,* and in the *Upaniṣads*. Before the Vedas, there was a time when Brahma, the Supreme Creator was once in deep meditation and the subtle inner vibration of *Gāyatrī* revealed itself to Him. It was later revealed to the Vedic sage Viśvamitra, a preceptor of Śrī Rāma, incarnation of Lord Viṣṇu. As a reward for his many years of deep meditation and penance, the Supreme Being revealed to him the *Gāyatrī mantra.* This was to be a gift for all humanity.

It is beyond human competence to describe the glory of Gāyatrī.

Gāyatrī is the primordial mantra that destroys sins and promotes wisdom, and nothing in the world is more important than wisdom. The Gāyatrī Mantra has specifically manifested so as to destroy falsehood and establish truth.

Ādi Shaṅkarāchārya

The *Gāyatrī mantra* is the most sacred prayer of the *Ṛg Veda,* a prayer for light, for illumination. It is addressed to the Immanent and Transcendent Divine, which has been given the name Savitur, meaning 'that from which all is born'. The *Gāyatrī* may be considered as having three parts: (1) praise, (2) meditation, (3) prayer. First, the Divine is praised, then it is meditated upon in reverence, and finally an appeal is made to the Divine to awaken and strengthen the intellect. The *Gāyatrī* possesses both the power of *mantra* and the power of prayer, and so has both an intrinsic power through its mere utterance alone, and also an instrumental power, which is derived from the understanding of its meaning and philosophical significance.

Gāyatrī is the essence of all *mantras,* and all spiritual powers and potencies are contained within it. Of all *mantras* the *Gāyatrī* is supreme. *Gāyatrī* is the Mother of the Vedas

(*Vedamāta*), the source of Divine Wisdom. *Gāyatrī* is the bestower of all that is beneficial to the person who chants it with faith.

The *Gāyatrī mantra* contains all the important *bīja mantras*.

Oṁ – Symbolizes God; Absolute Reality.
Bhūr – Represents earth; the physical plane. It also refers to the body made up of the *pañcha bhūtas* (five elements) that constitute *prakṛti* (nature).
Bhuvaḥ – Represents *bhuva loka*, the middle world; the subtle or astral plane. It is also the life-force (*Prāṇa Śākti*) that animates the body, that comes from the power of the Self (*Ātma Śākti*).
Svaḥ – Represents the third dimension or celestial region, known as *svarga loka* and all the luminous *lokas* (spheres) above.
Tat – That, the essential essence.
Savitur – Luminous, bright, sun-like, inner power of spiritual light, which leads one to Self-realization.
Vareṇyaṁ – Finest, best, fit to be sought.
Bhargo – Effulgence; destroyer of obstacles.
Devasya – Divine, resplendent, shining.
Dhīmahi – We meditate.
Dhiyo – Our being of intelligence, intellect, understanding.
Yo – Who, which.
Naḥ – Our.
Pracodayāt – May enlighten, direct, inspire.

The *Gāyatrī* invokes the splendour and power that pervades the Sun and the Three Worlds to activate the *chakras*, and awaken and strengthen the intelligence.

The *Gāyatrī mantra* is chanted for the attainment of cosmic consciousness and for awakening the intuitive powers. It has the power to destroy all delusions, energize *prāṇa* and bestow health, longevity, radiance and illumination. Unless the intellect is illumined the Truth remains hidden and veiled by *tamas guṇa* (dark forces) and *rajas guṇa* (passion). The light of *Gāyatrī mantra* removes the obstructions of *tamas* and *rajas* from the mind's mirror, and reflects the Light of Truth in it by which the mind is illumined. The Radiant Light of *Gāyatrī* burns *karma* and blesses with liberation.

Meditation on the Gāyatrī

Among hymns, I am Brihat-Saman; among poetic metres, I am Gāyatrī.

Śrī Krishna, *Bhagavad Gītā*, 10.35

Through meditation on the *Gāyatrī,* one can become aware of the inner motivating principle of the *pañcha bhūtas* (five elements) that constitute *prakṛti* (nature), the five *prāṇas* or vital airs in the body, and the five sheaths (*kośas*), which enclose the soul (*ātma*).

The best times to repeat the *Gāyatrī* are at dawn, noon and dusk. These times are known as the three *sandhyas*. These auspicious times are beneficial for spiritual practices. But the repeating of *Gāyatrī* is not limited only to these times. As long as the mind and heart are pure when repeating *Gāyatrī*, and it is pronounced clearly and correctly with concentration, and without haste or hurry, it can be repeated at any time of the day or night, and everywhere.

This *mantra* should not be repeated in a mechanical way with the mind wandering on other thoughts. The *Gāyatrī mantra* is synonymous with the Divine and therefore it should be repeated with reverence, faith and love. In this way, if the *Gāyatrī mantra* is chanted correctly, the atmosphere in which you are chanting it will be illumined by the vibrations produced by the *mantra*. The *Gāyatrī mantra* will illumine your intellect and light your spiritual path.

To realize the *Gāyatrī mantra*'s blissful effect one needs to chant it regularly for a considerable period of time. *Gāyatrī* activates the nerve ganglia and the *nāḍīs*, activating the power that yields spiritual knowledge. Repetition of the *Gāyatrī mantra* produces notes which mingle with the vibrations already existing in nature. This activates the centres of power in the *chakras* and the brain. Divine spiritual light and power are infused into the *chakras*, connecting them to the higher spiritual realms, aligning us with the forces of nature, both subtle and gross, and increasing our connection to the vital force of the sun. The mind becomes infused with solar spiritual energy, and our spiritual perceptions increase.

Gāyatrī Mantra Sādhanā (Spiritual Practice)

When you sit for meditation, if possible chant the *Gāyatrī mantra* 108 times. This is one *mālā* (a rosary of 108 meditation beads). You can use your *mālā* beads to count, using one bead for each recitation of the *Gāyatrī mantra*. This will take approximately 15 minutes to recite. The maximum benefit of chanting the *mantra* is said to be obtained by chanting it 108 times. However, one may chant it for 3, 9, or 18 times when pressed for time.

For your spiritual practice of meditation on the *Gāyatrī mantra*, start by chanting one *mālā* every morning. If you can devote more time, then chant 3–5 *mālās*. If you are on a personal spiritual retreat you may wish to chant 10 *mālās*, which will take about 2½ hours. You can also do a 40-day discipline of chanting 10 *mālās* each morning for 40 days. This is called a *Gāyatrī purascharana*. Or you can choose a number of repetitions per day, and chant that for 40 days.

An extended practice of chanting the *Gāyatrī mantra* (135,000 repetitions, equivalent to 1,250 rounds of a *mala*) is said to give the meditator a noticeable level of *mantra siddhi* (power of the *mantra*).

By chanting the *Gāyatrī mantra* for many repetitions over a period of time, the *chakras* become tuned to the energy of each of the seven planes of light. Eventually, after long devoted practice, the entire subtle body becomes attuned with all the planes of spiritual light, making the aura radiant.

If one practises this spiritual discipline sincerely, one realizes God in a very short time. So, practise this Gāyatrī Mantra meditation regularly and attain illumination.

Practice of Gāyatrī meditation destroys all karmas and sins. By purifying the heart and the mind, it opens the third eye of illumination.

Sadguru Sant Keshavadas

The *Gāyatrī* is a cosmic rhythm consisting of 24 syllables arranged as a triplet of eight syllables each. The individual syllables contain an energy seed for each of the seven celestial planes of light. The syllables of the *Gāyatrī mantra* are constructed and arranged in such a way that the major portion of *vāyu* (air) inhaled during the process of chanting moves downward towards the seat of *kuṇḍalinī śākti.* The escape of *vāyu* is minimized by the nature of the chest cavity's contraction caused by the systematic chanting of the *mantra*. The collected *vāyu* descends to the *mūlādhāra chakra* and the heated *prāṇa vāyu* strikes the *kuṇḍalinī*, activating it to ascend upward through the *chakras*.

Chanting the syllables of the *Gāyatrī mantra* positively affects all the *chakras* in the subtle body. The cyclic chanting of the *Gāyatrī mantra* stimulates the subliminal power centres in the subtle body. The pressure of the tongue, lips, vocal cords, palate and the connecting regions in the brain generated by continuous chanting of the 24 syllables of the *Gāyatrī mantra* creates a resonance or a vibration in the *nāḍīs* of the subtle body. This awakens the *chakras* and a sublime magnetic force arouses in the meditator that attracts the vital currents of *Gāyatrī śākti* immanent in the Infinite realms.

The Practice of Gāyatrī Mantra Meditation

There are two forms of *Gāyatrī Mantra* – the short form and the long form.

Meditation on the short form of Gāyatrī Mantra

Oṁ bhūr bhuvaḥ svaḥ
tat savitur vareṇyaṁ
bhargo devasya dhīmahi
dhiyo yo naḥ pracodayāt

We meditate upon the splendour of the Divinity, the Spiritual Effulgence of that Adorable Supreme Divine Reality, the Source of the Physical, the Astral and the Heavenly Spheres of Existence. May that Supreme Divine Being enlighten our intellect so that we may realize the Supreme Truth.

Sit facing east or north in a comfortable and relaxed meditation posture, with the head, neck and spine aligned. Close your eyes and bring your focused attention to the midpoint between the eyebrows at the Spiritual Eye, on the Light of Truth.

Chant the *Gāyatrī mantra* clearly and rhythmically without strain.

Begin first by inhaling and then chant *Oṁ*.
Pause . . . inhale again, and chant *bhūr bhuvaḥ svaḥ*.
Pause . . . inhale, and chant *tat savitur vareṇyaṁ*
Pause . . . inhale, and chant *bhargo devasya dhīmahi*
Pause . . . inhale, and chant *dhiyo yo naḥ pracodayāt*

When you have chanted all the syllables of the *mantra*, meditate upon its meaning with feelings of joy, devotion and faith.

Meditation on the long form of Gāyatrī Mantra

Oṁ bhūr	1st *chakra* (*mūlādhāra*)
Oṁ bhuvaḥ	2nd *chakra* (*svādhiṣṭhāna*)
Oṁ svaḥ	3rd *chakra* (*maṇipūra*)
Oṁ manaḥ	4th *chakra* (*anāhata*)
Oṁ janaḥ	5th *chakra* (*viśuddha*)
Oṁ tapaḥ	6th *chakra* (*ājñā*)
Oṁ satyam	7th *chakra* (*sahasrāra*)

Oṁ bhūr bhuvaḥ svaḥ
tat savitur vareṇyaṁ
bhargo devasya dhīmahi
dhiyo yo naḥ pracodayāt

I invoke the Earth Plane, the Astral Plane, the Celestial Plane, the Plane of Spiritual Balance, the Plane of Human Spiritual Knowledge, the Plane of Spiritual Austerities, the Plane of Ultimate Truth.

We meditate upon the splendour of the Divinity, the Spiritual Effulgence of that Adorable Supreme Divine Reality, the Source of the Physical, the Astral and the Heavenly Spheres of Existence. May that Supreme Divine Being enlighten our intellect so that we may realize the Supreme Truth.

Sit facing east or north in a comfortable and relaxed meditation posture, with the head, neck and spine aligned. Close your eyes and bring your focused attention to the midpoint between the eyebrows at the Spiritual Eye, on the Light of Truth.

Chant the *Gāyatrī mantra* clearly and rhythmically without strain.

In this longer form of the *Gāyatrī mantra* you can also concentrate on the *chakra* that correlates with each *mantra*. For example, chant *Oṁ bhūr* while concentrating on the *mūlādhāra chakra*, and so on.

The practice of prāṇāyāma with the Gāyatrī Mantra

The short form of the *Gāyatrī mantra* can be practised in conjunction with *nāḍī śodhana prāṇāyāma* – subtle channel purifying breath or alternate nostril breathing.

Nāḍī śodhana prāṇāyāma opens the channels of prāṇic energy and purifies them; balances the left and right brain hemispheres; activates all the brain centres; has a soothing effect on the nervous system; helps in stilling the mind in meditation and in activating *kuṇḍalinī śākti*.

The two nostrils directly influence through the breath the subtle *iḍā* and *piṅgalā nāḍīs*. The balance in terms of the relative dominance at any time between the left *iḍā* and right *piṅgalā* currents strongly influences our inner and outer experience through the mind and senses. When these two currents are in balance, and both are flowing equally, the *prāṇa* begins to move into the central *suṣumnā nāḍī*, as the *kuṇḍalinī*.

The chanting of the *Gāyatrī mantra* in conjunction with *nāḍī śodhana prāṇāyāma* should not be attempted until you have perfected the timing of the breath ratio (inhalation, retention and exhalation). Those who are not experienced in *prāṇāyāma* should begin by purifying the *nāḍīs* using the basic beginners' method as follows:

First Stage (15 days): Sit in a comfortable meditation posture with the head, neck and spine aligned.

Close the right nostril with the right thumb. Inhale deeply through the left nostril and exhale. *Repeat five times.*

Then, close the left nostril with your ring (third) finger and open the right nostril. Inhale and exhale deeply. *Again, repeat five times.*

This completes one cycle. Practise five cycles for the first five days, then 15 cycles for the next five days. For the last five days practise 25 cycles.

Second Stage (15 days): Close the right nostril and inhale through the left. Then, close the left nostril and exhale through the right. *Repeat five times.*

Now reverse the sequence by inhaling through the right nostril and exhaling through the left. *Repeat five times.*

This completes one cycle. Practise five cycles for the first five days, then 15 cycles for the next five days. For the last five days practise 25 cycles.

Third Stage (15 days): Following the 1:2:2 ratio for beginners you can begin with a count of 4:8:8. The internal breath retention and the exhalation are both double the inhalation. Inhale for a slow count of four, hold the breath in. for a slow count of eight, and exhale for a slow count of eight. (If you find this difficult and you are straining to hold the breath then decrease to 2:4:4. You must never force or strain the breath and lungs.)

Close the right nostril and inhale through the left for a count of four. Close both nostrils and hold the breath for a count of eight. Open the right nostril and exhale for a count of eight.

Now reverse the sequence by inhaling through the right nostril for a count of four, holding the breath for eight, and exhaling through the left for eight. *Repeat five times.*

This completes one cycle. Practise five cycles for the first five days, then 15 cycles for the next five days. For the last five days practise 25 cycles.

When you become proficient in this practice and feel comfortable with the 4:8:8 count you can gradually increase the duration of inhalation (*pūraka*), inner breath retention (*antar kumbhaka*) and exhalation (*recaka*).

Over a period of time, you will be able to change the breath ratio from the beginners' 1:2:2 to the advanced 1:4:2. The first stage of the advanced ratio is 4:16:8 which we will use in conjunction with chanting the short form of the *Gāyatrī mantra.*

Nāḍī śodhana prāṇāyāma with Gāyatrī Mantra

Use the breath count 4:16:8. Sit facing east or north in a comfortable and relaxed meditation posture, with the head, neck and spine aligned. Close your eyes and bring your focused attention to the midpoint between the eyebrows at the Spiritual Eye, on the Light of Truth.

Place your right hand in the *viṣṇu mudrā*, so that the index and middle fingers are curled into the palm of the hand, and use the thumb and the ring finger to regulate the nostrils (by opening and closing them).

Close the right nostril and inhale through the left for a slow steady count of four. While inhaling mentally chant *Oṁ*.

Close the left nostril with the ring finger while keeping the right nostril closed with the thumb. Hold the breath for a slow steady count of 16 in silence.

Keep the left nostril closed and exhale through the right for a slow steady count of eight, and mentally chant: *bhūr bhuvaḥ svaḥ*, allowing the syllables of the *mantra* to flow out with the breath rhythmically and harmoniously.

Inhale through the right nostril for a slow steady count of four, and mentally chant *tat*.

Close both nostrils and hold the breath out for a slow steady count of 16 in silence.

Exhale through the left nostril for a slow steady count of eight while mentally chanting: *savitur vareṇyaṁ*.

Then, relax by breathing normally through both nostrils.

Slowly and steadily inhale through both nostrils, then close the right nostril with your thumb and exhale through the left for a slow steady count of four mentally chanting: *bhargo*.

Close both nostrils and hold the breath out (external breath retention) for a slow steady count of 16 in silence.

Inhale through the right nostril for a slow steady count of eight while mentally chanting: *devasya dhīmahi*.

Exhale through the right nostril for a slow steady count of four while mentally chanting: *dhiyo*.

Close both nostrils and hold the breath out for a slow steady count of 16 in silence.

Inhale through the left nostril for a slow steady count of eight while mentally chanting: *yo naḥ pracodayāt*.

Then exhale through both nostrils, and return to normal breathing. Sit quietly and meditate on the inner meaning of the *Gāyatrī mantra.*

In the initial development of your spiritual practice these 12 stages may be repeated two or three times, which can be increased later as you make gradual progress.

Kuṇḍalinī Chakra Meditation with the Gāyatrī Mantra

In the *Gāyatrī mantra* there are seven rhythms (*vyāhṛtis*): *Oṁ Bhūr, Oṁ Bhuvaḥ, Oṁ Svaḥ, Oṁ Manaḥ, Oṁ Janaḥ, Oṁ Tapaḥ,* and *Oṁ Satyam*. These seven rhythms correspond with the seven chakras in the subtle body.

Gāyatrī chart

Rhythm (*Vyāhṛti*)	Principles (*Tattvas*)	Subtle properties of elements (*Tanmātras*)	*Chakra*	Number of lotus petals
Oṁ Bhūr	*Pṛithvī* (Earth)	*Gandha* (Smell)	*Mūlādhāra*	4
Oṁ Bhuvaḥ	*Jala* (Water)	*Rasa* (Taste)	*Svādhiṣṭhāna*	6
Oṁ Svaḥ	*Agni* (Fire)	*Rupa* (Form)	*Maṇipūra*	10
Oṁ Manaḥ	*Vāyu* (Air)	*Sparśa* (Touch)	*Anāhata*	12
Oṁ Janaḥ	*Ākāśa* (Ether)	*Śabda* (Sound)	*Viśuddha*	16
Oṁ Tapaḥ	*Mahat* (Intelligence)	*Buddhi* (Cosmic Mind)	*Ājñā*	2
Oṁ Satyam	Puruṣa (Consciousness)	*Prakṛti* (Primordial energy)	*Sahasrāra*	1,000

Meditation Practice – Chakras/Gāyatrī

Sit in a comfortable and stable meditation posture with the head, neck and spine aligned. Relax the mind and body by taking a few deep breaths. Inhale deeply and tense the whole body, then exhale and let go of all tension from the body and relax. Place your hands, palms down, on the knees in *jñānā mudrā* (gesture of knowledge). Close your eyes and relax, with your awareness on the natural breath.

Bring your focused attention to the base of your spine at the perineum, the location of the root *chakra, mūlādhāra.*

1. Inhale deeply and retain the breath, and visualize a deep red, four-petalled lotus at the base of the spine in *mūlādhāra chakra,* with its petals symbolizing its petalled rays of energy turning upwards toward the brain. As you exhale chant *Oṁ bhūr.*
2. Feel that the energy is awakened and offer the current of energy up to the *svādhiṣṭhāna chakra,* at the genital centre. As you inhale deeply and retain the breath, visualize a vermilion-coloured six-petalled lotus with its petalled rays of energy turning upwards toward the brain. As you exhale, chant *Oṁ bhuvaḥ.*
3. Now feel the energy of *kuṇḍalinī śākti* rising from the second *chakra* to *maṇipūra,* the third *chakra* at the navel centre. As you inhale deeply and retain the breath, visualize a bright yellow ten-petalled lotus, with its petalled rays of energy turning upwards toward the brain. As you exhale chant *Oṁ svaḥ.*
4. Feel the energy of *kuṇḍalinī śākti* rising from the *maṇipūra* to *anāhata,* the fourth *chakra* at the heart centre. As you inhale deeply and retain the breath, visualize a blue 12-petalled lotus, with its petalled rays of energy turning upwards toward the brain. As you exhale chant *Oṁ manaḥ.*
5. Feel the energy as the Divine *Śākti* enters the fifth *chakra, viśuddha,* at the throat centre. As you inhale deeply and

retain the breath, visualize a smoky grey-violet-coloured 16-petalled lotus, with its petalled rays of energy turning upwards toward the brain. As you exhale chant *Oṁ janaḥ.*

6. Now with your eyes still closed, concentrate deeply with your gaze at the midpoint between the eyebrows at the beautifully white, like the full moon, two-petalled lotus, *ājñā chakra,* the Spiritual Eye centre. As you inhale and retain the breath, meditate on the Divine *Śākti* and feel the energy in the *chakra*. As you exhale chant *Oṁ tapaḥ.*

Continue concentrating at the Spiritual Eye. As you inhale and retain the breath, meditate on the inner light and feel the energy flowing upwards toward the brain, in the *sahasrāra chakra,* the thousand-petalled lotus at the crown of the head, lustrous and whiter than the full moon. As you exhale chant *Dhiyo yo naḥ pracodayāt* ('Illumine our intellect').

Sit in the stillness of silent meditation for some time. Then prepare to let your consciousness begin the descent down through all the *chakras*. Feel that you are bringing the *Kuṇḍalinī Śākti* back to Her abode at the base of the spine. Chant *Oṁ* and feel that the *kuṇḍalinī śākti* energy is returning to the two-petalled lotus of the sixth centre, *ājñā chakra,* from the thousand-petalled lotus, at the crown *chakra*. Now feel the energy descend to *viśuddha,* the throat *chakra,* and chant the *bīja mantra 'haṁ'*. Continue down to the 12-petalled heart *chakra,* and chant the *bīja mantra 'yaṁ'*. Now bring your consciousness down to the ten-petalled lotus of the solar plexus, *maṇipūra chakra,* and chant the *bīja mantra 'ram'*. Continue the descent into the six-petalled lotus of the second centre, *svādhiṣṭhāna chakra.* And finally *Kuṇḍalinī Śākti* returns to Her abode in the four-petalled lotus *mūlādhāra chakra,* at the base of the spine, in the centre of the root *chakra*. Chant the *bīja mantra 'laṁ'*. The *kuṇḍalinī* prāṇic energy coils up at the base of the spine bringing a sense of completion and groundedness to the purification and balance of the *chakras*.

Again, sit in the stillness of silent meditation. Feel the

re-energized and revitalized body of your energy system. Remain with your attention and awareness focused at the Spiritual Eye and in the higher regions of the brain.

Pray sincerely from the essence of your being. Feel that your are one with the wholeness of ultimate Reality:

'Infinite Spirit, help me to clarify my mind and awareness. May my consciousness be illumined and be fully awakened to Self-Realization. *Oṁ*, peace, Amen.'

As you relax the mind and go deeper into meditation, begin to be aware of your eternal form, your spiritual form of light . . . you the spiritual being, with awareness, with recognition, are in charge of your mind, body and senses. Feel the unlimited capacity of your own mind, and as the master of your mind, focus this unlimited energy on peace and on Truth. The kingdom of God is just behind the darkness of your closed eyes, and the first gate that opens to it is your peace.

Exhale, and as you relax, feel your consciousness expanding into the Infinite. In your calmness, feel peace spread everywhere – within and without. Immerse yourself in that ineffable peace. Peace is your natural state of being, in this state of purity and peace you rediscover the love that is within you . . . a love for yourself, love for each member of your human family, and love for God, the ultimate Reality.

Centred in the stillness of peace, develop a deeper awareness of the Divine within you. Completely relax into the present-moment stillness and allow the love of the Divine to fill your entire being. Mentally affirm divine calmness and peace: 'I am an instrument of peace and a channel through which Divine Love flows.'

Pray for universal peace and send out thoughts of love and goodwill to all. While keeping your concentration at the Spiritual Eye, visualize cosmic energy surrounding and entering your body through the medulla and the Spiritual Eye, then flowing into the spine. Feel the energy flowing down through the whole length of your arms into your hands. Rapidly rub the palms of your hands together to create warmth and healing energy in them. Then raise the arms upwards with the opened hands in front of you, feeling the life current of prāṇic energy flowing from the medulla into the spine, especially through both palms, with a warm tingling sensation. Then chant *Oṁ* three times, sending the healing energy and blessings into and around the world. Visualize the healing energy as a powerful stream of God's Light sending healing, harmony, divine peace and pure love into the world.

Then finish your meditation by chanting *Oṁ* three times, followed by *Oṁ shanti, shanti, shanti, peace, Amen.*

After finishing, remain sitting quietly in the stillness and peaceful energy for some time, before returning to the activities of the day. Try to practise the presence of God, living in the awareness and consciousness of the Divinity within you, by remaining peacefully and calmly present in the moment as you go about your activities and work. As Paramhansa Yogananda said: 'Be actively calm and calmly active.'

You are not far from the Kingdom of God.

Mark 12: 34

For in Him we live and move and have our being.

Acts 17: 28

Kuṇḍalinī Prāṇāyāma with Oṁ Mantra

Sit in a comfortable and stable meditation posture with the head, neck and spine aligned. Relax the mind and body by taking a few deep breaths. Inhale deeply and tense the whole body, then exhale and let go of all tension from the body and relax. Place your hands palms down on the knees in *jñānā mudrā* (gesture of knowledge). Close your eyes and keep your inner gaze at the Spiritual Eye. Allow your body and mind to relax and let go. Relax, with your awareness on the natural breath for a few minutes, then bring your awareness and concentration to the *mūlādhāra chakra* at the base of the spine.

Raise your right hand and position it in the *viṣṇu mudrā* for practising alternate nostril breathing. Close the right nostril with the right thumb, exhale and inhale through the left nostril to the count of three *Oṁ*s. As you inhale feel that you are drawing in prāṇic energy.

Close both nostrils and hold the breath for a count of 12 *Oṁ*s. As you retain the breath, feel that you are sending the current of prāṇic energy down the spine into the *mūlādhāra chakra.* Feel the current striking against the lotus in the *mūlādhāra chakra.*

Exhale slowly through the right nostril to the count of six *Oṁ*s. Now inhale through the right nostril, repeating the process in reverse. Practise five complete rounds.

After finishing, remain sitting quietly in meditation in stillness for as long as you are able to.

Chapter 17

Spiritual Eye Meditation/ Hong-Sau Mantra

The purpose of the Hong-Sau technique is to help you to free your attention from outwardness, and to withdraw it from the senses, for breath is the cord that keeps the soul tied to the body . . . By dispassionately watching the breath coming in and going out, one's breathing naturally slows, calming at last the peace-disturbing activity of the heart, lungs and diaphragm.

Paramhansa Yogananda, *The Wisdom of Yogananda*

Hong-Sau – Introduction

Hong-sau (pronounced 'hong-saw') is an ancient Sanskrit *mantra* for focusing and calming the mind, and deepening the concentration for meditation. It stills the restless thoughts, withdraws the mind from the senses, and calms and interiorizes the prāṇic energy in the body. *Hong-sau* is another way of pronouncing the *mantra 'haṁsa'*, which means 'I am He,' 'I, the manifest Self, am He, the Unmanifest Spirit (the Absolute).' When *haṁsa* is repeated continuously it becomes *So-ham,* which means 'He (the Absolute) am I.' Repeated either way the meaning is the same. By consciously repeating mentally the seed-syllable *mantra 'hong-sau'*, in conjunction with the concentration on the breath, you affirm that the individual self is one with the Infinite Spirit. *Hong* as the inhaling breath, represents the contraction of consciousness into finitude. *Sau* as the exhaling breath, represents the expansion of consciousness and the reabsorption of differentiation into pure unity.

Hong-sau possesses a vibratory connection with the breath. It is the natural, subtle sound of the breath – *hong* vibrates with the inhalation, corresponding to the ascending current in the *iḍā nāḍī*. *Sau* vibrates with the exhalation, corresponding to the descending current in the *piṅgala nāḍī*. Throughout the 24 hours of the day the breath flows in and out 21,600 times in a continuous *mantra* of *hong-sau*. Unknowingly, we are all repeating this *mantra* in a process of automatic and continuous recitation. In Yoga, continuous recitation of a *mantra* is called *ajapā-japā*. The *japā* becomes *ajapā* when the *mantra* gets repeated in the mind on its own. The difference between *ajapā-japā* and *japā* is that *ajapā-japā* goes on subconsciously all the time,while *japā* is done consciously.

In an early Śaiva Tantra (7th century CE) it is stated that *ha* is the inhaling breath, representing Śākti, and *sa* is the exhaling breath, representing Śiva. The syllables *ha* and *sa* are joined by the nasal sounding *ṁ*, which represents the individual soul (*jīva*). Joined together *ha* plus *ṁ* plus *sa* form the *mantra haṁsa*.

In the *Vijñānabhairava*, an old meditation text, each complete breath is described as an automatic repetition of the *mantra 'haṁsa'*, or *so-ham* when the exhalation is emphasized. The syllable *haṁ* vibrates with the experience 'I am', and the syllable *sa* or *so* vibrates with the expansive experience of 'That' (the Absolute). Therefore, when we repeat *haṁsa* or *so-ham* with awareness, we affirm 'I am That'.

If the technique of *hong-sau* is practised correctly and regularly, it will eventually bring you to a state of mental calm and stillness, withdrawing your energy inward, and leading you naturally into a breathless state as the pauses between your breaths naturally lengthen. In the breathless state the twofold vibration of *hong* and *sau* merge into the single omnipresent vibration of *Oṃ*.

When Paramhansa Yogananda was a young boy, whose name then was Mukunda, he would sit alone in meditative silence practising *hong-sau* for four hours in one sitting. Observing his breath, while gazing at his Spiritual Eye, he would interiorize his consciousness so deeply into his subtle spine that he was without breath, or in the 'breathless state'. He called *hong-sau*, the 'baby Kriyā', in which he was referring to the supreme Kriyā meditation technique that was originally passed down through a succession of enlightened Kriyā Yoga Masters from Mahāvatar Babaji to himself. Yogananda once said, 'One hour of *hong-sau* practice equals twenty-four hours of sitting in the silence.'

Meditation – Hong-Sau

Preparation – Ujjayi Prāṇāyāma

Before we begin this meditation, it is useful to learn the *prāṇāyāma* technique of *ujjayi* breathing (*ujjayi* – 'victory from expansion'), as you will use this *prāṇāyāma* to breathe in your spine to direct the energy upward in the spine to your Spiritual Eye. *Ujjayi* breathing creates the expansion and upward movement of the prāṇic energy through the *suṣumnā nāḍī*. The two distinctive characteristics of *ujjayi* breathing are an action in the throat that produces a soft snoring-like sound of 'haaa' in the vocal diaphragm and epiglottis, and a smooth and even flow of the breath in both the inhalation and the exhalation. This is a very soothing and calming breath that keeps your awareness and attention on the breath. To breathe in *ujjayi*, close your mouth and breathe in through the nose, so that your breath moves upwards along the back of your throat with the smooth, continuous and steady 'haaa' sound, and out through your nose with a continuous and steady, sibilant sound of 'saaa'. The purpose of the *ujjayi* sound is to attune your attentive awareness to each breath.

Ujjayi breath warms and filters the air entering the nostrils, producing a calming and relaxing effect in the brain. On a subtle level it generates prāṇic energy within the body and induces meditation.

Stage 1: Tensing and Relaxing

Sit in a comfortable and steady meditation posture with your head, neck, and spine aligned. To relax your mind and body, inhale deeply, hold the breath, and tense all the muscles in your body. Hold both the breath and the tension in your muscles for a few seconds, then simultaneously release the breath and the tension and relax. Repeat the process of tensing and relaxing three times, then finish by completely relaxing. Feel the relaxation and the flow of energy into your body.

Stage 2: Loma Prāṇāyāma

Now continue to remain relaxed as you practise a minimum of nine rounds of *loma* ('natural force') *prāṇāyāma*. This is a three-part equal ratio, breathing through both nostrils. Inhale for a count of 12, hold your breath for a count of 12, exhale for a count of 12 (12:12:12). If this is not within your lung capacity, keep the ratio, but halve the count to 6:6:6. The number of rounds can be gradually increased over a period of time to 27 rounds.

Stage 3. Inhaling in the Spine

Continue to sit in a comfortable and stable meditation posture with your head, neck and spine aligned. Place your hands palms upward in *chin mudrā* (gesture of consciousness) on your knees Relax your mind and body by taking a few deep breaths. Close your eyes and relax, with your awareness on the natural breath.

Now as you inhale smoothly and continuously in *ujjayi* breath feel a cool current of prāṇic energy slowly rising up the spine from *mūladhāra chakra* to the medulla oblongata and then through the brain to the Spiritual Eye. While gazing with your attentive awareness into the Spiritual Eye, mentally chant *Oṁ* three times, and then, breathing smoothly and continuously in *ujjayi* breath, slowly exhale and feel a warm current of prāṇic energy descending back down through the spine to *mūladhāra chakra*. In this way, continue several times breathing up and down the spine until you feel the warmth and sensation of a tingling current of energy in your spine. Then, on the next inhalation, draw the breath up the spine to the medulla, and then through the brain to the Spiritual Eye.

Stage 4: Sit Calmly for Meditation

Remain sitting still and concentrate your relaxed attention at the point between the eyebrows. Let go of all thoughts and be totally centred in the present here and now moment. Place your hands palms upward on your knees in *chin mudrā*. Close your eyes and relax, with your awareness on the natural breath. Keep your body still and bring your attention and awareness to the frontal part of your brain at the Spiritual Eye. If your mind wanders, gently bring it back to the practice of watching your breath with awareness. Watching the breath is a present-moment experience. Focus and interiorize your mind by deepening your attentive awareness and concentration.

Hong-Sau Technique

Step 1: Now with your body and mind still, uniting your mind with the present moment, begin the practice of *hong-sau*. With closed eyes and without straining, gently lift your gaze upward to the point between the eyebrows, and with steady concentration and inner calmness look into the Spiritual Eye, the seat of intuition and omnipresent perception.

Step 2: Feel the natural breath flow in and out of your nostrils. Feel the tactile sensation of the breath, and try to feel where the flow of breath is strongest in your nostrils. The sensation of breath is subtle, and yet it is quite distinct when you learn to tune into it. Once you have found the point where the breath is strongest in your nostrils (usually just inside the tip of the nose) then concentrate on the breath at that point. It is from this point that you will follow the whole passage of your breath.

Step 3: Use this single-point sensation inside the nose to keep your attention fixed. Observe each breath as it flows in and out with attention and precision in present-moment awareness, taking it one split second on top of another. In this way, continuous and unbroken awareness will eventually result.

Step 4: Then as your breath becomes quieter, begin to feel the sensation of the air that passes in and out of your nostrils higher up in the nasal passages at the point between your eyebrows. Concentrate at this point. As your concentration deepens, your breathing will begin to slow down, and you will be able to focus on it more clearly, with fewer and fewer interruptions.

Step 5: As you concentrate on your breath, make no attempt to control the breath. This is not a yoga breathing exercise. With focused awareness just let go, and allow this natural process of subtle breathing to move in its own rhythm.

Step 6: First inhale deeply, then slowly exhale. Then as the next inhalation naturally arises and flows into your nostrils, feel the breath where it enters the nostrils, and with your inner focus, mentally follow the breath with the *bīja mantra 'hong'*. Imagine that the breath itself is making this sound.

Step 7: And as your breath flows out naturally, mentally follow it with the *bīja mantra 'sau'*. Remember, make no attempt to control your breath; you are only observing it, so just allow its flow to be completely natural. The process of *hong-sau* is not a breathing technique, it is simply being consciously aware, with your concentration on the *hong-sau mantra* as the breath flows. Feel that your subtle breathing is silently making the sounds of *hong-sau*. By simply observing your breath it will become calm.

Step 8: Continue focusing on your Spiritual Eye and as the breath naturally flows in mentally follow it with the *mantra* '*hong*'. As the breath flows out, mentally follow it with the *mantra* '*sau*'. By concentration on the breath, the breath gradually diminishes. This gradual subtle refinement leads naturally to an interiorized calm meditative state. When the mind is united with the breath flowing all the time, you will be able to focus your mind in the present moment.

Step 9: If your mind begins to wander on to other thoughts, gently bring it back to the awareness of watching the breath in unison with *hong-sau*.

Step 10: As you go deeper into the practice of watching your breath in unison with *hong-sau,* the breathing becomes more subtle and the mind becomes very calm and still. You may notice that between each inhalation and exhalation, there is a natural space or pause, a point of complete stillness, where the form of the breath is briefly suspended. This is the space of the innermost Self. Softly focus your attentive awareness on those pauses, where the inhalation subsides and the exhalation arises. And, as your mind becomes more calmly interiorized, notice the spaces gradually extending between your breaths, into a breathless state, and enjoy that experience of expansion into the freedom of infinite spaciousness while inwardly gazing into your Spiritual Eye. Then, when the breath naturally returns, continue with the practice of *hong-sau*.

During and after practising *hong-sau,* remain in the inner calmness for as long as possible. Remember and feel that inner calmness from your meditation, and remain calmly centred within your Self, allowing the calmness to permeate your everyday consciousness as you go about your daily activities.

The Breathless State

By silently observing the breathless state, you let go of the identification with your body, and realize that you are something other than mind–body–senses. You realize that your body is sustained by something other than the gross breath. In the perfect stillness in between the breaths of the breathless state, you perceive the reality of pure consciousness within you.

This breathless state, in which there are long pauses between the breaths, happens naturally. There is no need to be anxious or alarmed, for the breath returns automatically when the body needs to breathe again. Just remain calm and aware in the meditative stillness and inner freedom from body-consciousness, and allow the breath to flow effortlessly, and stop and start naturally, without any control by you.

Chapter 18

The Inner Spine – Tunnel of Light

'I saw the light at the end of the tunnel' is an expression that you have probably heard in relation to 'out of body experiences', or 'near-death experiences', which I discussed in my earlier chapter on the subtle bodies. This experience of seeing the light at the end of the tunnel is buried deep in our subconscious minds. It is the long-lost memory of an absolute fact that has to do with our birth into the physical body and the final transition from embodiment at the moment of death. However, we do not have to experience a serious accident or suffer a serious illness and die to discover the divine light. We do not have to wait for the after-life. God as Light and the Kingdom of God are within us. That eternal light is within us all, present here and now. Through deep scientific meditation, like Kriyā Yoga meditation, we can discover and experience the Inner Light and consciousness of God within us; as Jesus said: 'The Kingdom of God is within you' (Luke, 17: 21).

Behind the wave of your consciousness is the sea of God's presence.

Paramhansa Yogananda

The subtle or astral inner dimensional tunnel of light, is the main energy channel flowing from the upper brain to the base of the spine, referred to as the *suṣumnā.* The seven dimensions of reality, energy and consciousness, known as *chakras*, intersect along the *suṣumnā*.

The primordial energy, *kuṇḍalinī śākti*, when awakened from her dormant state at the base of the spine in the form of the life-force, can awaken the *chakras*. For our consciousness consciously to make the return journey through the tunnel of light (*suṣumnā*) to the crown *chakra, kuṇḍalinī*, must be awakened. The *suṣumnā* must be cleared of blocked energy, psychological barriers, and the *vṛttis*. The *chakras* have to be activated and opened, so that the true Self can be completely expressed. A strong upward flow of energy dissolves the *vṛttis*.

The inner-dimensional tunnel of light corresponding to our spinal column is our 'tree of life'. All souls travel to and from the Light of God, the Ultimate Reality, through this tunnel of light into the Kingdom of God. The spine is the inner-dimensional tunnel through which consciousness ascends to superconsciousness.

By concentrating at the point between the eyebrows at the Spiritual Eye, which is a reflection of the energy that enters the body through the medulla in meditation, you can enter the tunnel of divine Light.

Concentration on this point acts like a magnet, drawing the prāṇic energy flow upward, interiorizing the energy in the higher brain centres.

During deep Kriyā Yoga meditation, meditators who have concentrated their inner gaze on the astral Spiritual Eye of intuitive perception, have beheld a bright gold ring of light forming around the entrance of a deep blue tunnel of light, and a brilliant silvery-white, five-rayed star of divine light suddenly appearing off in the distance, towards the end of the tunnel. This is the gateway to Cosmic Consciousness.

The gold ring of light represents Cosmic Energy. The blue light represents the omnipresent Intelligence of the Christ Consciousness. The silver-white star represents Infinite Spirit or Cosmic Consciousness.

Meditation – Spiritual Eye

Sit in a comfortable meditation posture with the head, neck and spine upright. To relax completely, first inhale deeply and hold the breath, then tense all the muscles in your body. Then, with a deep exhalation, completely relax your whole body. Repeat this exercise three times.

Close your eyes and, with a steady inner gaze, concentrate at the midpoint between the eyebrows, at the Spiritual Eye. Then become aware of your natural breath; do not try to control it in any way but just be aware of each breath as it flows in and out. Be still, and remain calmly centred within as you continue to gaze into the Spiritual Eye.

In the calmness of your soul become aware of the point in the centre of your brain, the pituitary gland – centred inward from the root of the nose, between the two temples, and downward from the crown of your head. This is the divine centre of consciousness, *ājñā chakra.* Light particles moving outward from this divine centre of consciousness at the pituitary centre, through the optical nerves into your eyes, will begin to project images. The tunnel of light will begin to appear on the screen before your gaze. Realize that your eyes are projecting before you the image of the place in which your consciousness is existing at the moment, within your astral spine, the *suṣumnā.*

The light of the body is the eye: if therefore thine eye be single, thy whole body shall be full of light.

Matthew 6: 2

As your meditation deepens, the inner light will be seen reflected at the Spiritual Eye as a tunnel of light. First feel yourself surrounded by a great sense of joy and freedom as you journey through and bathe in the gold ring of light of Cosmic Energy. Then, passing through the deep blue light of omnipresent Intelligence, feel the inner freedom of non-attachment to all worldly thoughts. As you continue your journey through the tunnel of light feel your consciousness expanding into infinite joy. As the blue light becomes lighter, enter the radiant white light of the five-rayed star – gateway to the Infinite Spirit – and let any remaining perception of existing apart from the reality of pure Consciousness dissolve. Calmly and joyfully remain in the present, in the stillness, in the timeless dimension of here and now . . . And like the wave or a bubble dissolving into the ocean, remain in the limitless awareness of your essential spiritual Self united in oneness with Cosmic Consciousness.

The light of God shines at the Spiritual Eye, the inner door that leads the soul's awareness into the realm of divine glory of God. The reality of God that dwells in each person can be known by entering the sanctuary of illumined consciousness.

Lahiri Mahasaya

Meditation at Sahasrāra, the Crown Chakra

After meditating at the Spiritual Eye, bring your attention and awareness to the crown of your head and continuously repeat the *Śākti mantra 'hrīṁ shrīṁ klīṁ param īśvari svāhā'*.

Concentrating at the crown of your head and repeating this powerful *mantra* will move the energy up to the crown *chakra*. As you repeat the *mantra* feel the sound resonating at the crown *chakra,* energizing the thousand-petalled rays of *sahasrāra*.

The energy of *sahasrāra* is Pure Consciousness, it is all-pervasive, it permeates all dimensions of reality. As you meditate at the crown *chakra,* continue to keep your inner gaze at the Spiritual Eye while concentrating at the crown of your head or just above the crown. Remain in the stillness in *sahasrāra* for as long as you can, and listen for the inner sound reverberation of *Oṁ*. Feel your oneness with the omnipresent Spirit. Visualize and feel your consciousness expanding in Divine Consciousness. Feel God's light and joy flowing through you and become absorbed in the vibration of God's ineffable peace, and know that in essence you are the Infinite.

Chapter 19

Bhrāmarī Kriyā Meditation in Sahasrāra

By this yogic practice of Bhrāmarī, yogis with their minds absorbed in bliss, feel an indescribable joy in their hearts.

Hāṭha Yoga Pradīpikā, 2: 68

Bhrāmarī comes from the Sanskrit word, *bhrāmarā*, meaning 'bumblebee'. This is because the humming breath sounds like the drone of a bee. Through concentration on this sound the mind reaches a state of self-absorption.

The practice of *bhrāmarī prāṇāyāma* calms the nervous system and the mind, and has a direct effect on the *viśuddha chakra*. According to tantric texts, there is a subtle centre called *talu chakra* which controls the pineal and pituitary glands. When the nerve endings in the upper part of the throat and the roof of the mouth are stimulated by *bhrāmarī*, the *talu chakra* is affected too. *Bhrāmarī* also promotes concentration, and prepares you for meditation, bringing you into contact with your inner Self.

Practising *bhrāmarī* involves vibrating the vocal cords as in humming, but with additional resonance in the nasal cavity. As the tongue is slightly pressed toward the roof of the mouth, the sound shifts from the throat to the nasal cavity.

Step 1: Sit relaxed in a comfortable meditation posture with the head, neck and spine aligned. Rest your hands on the knees in either *jñanā mudrā* or *chin mudrā*, and close your eyes and relax the whole body.

Step 2: Inhale deeply through the nose using *ujjayi* breath, creating a mild suction effect in the throat. Feel a cool sensation in the throat and relate the cool sensation to the spine as you draw the current of energy up from the base of the spine to the medulla.

Step 3: Hold the breath in and apply *mūla bandha,* followed by *jālandhara bandha*. Bring your focused attention and awareness to the Spiritual Eye and, while holding the breath in, mentally chant *Oṁ* six times at the Spiritual Eye.

Raise your hands to the level of your ears. Press the ear-flaps closed with your thumbs and rest the fingers of each hand on your forehead.

Then, release the chin lock followed by the anal lock, and slowly exhale with your mouth and lips closed, but with the teeth slightly separated, and make a long, deep, continuous, steady humming sound like that of a bee for the duration of your exhalation. Feel the humming-bee sound vibrating throughout your brain.

Take one or two normal breaths in between each round. Practise five rounds, increasing to 12 rounds as you progress with this technique.

Meditation

Now sit with the body still and relaxed. The perception of God begins when the body and mind are still. Continue to sit in the stillness with your eyes closed and your inner gaze at the Spiritual Eye. Feel the resonance and vibration from the *bhrāmarī kriyā* in your brain. Feel this vibration expanding to the crown of the head, then to about 8 cm (3 in.) above your head. Meditate in the tranquil silence, being aware of your Self as pure existence-being. Remain in this still state of absorbed meditation for as long as it persists.

Mentally affirm: 'The Spirit of God vibrates and resonates within me as pure joy.'

After-Effects-Poise

Remain sitting in the stillness of calm meditative silence for as long as you can. Lahiri Mahasaya, the great Kriyā guru of Swami Śrī Yukteswar, referred to this stage as the 'after-effects-poise' of Kriyā. Feel that superconscious forces are entering the mind, brain, nervous system and body. Feel that these subtle forces are cleansing and purifying the physical and subtle systems, renewing and vitalizing you.

Then continue your day, maintaining present-moment awareness of the Reality of God within you.

Navi Kriyā – Awakening Energy at the Maṇipūra Chakra

Navi kriyā (pronounced as 'nabi kriya') is one of the original Kriyā Yoga techniques that was taught by Lahiri Mahasaya. The purpose of this technique is to stimulate and awaken the prāṇic energy at *maṇipūra chakra,* at the navel centre, and then to draw the energy from *maṇipūra* up the spine to the Spiritual Eye of the *ājñā chakra.* While practising this technique, a calm energy is experienced in the lower part of the abdomen (the prāṇic current there is called *samāna vāyu*). By directing prāṇic energy up the spine, *navi kriyā* is a good preparation technique for meditation.

To practise *navi kriyā,* sit upright with the head, neck and spine aligned in a comfortable meditation pose. Relax your whole body and, with your eyes closed, bring your focused attention to the point between the eyebrows at the Spiritual Eye.

Now, starting from *mūlādhāra chakra,* as you slowly inhale, mentally chant *Oṁ* successively at each of the five *chakras* up through the spine to the sixth centre, *ājñā chakra.* Mentally chant *Oṁ* at the medulla (negative pole of *ājñā chakra*), then mentally chant *Oṁ* at the Spiritual Eye (positive pole of *ājñā chakra*).

Slowly tilt the chin down towards your throat cavity to perform chin lock. Concentrate at the *maṇipūra chakra* (navel centre) on the front of the body, and while breathing normally, mentally chant *Oṁ* 100 times to stimulate that centre. You can count *Oṁ* 100 times on your *mālā* beads.

Then raise the chin and slowly tilt the head back and, without strain, gently contract the muscles at the back of the head. Feel the energy move to the medulla oblongata, and then down through the spine to the *maṇipūra chakra*. While breathing normally, mentally chant *Oṁ* 25 times on the counterpart of the navel on the back of the body to stimulate that centre.

Then slowly raise your head to its normal upright position, and, with concentration, mentally chant *Oṁ* successively at each of the five *chakras* from the Spiritual Eye at the point between the eyebrows down to *mūlādhāra chakra* at the base of the spine.

This completes one round of *navi kriyā*. Practise six to 12 rounds.

Meditation

After your practice of *navi kriyā*, focus your attention within, in the stillness of your inner Self. As you meditate, keep your inner vision at the Spiritual Eye. Feel the upward flow of energy in the *suṣumnā* in the subtle spine flowing to the medulla oblongata. Concentrate there first for a short while, then feel that you are dissolving the ego-consciousness (seated at the medulla) into superconsciousness at the Spiritual Eye. With a steady inward gaze, concentrate your attention deeply at that point between the eyebrows. Then, feeling that joy within, expand that blissful consciousness into the Infinite.

Mentally affirm: 'I am pure consciousness awakening in God.'

Chapter 20

Oṁ – The Cosmic Vibratory Sound

Patañjali speaks of God (in the Yoga sutras) as the actual Cosmic Sound of Aum heard in meditation. Aum is the Creative Word, the sound of the Vibratory Motor. Even the yogi-beginner soon inwardly hears the wondrous sound of Aum. Receiving this blissful spiritual encouragement, the devotee becomes assured that he is in actual touch with divine realms.

Paramhansa Yogananda, *Autobiography of a Yogi*

Tasya vācakaḥ Praṇavaḥ. [The expression of Īśvara (Supreme Lord) is Aum (*Praṇavaḥ*).]

Patañjali, *Yoga Sūtras*, 1.27

That indwelling omnipresent sole reality is verbally alluded to as Oṁ, which is the ever-new and eternal cosmic sound that is heard in all natural phenomena (thunderclap, roaring of the ocean, wind rustling trees in the forest) and even in the reverberations of the musical instruments, the hum of engines, and the distant din of the carnival crowd.

Swami Venkatesananda

Oṁ (pronounced as Aum) the *Praṇava,* is the Divine Cosmic Vibration that is God. In the Bible, the Word that St John refers to is the Creative Vibration: 'In the beginning was the Word, and the Word was with God and the Word was God' (John 1: 1). From the centre of God's consciousness of absolute stillness and oneness, vibrated the Cosmic Sound, *Oṁ* into Creation.

Kriyā prāṇāyāma and contemplation of Aum are the keys to effective meditation practice. Practise of these methods makes possible the fulfilment of one's highest aspirations.

Lahiri Mahasaya

The Significance of Aum

The sacred sound syllable *mantra 'Oṁ'* (Aum), the vibration of consciousness that is always in the present, eternal, and infinite, signifies the Supreme Being. In ancient times *Oṁ* was referred to as *Praṇava* (reverberating; sounding).

Oṁ is the Primal Sound, the Cosmic Vibration and energy of creation that exists prior to the manifest activities of the three constituent aspects or *gunas* that originate from *Prakṛti* (Primordial nature): *sattva* (luminosity, goodness, purity) *rajas* (activity, desire, passion), *tamas* (darkness, inertness, ignorance).

The relationship between Īśvara and *Oṁ* is eternal; the Creator and the energy of creation cannot be separated.

Sound is an evolute of *Prakṛti*. On this level *Oṁ* remains a sound vibration and Īśvara remains a special and distinct transcendental being. But on another level *Oṁ* is non-different from Īśvara, it is permeated by Īśvara and so it manifests the qualities of Īśvara.

The mind which is also an evolute of *Prakṛti* is unable to comprehend that which is more subtle than itself. The mind can only come into direct contact with Īśvara through the cosmic vibratory sound *Oṁ*, with which Īśvara's divine presence, grace, and potency are permeated and empowered.

In the *Yoga Sutrās* (1: 28), Patañjali states: '[R]epetition [of the cosmic vibratory sound *Oṁ*] can lead to the realization of its meaning.' We can experience Īśvara's Divine Presence by continually repeating [*japā*] His Name, the *mantra 'Oṁ'* (Aum). To invoke awareness of the presence of the Divine and to go deeper in meditation *Oṁ* should be recited with deep concentration, devotion and reverence, in inner silence, while meditating on its meaning, and listening to the inner subtler sound behind the audible Vibratory Sound of *Oṁ*.

Aum and Oṁ – Sounding the Mantra

Aum is an extension of the *Oṁ* energy. *Oṁ* extended becomes Aum, which has a greater power to expand, with a greater force, and *prāṇic* energy to it.

The *mantra* 'Aum' may be sounded aloud, whispered, or repeated mentally. In sounding the word Aum the three syllables are sounded equally. The 'a' and 'u' become blended into 'o'.

The long vowel letter 'Ā' (pronounced like aw in dawn) on an energetic level, represents Self-expansion and awareness of the Absolute. It starts at the back of the mouth, with the tongue lying relaxed on the lower palate, the sound resonating deeply from the lower abdomen. Repeat a long 'aaw', like opening your mouth to reveal your tonsils. This will expand and release the prāṇic energy.

The strongest of the three primal vowels, the short vowel letter 'u' represents the Divine Force unfolding and expanding in a creative and energizing way. It is formed in the middle of the mouth with a long 'uuu' sound, and has a strong expansive power. The letter 'm' is produced by closing the lips. As the full range of the mouth is used, it is said that *Oṁ* contains all sounds.

The correct pronunciation of *Oṁ* is like the 'ong' in 'song' but drawn out and with the 'o' pronounced like its alphabet name. *Oṁ* is a pure vowel sound and the 'm' is silent, because the 'o' sound is prolonged.

Aum – Inner Sound Meditation Technique

The Aum Technique will help you to attune inwardly with the Vibratory Sound of Cosmic Consciousness. Aum is the connecting link between human consciousness and Divine Cosmic Consciousness.

The Aum Technique can be practised at any time after the preliminary techniques: *mahāmudrā, hong-sau,* and *navi kriyā,* or it can be practised alone. Practising during the peaceful energy of the night is a particularly good choice when performing the Aum Technique and *jyoti mudrā.*

This meditation of listening to the inner vibratory sound of Aum is best practised when the mind is calm and focused in the stillness after practising *hong-sau* meditation. Practise *hong-sau* for at least three months to help you deepen your concentration and calm the restlessness of the mind, before you start to practise the Aum inner sound meditation. Then you will be able to go deeper in your meditation to feel a profound sense of inner calmness, and attunement in oneness with the Divine Self.

Preparation

Before you practise the Aum meditation technique begin with three rounds of *mahāmudrā,* and few rounds of *nāḍī śodhana prāṇāyāma.* Then focus and calm your mind by practising the *hong-sau* technique for 10–15 minutes, or until you are calmly centred within in inner stillness.

Aum Technique

Step 1: Sit in a meditation posture that is comfortable and steady, with your head, neck, and spine aligned straight. Place your upper arms on a T-shaped armrest, or sit with your knees together, pulled up against your chest, and rest your elbows on your knees. When using the T-shaped armrest, make sure your upper arms are resting parallel to the floor with your elbows in line with your shoulders. Make sure your arms and shoulders are at a comfortable height; there should be no strain on your hands, arms, back, or neck.

Step 2: Raise your hands up to your head and position your fingers in the Aum *mudrā*: first close your ears by gently pressing the earflaps (*tragi*) inward with your thumbs. Rest your little fingers gently and lightly on the outer corners of each closed eyelid to stabilize the eyeballs. Rest your other fingers upward on your forehead, pointing inward toward the eyebrow centre, to direct energy toward the Spiritual Eye.

Step 3: Breathe normally while holding the position of the Aum *mudrā*, and with your eyes closed, gaze with deep attentive awareness into your Spiritual Eye. Then, in a natural rhythm, mentally chant 'Aum, Aum, Aum, Aum . . .' continuously at the spiritual eye, so that the *mantra* vibrates and resonates in that centre.

Step 4: As you gaze inwardly, into the Spiritual Eye mentally chanting Aum, with intuitive awareness, simultaneously listen in your right ear for the subtle sound-frequencies of your *chakras*. If you hear one distinct sound, focus your awareness totally on that one sound. As sensitivity develops, another fainter sound will be heard behind it. Leave the first sound and transfer your awareness to the fainter sound. Again, a third sound will begin to emerge behind the second sound. With awareness continue discarding the grosser sounds for the more subtle sounds. Your aim is to reach the source of all sound – the primordial vibratory sound, Aum.

Step 5: Try to hear the Aum sound first in your right ear, then going deeper, hear it in both your ears, until you hear it in the centre of your brain. Then, feel it gradually descending down to permeate every cell in your whole body, and then expanding outward. As your listening to Aum deepens, your consciousness expands, and you begin to feel omnipresent, beyond the ego, mind, body, and senses. Your consciousness dissolves into that omnipresent Aum sound-current of the power of consciousness, and you feel complete oneness with Aum, experiencing bliss in the Supreme Consciousness.

Mentally affirm: 'The quiet stillness of the Infinite permeates my being. I melt into the ocean of bliss.'

After listening to the inner sound vibration of Aum, remain sitting for some time, calmly and joyfully in the stillness of your meditation and experience pure awareness of Being or a perception of oneness with the Divine.

The Inner Sounds of the Chakras

As a beginner, when you first practise the Aum inner sound meditation you may only hear the inner sounds of the physical body: heartbeat, blood circulation and breathing. You may also hear a very high pitched electrical sound from the electrical field of energy of the astral body. If you hear any of these distinct sounds, concentrate on them until they recede into the background, then transfer your awareness to the next fainter sound that you hear, and then to the more subtle astral sounds. If your mind is deeply interiorized and calm while listening to these inner sounds, you will eventually be able to tune into and hear the subtle sounds of the *chakras*. Listening to the inner *chakra* sounds will lead you to hear the primordial sound vibration, *Oṁ*.

The Chakra Sounds as Heard in Meditation

Mūlādhāra chakra – The humming or drone of bees, a low vibratory sound. When heard less perfectly it may sound like a motor or a drum.

Svādhiṣṭhāna chakra – Like a flute. When heard less perfectly it may sound like crickets, or running water.

Maṇipūra chakra – Stringed instrument sound, like a sitar or harp.

Anāhata chakra – Like the flowing peal of deep bells, or a gong. Less perfectly it sounds like tinkling bells.
Viśuddha chakra – Thunder or the ocean's roar. When heard less perfectly it may sound like wind or a waterfall.
Ājñā chakra – A symphony of sounds; *Oṁ*.

Chapter 21

The Pañchamahābhūtas – The Five Great Elements

Pañchabhūta or *Pañchatattva* (the two words are synonymous) both mean 'the five elements'. *Pañcha* means 'five', and *bhūta* and *tattva* both mean 'elements', as we have seen. These elements should not be confused with the physical or chemical elements, as known to modern science. In fact, the *pañchabhūtas* or *mahābhūtas* are the essential states of matter, from which even the elements of modern science are derived. The *pañchabhūtas* are manifested as a consequence of light and sound emanations, created by vibratory *prāṇā*.

The philosophies of Tantra, Sāṁkhya, and Ayurveda, are based on the universal theory of *pañchabhūta*. The ancient *Ṛg Veda* does not use the word *pañchabhūta*, however. The theory of *pañchabhūta* actually developed in the post-Vedic period especially during the time of the *Upaniṣads*.

The *pañchabhūta* originate from the five *tanmātrās* (the essences emanating from *ahaṁkāra*: the essences of sound (*śabda*), touch (*sparśa*), form and colour (*rūpa*), taste (*rasa*) and smell (*gandha*).

The Vedic *rishis* (seers) of India perceived that life was created from within the eternal, Divine, unmanifested existence that is ever present, like a thread that comes from within a spider and is spun into a web. Eventually creation is dissolved back into the Divine like the spider returning the web into itself. In the beginning the universe remained in an unmanifested state of consciousness, until the subtle vibrations of the cosmic sound *Oṁ* manifested. Its vibration caused the ether element to appear, and as it began to move, its subtle movements created the air element. The movement of air produced friction that generated heat, and particles of the heat energy combined to create intense light. From the light, the fire element was manifested. The heat from fire produced moisture, creating the water element. Finally, water solidified to form the earth element. From these five great elements (*pañchamahābhūta*), ether, air, fire, water, and earth, all creation, including the human body, is made. These subtle elements are finer than the molecular and subatomic particles of matter.

The five human senses (*indriyās*) correspond to the *pañchabhūta* – 'the building blocks of existence' – and it is out of these that all things we observe, and all that is in the cosmos, are formed. The *bhūtas* are present in each and every substance around us. The phenomenal world is experienced through the senses, and each sense has the power to reveal to our perception something about the world.

The reason why there are only five *bhūtas* is because God has endowed us with only five senses and the external world can only be perceived by us through these five instruments of perception. There is no other source which can give any information about the matter which constitutes the physical world. For one particular *indriyā*, there is only one sense organ. The sense of hearing can appreciate only the quality of sound. Sound, touch, form and colour, taste, and smell are the five sense-objects corresponding to the five senses. These are *gunas* (qualities) and as such cannot exist independently by themselves, but must have some receptacles. In this way we get five receptacles, the five *bhūtas*.

All material substances are derived from a combination of the five *bhūtas* and the predominance of any one of them in a particular substance determines its character. For instance, those parts of the body which are solid, heavy and hard like nails, bones, teeth and muscles, as well as the smell of the body and the soil, have an earthy character. Whereas those parts of the body which are liquid, inactive, viscid and soft, and can flow, like blood, lymph, chyle, urine and sweat, are of a watery character.

Each of our five senses is the main organ of perception for a basic element. No element ever appears in its pure form but always intermixed. All the sense organs are involved in each act of perception. One of these takes the lead in perceiving the effects of a particular element.

- The sense of hearing (*śabda*) is associated with the element ether (*ākāśa*). There is no sound without space.
- The sense of touch (*sparśa*) is perceived through the element air (*vāyu*), whose characteristic is motion. We can feel the pressure of air on our skin from a breeze or a wind blowing.
- The sense of vision (*rūpa*) is perceived through the element fire (*tejas* or *agni*), whose characteristic is that we can see by the light of the fire element. Due to the activity of light-sensitive cells in the retina we are able to see form, shape and colour.
- The sense of taste (*rasa*) is perceived by the presence of the element water (*apās*). The watery saliva on the tongue helps us to taste flavours, which are only detectable when the tongue is wet.
- The sense of smell (*gandha*) is the principal apparatus for perceiving the element earth (*pṛithvī*).

The physical matter we perceive as tangible in the physical world only comes into existence after the process of *pañchikārana* (quintuplication) between the five *mahābhūtas* takes place. Each of the five *mahābhūtas* is divided into two equal parts. Then one of the halves of each *mahābhūta* is split into four equal parts. Then one quarter of each of the remaining four *mahābhūtas* is added to the undivided half of each *mahābhūta*. The final result of this quintuplication process of the *mahābhūtas* is that in each *mahābhūta* there will be a constituent part of all five original *mahābhūtas* in definite proportions. Without this compounding process, the *mahābhūtas* cannot produce the physical world and the physical objects within it.

Although innumerable forms arise, it is one pure Consciousness which is the substance of all things.

Jñaneshvar, 13th-century Indian mystic-poet

Spiritually there is One life that is pervasive in everything, an Intelligence that is omnipresent, omniscient, and omnipotent. The sages call it Brahman, which is derived from the Sanskrit root *brha*, meaning 'expansion, knowledge, all-pervasive'. Brahman is the Absolute Reality beyond all duality. It is the Supreme Consciousness, and it is the nature of your true Self. We are spiritual beings, soul-consciousness, that has descended and become embodied in matter. Due to misidentification with the mind and body, and the objects of the world, we have forgotten our true essential nature as spiritual beings. This has caused a veil of ignorance to cover our consciousness, and unless we awake spiritually and remove the covering of ignorance and illusion, the light of the Self or pure consciousness cannot shine. The soul needs to remember its true identity and start ascending to its lost higher plane of consciousness – the journey from matter to Spirit. Paramhansa Yogananda said, 'Spirit is that vast stillness which is beyond all created things.'

Purification of the Five Elements

One who has conquered the five-fold elements: ether, air, fire, water and earth through the practice of yogic meditation, attains a body purified by the fire of yoga and he is not touched by disease, old age, or death.

Śvetāśvatara Upaniṣad, 2: 12

There is an ancient yogic purification–meditation practice from the tantric and *kuṇḍalinī* traditions of yoga, called *bhūta śuddhi*, or *tattva śuddhi*. *Tattva* has two syllables: *tat* means 'that' and *twa* means 'ness'. *Tattva* means 'Thatness' or the essence that creates the feeling of existence. *Tattva śuddhi* or *bhūta śuddhi* mean 'purification of the elements'. *Bhūta śuddhi* purifies the subtle elemental energies of the *chakras* – earth, water, fire, air, and ether – preparing the aspirant for awakening *kuṇḍalinī*, the life-force. *Bhūta śuddhi* works on purifying not only the physical body but also the subtle body (*sūkshma sharīra*) and the causal body (*kāraṇa sharīra*). Without purification of the subtler levels of the mind, it is impossible to attain higher states of consciousness.

This practice systematically focuses on each of the *chakras* in the *suṣumnā*, while using *yantra* visualization, *prāṇāyāma*, and the repetition of the *bīja mantras*. (*Ājñā*, the sixth *chakra*, and *sahasrāra*, at the crown [and above the head], are beyond the elements. *Ājñā chakra* is concerned with realization or enlightenment, and *sahasrāra* is concerned with liberation.)

Benefits

Bhūta śuddhi purifies the heart and mind, and unblocks the energy channels. It calms the mind and trains it to concentrate deeply, leading to one-pointed, effortless meditation in stillness. This makes it a very effective practice of inner purification for Kriyā Yoga and Rāja Yoga meditators.

Prerequisites

Before undertaking the practice of *bhūta śuddhi* it is advised that you have a basic knowledge and understanding of yoga philosophy and the location of the *chakras* in the body, and experience of having practised fundamental yoga *āsanas*, *mudrās*, *bandhas* and *prāṇāyāma*, and *mantra* repetition.

In addition to this, you need to have been regularly practising meditation for some time, so that you are able to sit with the body steady, and enter into a state of inner calm and stillness.

Contraindications

People suffering from heart conditions, high blood pressure, nervous disorders or schizophrenia should avoid this practice. Consult an experienced and competent teacher.

Preparation

The first step of purification is cleansing the physical body and strengthening the nervous system. The second step is concerned with the purification of the subtle body, which uses the mind and *prāṇa*, from which the elements (*tattvas* or *bhūtas*) have arisen. The causal body, which is not influenced by the conscious mind, is more difficult to purify. It requires the powerful force of concentrated energy by repetition of the *tattva bīja mantras* and visualization of their respective *yantras* to create a transformation.

Tattva Śuddhi – Purification of the Elements

Stage 1: Preparation

To prepare for the practice of *tattva śuddhi*, first perform three rounds of *agnisāra kriyā*, and then practise the following *prāṇāyāma* techniques to steady the mind:

Kapālabhāti (three rounds of 60 breaths, resting with two or three normal breaths in between each round).
Nāḍī śodhana (five rounds of alternate nostril breathing – breath count 3:12:6).

Breathing through the chakras

Now, with your eyes closed, sit in stillness for a few minutes, with your inner gaze at the Spiritual Eye. Then, when your body is still and your mind is calm and steady, bring your attention and awareness to the first centre in the spine, *mūlādhāra chakra*. Then mentally feel your inner consciousness travel up and down the *suṣumnā* several times, from the coccygeal plexus at the base of the spine to the point between the eyebrows.

Now, as you inhale using *ujjayi* breathing, visualize and feel the breath ascending through the *suṣumnā*. Feel the coolness of the breath touching each *chakra* from *mūlādhāra* at the base of the spine, to *viśuddha* in the throat, then the medulla, until it reaches the Spiritual Eye. After mentally repeating *Oṁ* with your awareness totally focused at the Spiritual Eye, begin to exhale in *ujjayi* breath back to the medulla, and then down through the *chakras* from *viśuddha* to *mūlādhāra*, feeling the warm sensation of the breath touching each *chakra* as it passes through it.

Repeat this circuit of rotating your consciousness up and down the spine through the *chakras* six times, or until you feel that your consciousness is transferred from the body to the subtle astral spine.

Practice of hong-sau mantra in the spine

Focus on the natural flow of prāṇic energy rising and falling in the spine with each inhalation and exhalation. As you inhale, feel the energy naturally rising from the base of the spine to the *sahasrāra chakra* at the crown of the head. As you exhale, feel the energy naturally descending from the *sahasrāra chakra* to the base of the spine. Then, as you feel the energy and consciousness moving up and down the spine, mentally repeat the *mantra* '*hong*' with the inhalation and the upward movement of the energy, and '*sau*' with the exhalation and the downward movement of energy. As you continue synchronizing your breathing with the *mantra* up and down the *suṣumnā* with each breath, feel yourself becoming united with Supreme Consciousness.

When your practice deepens you may find that the spaces between your breaths widen. You will be breathing less. If this happens, leave the technique and enjoy the calmness in these still moments. You can continue the practice when the breath begins again.

Stage 2: Creation

Now bring your awareness to the lower part of your body, the area between your toes and your knees, and visualize the symbol of the earth element (*pṛithvī tattva*) as a large, bright yellow square. See this luminous yellow square and feel its stability and solidness. As you visualize this bright yellow square, the symbol for the *mūlādhāra chakra,* repeat the *bīja mantra* 'laṁ' 16 times (you can use *mālā* meditation beads to count the 16 repetitions), and feel it resonating in the area between your toes and knees.

Next, bring your awareness to the area between your knees and your navel, and visualize a luminous white crescent-shaped moon lying horizontally. At each end of the crescent moon, there is a full-bloom white lotus, with its petalled rays of light pointing upward. Surrounding the crescent moon with the two white lotuses is a circle of water. This is the subtle element of water (*apās tattva*). Visualize the white crescent moon with the two white lotuses and repeat the *bīja mantra 'vaṁ'* 16 times, and feel it resonating in the area between your knees and navel.

Now bring your awareness to the area between the navel and the heart, and visualize a bright red inverted triangle made of fire, and on each of the triangle's three outer sides is a gate or an entrance (in Sanskrit called a *bhupura*). By its appearance as light it gives definition to form. Visualize this bright red inverted triangle of fire, the fire element (*tejas tattva*) and repeat the *bīja mantra 'raṁ'* 16 times, and feel it resonating in the area between your navel and your heart.

Then bring your awareness to the area between your heart and your eyebrow centre, and visualize a smoky blue-grey hexagon formed inside two intersecting triangles overlapping to make a six-pointed star. Its smoky interior has a mysterious glow of light. This is the subtle air element (*vāyu tattva*). As you visualize the smoky blue-grey hexagon, repeat the *bīja mantra* '*raṁ*' 16 times, and feel it resonating in the area between your heart and your eyebrow centre.

Now bring your awareness to the area between your eyebrow centre and the crown of your head, and visualize a dark blackish-blue circle. This is the subtle ether element (*ākāśa tattva*) that cannot be perceived by the external senses. As you visualize and gaze into the deep space of the dark blackish-blue circle, repeat the *bīja mantra* '*haṁ*' 16 times, and feel it resonating in the area between your eyebrow centre and the crown of your head.

Stage 3: Dissolution

Now reverse the process of creation by bringing your awareness back down to the earth element, symbolized as a large, bright yellow square. Visualize the earth element dissolving into the water element, then water dissolving into fire, fire dissolving into air, and air dissolving into ether, space.

Then, imagine and feel that the ether element is dissolving back into its cause, the ego (*ahaṁkāra*). The *ahaṁkāra* dissolves into *mahat* (cosmic consciousness), this then dissolves into *prakṛti* (the eternal principle of matter), which merges into *Puruṣa* (the Supreme Self, the eternal principle of consciousness). In total stillness and oneness feel you are that Pure Consciousness. Feel now that everything in the universe is reflected within you. That you are an essential and necessary part of the whole that continues to expand ever outward, and that Supreme Consciousness is eternally and lovingly aware of your presence.

After your meditation continue to sit for some time in the inner calmness, joy and stillness.

Bhūta Śuddhi – Advanced Practice

Stage 1: The ascent through the chakras

Step 1: Sit in a comfortable meditation posture with the spine erect, so that the pelvis, chest, neck and head are vertically aligned. To relax completely, first inhale deeply and hold the breath, then tense all the muscles in your body. Then, with a deep exhalation, completely relax your whole body. Repeat this exercise three times.

Close your eyes and with a calm and steady inner gaze, concentrate at the Spiritual Eye. Then become aware of your natural breath; do not try to control it in any way but just be aware of each breath as it flows in and out. Be still, and remain calmly cèntred within as you continue to gaze into the Spiritual Eye while being aware of your breath.

Step 2: Now bring your awareness and concentration to the first spinal centre, *mūlādhāra chakra*. It is related to the earth element, and is the seat of *kuṇḍalinī*, the life-energy. Visualize *mūlādhāra chakra* in the form of a deep red lotus flower having four petals. Within the lotus is a bright yellow square, representing the earth element energy. In the centre of the bright yellow square is a bright red equilateral triangle pointing downwards, and within the triangle is a smoky-coloured *Śiva lingam* encircled by a brilliant golden-coloured sleeping serpent, known as *kuṇḍalinī śākti*, the life-force.

Step 3: As you concentrate on *mūlādhāra chakra* apply *mūla bandha* by slowly contracting the anal and perineal muscles and pulling them upward. Breathe normally and with your concentration at the centre of the contracting muscle; be totally aware of the physical sensation at that central point. As you focus your mind at that point on the *kuṇḍalinī śāti*, mentally repeat *laṁ*, the *bīja mantra* of the earth element, 16 times.

Step 4: Now, visualize the *kuṇḍalinī* energy awakening and feel it rising from the *mūlādhāra chakra* to the second spinal centre, related to the water element, *svādhiṣṭhāna* *chakra,* at the level of the pubic bone and coccyx. Visualize it in the form of a six-petalled vermilion lotus. In the centre of the lotus is a blue circle representing the water element. At the centre of the blue circle is a luminous white crescent moon. While visualizing this image, mentally repeat *vaṁ,* the *bīja mantra* of the water element, 16 times.

Step 5: Next, feel and visualize the *kuṇḍalinī* energy moving up to the third centre, related to the fire element, *maṇipūra chakra,* at the navel centre. Visualize a ten-petalled, bright yellow lotus. Within the lotus is a red inverted triangle. While visualizing this image, mentally repeat *raṁ,* the *bīja mantra* of the fire element, 16 times.

Step 6: Now feel and visualize the *kuṇḍalinī* energy rising up to the fourth centre, related to the air element, *anāhata chakra,* at the level of the heart centre. Visualize a twelve-petalled blue lotus. Within the blue lotus are two smoky-blue-coloured intersecting triangles, forming a six-pointed star. Focusing in the space at the centre point of the two intersecting triangles, visualize light in the form of a flame; this is the seat of the soul. While visualizing this image, mentally repeat *yaṁ,* the *bīja mantra* of the air element, 16 times.

Step 7: The *kuṇḍalinī* energy now rises up to the fifth centre, the centre of purification related to the ether element, *viśuddha chakra,* at the base of the throat centre. Here all the elements of the lower *chakras* are refined and transmuted to their purest essence, into ether. Visualize a 16-petalled violet lotus. In the centre of the violet lotus is a silver crescent within a white circle shining as a luminous full moon. While visualizing this image, mentally repeat *haṁ,* the *bīja mantra* of the ether element, 16 times.

Step 8: Now feel and visualize the *kuṇḍalinī* energy flowing up to the sixth centre, the *ājñā chakra,* the Spiritual Eye of intuition, the centre of spiritual realization that is beyond the elements. Visualize a two-petalled luminescent bluish or white lotus. In the centre of the two-petalled lotus is a yellow or gold triangle surrounded by a luminous white circle, like a full moon. At the centre of the yellow triangle is a bright white flame. While visualizing this image, mentally repeat the primal Sound Vibration *Oṁ*, 16 times.

Step 9: Continue feeling the *kuṇḍalinī* energy rising up from the *ājñā chakra* to the highest centre at the crown of your head, the *sahasrāra chakra*. Beyond the comprehension of the mind, *sahasrāra* is the spiritual realm of Pure Consciousness that contains all the other *chakras* within it. *Sahasrāra* is beyond all colours, forms and shapes. It is in *sahasrāra*, the highest spiritual centre, that *Śiva* or consciousness resides. The ultimate union of energy (*Śākti*) and consciousness (*Śiva)* takes place in *sahasrāra*. Here the illusion of the individual self is dissolved and transcended.

Traditionally, *sahasrāra* is conceived as a thousand-petalled rayed lotus of white light tinged with a pink aura. Feel and visualize this multi-rayed luminous lotus slightly above the crown of your head, and mentally repeat the *mantra 'haṁsa'*, which means 'I am He.' *Haṁsa* is the ever-perfect Self. One who dwells in this consciousness is called a *Parāmhaṁsa*.

Stage 2: Prāṇāyāma, mantra, visualization

Step 10: Remain with your eyes closed with your inner gaze fixed at the Spiritual Eye. Keep your consciousness at the crown of the head in the luminous light of the *sahasrāra chakra*.

Raise your right hand to your face and position it in the *viṣṇu mudrā* for alternate nostril breathing. Close the right nostril with your thumb and inhale slowly and evenly through your left nostril for a slow count of eight, while mentally repeating *yaṁ* (the *bīja mantra* of the air element), eight times, and visualizing a smoky colour in the left nostril . . . Close both nostrils, and while holding the breath, repeat the *mantra 'yaṁ'* 32 times, and feel that your heart region is filled with the air element, drying up all the impurities in the body . . . Keep the left nostril closed with your ring finger, and exhale slowly through your right nostril, repeating the *mantra* '*yaṁ*' 16 times.

Step 11: Now keep the left nostril closed, and inhale through the right nostril while repeating *raṁ* (the *bīja mantra* of the fire element) eight times. As you do this, visualize a bright flame of light in the right nostril . . . Close both nostrils, and while holding the breath, repeat the *mantra* '*raṁ*' 32 times. Feel that the flame of light is burning all the impurities in the body.

Now slowly exhale through the left nostril, repeating the *mantra* '*raṁ*' 16 times. Visualize the light emanating from the heart region and expelling all the impurities of the body through the left nostril.

Step 12: Now close the right nostril with your thumb and inhale through the left nostril while mentally repeating *vaṁ* (the *bīja mantra* of the water element) . . . Close both nostrils and hold the breath and concentrate at the Spiritual Eye of the *ājñā chakra*, while repeating the *mantra* '*vaṁ*' 32 times. As you do this, feel a blissful light showering from this *chakra*, filling your body with light . . . Now exhale through your right nostril, repeating the *mantra* '*vaṁ*' 16 times.

Stage 3: The descent through the chakras

Step 13: Now prepare your consciousness to descend down through the *chakras*. In the beginning of this practice *kuṇḍalinī śākti*, the life-force, ascended up through the seven *chakras* purifying each of the elements and energies associated with them. Now as it travels back down, those elemental energies will have been purified and energized by *kuṇḍalinī śākti*.

Feel now that your consciousness is beginning the descent down from *sahasrāra*, the spiritual realm of Pure Consciousness, to the *ājñā chakra*, the two-petalled lotus behind the eyebrow centre. Leave the mind at its centre purified . . . Now descend to the fifth *chakra*, *viśuddha*, the 16-petalled violet coloured lotus . . . Feel its endless space and calmness . . . Feel *viśuddha*'s subtle element of ether purified. Ether, the vibration of space, is that which separates the material universe from the astral universe . . . Continue your journey down through the *chakras* into the fourth centre, *anāhata chakra*, the 12-petalled blue lotus, where our individual consciousness resides . . . Feel the expansiveness and freedom represented by the element of air in the heart *chakra* . . . Feel the *anāhata chakra*'s subtle element of air purified . . . Feel the heart purified and the love of the heart centre expanding into the oneness of all life . . . Now continue down to the third centre, the *maṇipūra chakra*, the 10-petalled bright yellow lotus located at the level of the navel. Feel *maṇipūra*'s dynamic subtle element of fire purified . . . Feel that its element of fire has burnt away all the obstacles, desires, habits and attachments that were keeping you from the truth . . . Continue travelling down to the second centre, *svādhiṣṭhāna chakra*, the six-petalled vermilion-coloured lotus . . . Now with the water element of this *chakra* purified you feel at home in the flow of life, accepting everything as it comes, with true discrimination and inner joy. Feel that you are flowing freely and fearlessly in the flow of divine grace . . . Continue down and finally return to the root centre at the base of the spine, *mūlādhāra chakra*, the 6-petalled deep red lotus . . . Feel the expansion of your awareness and a sense of having purified, balanced and energized your *chakras* . . . Feel the energy now, flowing freely through your body . . . Now gently return your awareness to your breath, and take a few long, slow, deep breaths in and out, feeling the cool air in the nostrils as you inhale, and warm air in the nostrils as you exhale . . . Then become aware of your physical body by slowly moving your fingers and toes, and gently stretching your arms and legs . . . Then, when you feel grounded in your whole body, and aware of the environment around you, slowly get up . . . The practice is now complete.

Now, guided by divine wisdom, soar to new heights of understanding. Uplifted in spirit, see your way over obstacles that you may have once thought blocked you from realizing your good. In this higher elevation of divine knowledge, you have an overview of the bigger picture. Mountains become ant hills, challenges become opportunities, the seemingly impossible becomes possible.

Chapter 22

Meditation on the Heart Chakra

Love is the highest state and final goal of spiritual realization. It therefore makes sense that you have to open your heart, as well as focus your mind, during meditation. Without love and devotion, your meditation practice would become mechanical, dry and of little worth. Practising meditation with love and devotion can lead the mind beyond mere intellectual knowledge to an experience of the blissful Self, which constitutes true knowledge. Love is the Divine within you. Love is your inner source and potential. Love is your true nature.

Just as you can only see the moon by reflected rays of light from the sun, similarly you can only see the Divine through the rays of love. By opening your heart and cultivating Divine Love within you, the dark clouds disperse. Then you will recognize that the same divinity resides in others as in yourself.

Method

Sit in a comfortable meditation posture with the head, neck and spine upright. To relax completely, first inhale deeply and hold the breath, then tense all the muscles in your body. Then, with a deep exhalation, completely relax your whole body. Repeat this exercise three times.

Close your eyes and with a steady inner gaze, concentrate at the midpoint between the eyebrows, at the Spiritual Eye. Then become aware of your natural breath, do not try to control it in any way but just be aware of each breath as it flows in and out. Be still, and remain calmly centred within as you continue to gaze into the Spiritual Eye while being aware of your breath.

Now, with your eyes closed, place your attention on your heart centre, and feel the greatest love that you ever felt for another person. Feel that love permeate every cell and atom of your being . . . Now expand that feeling of unconditional love . . . radiate waves of love like an encircling sphere, embracing your family, friends and all your loved ones . . . Feel God's unlimited love being channelled through you, consciously filling your heart and increasing your love to share with your family, friends and all your loved ones . . . continue to expand that love by including all the people in your neighbourhood . . . your city . . . your country . . . the world . . . Your love expands into our solar system, and beyond into the universe. Love has no boundaries, it encompasses everything. God's love is infinite . . . Feel the door of your heart open wide and let God's universal love flow continuously through you . . . Feel the infinite joy and blessing of being the instrument of God's love.

Affirmations

'As I radiate God's peace, light and love to others, I open the channel for God's love to flow through me.'

'I am ever-present, expressing myself in my eternal Divine nature. I am a creation of the Infinite Life which is Love, My heart and mind rest calmly in the realization of the omnipresent Love of God that permeates every single particle of substance that exists in the universe.'

Through all the dance of life and death, know that God is love. The only purpose of life should be to find that love. Once the love of all human beings, and, indeed, of all things living, is included in your heart's feeling, your heart will merge with and become one with the Heart of God.

Paramhansa Yogananda

Appendix 1

An Introduction to Sanskrit

The Sanskrit language, whatever be its antiquity, is of wonderful structure, more perfect than the Greek, more copious than the Latin and more exquisitely refined than either.

Sir William Jones, British orientalist, 1746–1794

Sanskrit is a Western term that originates from *saṃskṛta* (perfectly composed, refined). In the Western world Sanskrit, like Latin, is usually considered to be an unspoken language. However, Sanskrit is very much a spoken language today. In India there are nine Sanskrit universities, with about 600 branches, where all subjects are taught in the Sanskrit medium, and India publishes many magazines in the Sanskrit language and these address contemporary issues. The news service offered by the Government of India through television and radio continues to feature daily Sanskrit programmes dealing with international as well as local news. The grammar of Sanskrit has attracted scholars worldwide. It is very precise and up to date and remains well defined even today.

Sanskrit is a language for humanity and not merely a means for communication within a society. There is sufficient evidence available today that shows that Sanskrit is the oldest language in the world. In fact, Sanskrit is known as the 'Mother of all European Languages'. Among the current languages which possess an antiquity like Latin or ancient Greek, Sanskrit is the only language which has retained its pristine purity. It has maintained its structure and vocabulary even today as it did in the ancient past. Sanskrit distinguishes itself from other languages in that it is the only known language which has a built-in scheme for pronunciation, word formation and grammar.

The oldest surviving literature of the world – the *Vedas* – encompass knowledge in virtually every sphere of human activity. The early Brahminical texts of the *Ṛg Veda* written in the pre-Classical form of Vedic Sanskrit are the oldest, dating back to as early as 1500–1200 BCE. The oldest surviving Sanskrit grammar, which evolved from the earlier Vedic form, is Pānini's 'Eight-Chapter Grammar'(*Astādhyāyī*), consisting of 3,990 *sutras* (aphorisms), which define correct Sanskrit. About a century after Pānini (around 400 BCE), Kātyāyana composed *Vārtikas* on Pānini's *sutras*. Around the middle of the second century BCE the great sage Patañjali, who formulated the *Yoga Sutras*, also wrote the *Mahabhaśya* (the 'Great Commentary'), a commentary on the earliest extant Sanskrit grammar (the *Astādhyāyī* and *Vārtikas*) of Pānini. Patañjali, living three centuries after Pānini, formulated certain new grammatical rules (*ishtis*) to supplement the earlier ones; this would mean that Sanskrit had by now undergone changes.

Around the middle of the first millenium BCE, Vedic Sanskrit began the transition from a first language to a second language of religion and learning.

Sanskrit abounds in expressions related to philosophy and theology. There are so many words encountered within Sanskrit that convey subtly differing meanings of a concept that admits of only one interpretation when studied with other languages. The Sanskrit language thus has the ability to offer links between concepts using just the words. For every sound there is only one letter and for every letter there is only one sound. This principle is hardly seen in any other language. Also, in the Sanskrit alphabet, all the vowels are listed first and then all the consonants. This is different from the alphabets used for Western languages, which are mostly based on Egyptian hieroglyphics and the old Phoenician alphabet. The order a, b, c, d . . . mixes vowels and consonants indiscriminately and is generally unsystematic.

Sanskrit is a spiritual language full of spiritual significance. Like most things in Sanskrit, the grammar has roots tracing back to a divine origin. The mythological story of the seven great seers, the Saptarsi, describes how they went to Lord Śiva seeking the essence of language. Lord Śiva played his tiny two-ended drum (*damaru*), and from it came sounds that are known as the *Mahesvārasutrani*. These sounds were 14 *sutras* that became the basis of Sanskrit grammar as recorded by Pānini.

For those who are sincerely practising yoga, meditation, and chanting *mantras*, Sanskrit words give meaning and clearer explanation on a spiritual level. It is useful to understand the exact connotations of Sanskrit terms, as it can be difficult to equate certain Sanskrit terms with English words. For example, 'mind' and 'consciousness' are two words that get confused in translation. *Manas* in Sanskrit is usually translated as 'mind', but the connotations are certainly different. *Manas* is subtle material and objective, it is not the brain. The brain is gross matter and is an instrument of *manas*. The physical brain dies when the physical body dies, but *manas*, which is made of subtle matter, leaves the body at the time of death.

It is also worth taking some time to learn correct pronunciation of Sanskrit. Correct pronunciation helps to bring out the subtle effects in chanting *mantras*, adding a beneficial effect through its vibrations.

The Devanāgari script of Sanskrit is a phonetic alphabet that consists of 13 vowels (*svāra*) and 34 consonants (*vyanjana*). It is known as a syllabic script. Every letter has a unique sound and is a single syllable of each word. Each letter in the Devanāgari script has a mystic value.

According to the *bīja* code each letter of the Sanskrit *varnamāla* (alphabet) represents certain instincts. Since each letter has a different acoustic root, each one creates a different vibration which often impacts on the psyche of the persons being addressed. For students of the science of *mantra* it is important to know the acoustic root and the power of all letters used in Sanskrit.

The seed (*bīja*) syllable has a magical aura around it. According to the tantric tradition, every seed syllable must have a nasal sound which results in a divine union. Since Śiva and Śākti are considered to be two lips, their union leads to the birth of seed, or *bīja*.

The nasal sound (*anusvāra)* as in *ṁ*, is supposed to have the germ of a complete doctrine. By using *bīja-akśar* (seed syllables) a huge treatise can be compressed into a few lines. A seed syllable, by virtue of being short, is good for the repetitions of a *mantra* as it creates cerebral vibrations which keep reverberating. With the help of the nasal sound, one can transfer the seed syllable to the back of the head or between the eyebrows. At a later stage the accumulated energy of a *mantra* can be projected anywhere in order to achieve the desired result. *Mantras* chanted in Sanskrit reveal the mystery of sound. Their result can be multi-dimensional; some *mantras* can bring enlightenment, while other *mantras* bring disenchantment.

The aim of *mantra* is to experience the non-dualistic state. The great yogis have said that a *mantra* (in Sanskrit) does not give any results if it is not chanted properly, as it should represent *Śabda-Brahman*, 'cosmic sound waves'.

Sanskrit is the eternal spiritual language. The eternal syllable *Oṁ* is the Primordial Transcendental Sound, the divine sound vibration from which all other sounds originate. *Oṁ*, the *Praṇava*, is the root of all the *mantras*. From *Oṁ* emanated all the other sounds of the alphabet, including the seven primary notes of music: *ṣaḍja*, *ṛṣabha*, *gāndhāra*, *madhyama*, *pañcama*, *dhaivata* and *niṣāda* (known as *Sa*, *Re*, *Ga*, *Ma*, *Pa*, *Da*, *Ni*).

The word Oṁ should be used in the beginning. It is the Supreme Reality. It is used as a synonym for Brahman.

The Atharvaśikhopaniṣad

Guide to Sanskrit Pronunciation

Too often, in Western books on yoga, there is over-simplification when Sanskrit words are translated into English, in which the original meaning tends to get diluted, mistranslated or lost. In this book I have tried to keep as many Sanskrit words as possible in their original meaning.

Since the late 18th century, Sanskrit has been transliterated using the Latin alphabet. The system most commonly used today is the IAST (International Alphabet of Sanskrit Transliteration), which has been the academic standard since 1888/1912.

The following guide to pronunciation gives approximate equivalents in English of the Sanskrit sounds.

Diacritical marks used in this book: ā ī ū ṛ ḷ ḥ ṁ ṅ ñ ṇ ṭ ḍ ś ṣ.

Vowels

a ā i ī u ū r ṛ ṝ l ḹ e ai o au

These vowels are further divided into simple vowels (*a*, *ā*, and so on) and combined vowels (*e, ai, o, au*). The simple vowels are listed in pairs (*a-ā, i-ī* . . .). In each pair the first vowel is short and the second is exactly twice as long. In the English transliteration the long vowels are marked with a bar (¯). The dipthongs are also pronounced twice as long as the short vowels. Thus in the words *nī – la* 'blue' or *go – pa* 'cowherd', the first syllable is held twice as long as the second.

Simple

a short *a* as in '**a**bout'
ā long *a* as in 'f**a**ther'
i short *i* as **e** in '**e**ngland'
ī long *i* as in **ee** in 'f**ee**t'
u short *u* as in **oo** in 'f**oo**t'
ū long *u* as in 'r**u**le'
ṛ as in 'w**r**itten'(but held twice as long)
ḷ **le** as in 'turt**le**'
ḹ longer '**le**'

Dipthongs

e as in 'they'
ai as in '**ai**sle' '**i**ce' 'k**i**te'
o as in 'go'
au as in '**ow**l'

Aspiration

ḥ (*visarga*) a final 'h' sound that echoes the preceding vowel slightly, as in 'aha' for ***aḥ***, ***iḥ*** as ihi, ***uḥ*** as uhu.

Nasalized vowel

ṁ (*anusvāra* – marked with a dot) a nasal sound pronounced like *mm*, but influenced according to whatever consonant follows, as in 'bingo'. The nasal is modified by the following consonant: *sāṁkhya* as saankhya.

Consonants

Consonants are generally pronounced as in English, but there are some differences. Sanskrit has many 'aspirated' consonants; these are pronounced with a slight *h* sound. For example, the consonant *ph* is pronounced as English *p* followed by an *h* as in ha*ph*azard. The *bh* is as in a*bh*or.

k as in 'skip'
kh as in 'Ec**kh**art'
g as in '**g**ame'
gh as in 'do**gh**ouse'
ṅ as in 'si**ng**'
c as in 'ex**ch**ange'
ch as in '**ch**urch'
j as in '**j**am'
jh a in 'he**dg**ehog'
ñ as in 'ca**ny**on'
ṭ as in '**t**ub', the tongue curls back and hits the upper palate
ṭh as in 'ligh**t-h**eart', the tongue curls back and hits the upper palate
ḍ as in '**dove**', the tongue curls back and hits the palate
ḍh as in 'a**dh**ere', the tongue curls back and hits the palate
ṇ as in 'ti**n**t', tip of tongue touches the back of the upper teeth
t as in 'tub', tip of tongue touches the back of the upper teeth
th as in '**th**ick', tip of tongue touches the back of the upper teeth
d as in '**d**ove', tip of tongue touches the back of the upper teeth
dh as in 're**d-h**ot', tip of tongue touches the back of the upper teeth
n as in '**n**ame', tip of tongue touches the back of the upper teeth
p as in '**p**a**p**a'
ph as in 'ha**ph**azard'
b as in '**b**alloon'
bh as in 'a**bh**or'
m as in '**m**um'
y as in '**y**ellow'
r as in '**r**un'
l as in '**l**ove'
v as in '**v**ine'
ś as in '**sh**ell'
ṣ as in '**s**ilk'
h as in '**h**ill'

Double consonants

In double consonants, both letters are pronounced distinctly and separately.

śraddhā (faith) is pronounced *śrad-dhā*

icchā (desire) is pronounced *ic-chā*

jagannātha (Lord of the Universe) is pronounced *jagan-nātha.*

jña (to know) as in *jñanā yoga* (the path of wisdom or higher knowledge) is widely pronounced as 'gya'. More accurate is 'gnya', and best is to combine a correct *ja* with a correct *ña.*

Appendix 2

Properties of the Chakras

	Mūlādhāra	*Svādhiṣṭhāna*	*Maṇipūra*	*Anāhata*	*Viśuddha*	*Ājnā*	*Sahasrāra*
Location	Perineum, cervix	Sacral centre / sex organs	Lumbar centre / navel	Dorsal centre / heart	Cervical centre / throat	At the centre of the brain	At the crown of the head
Number of lotus petals	4	6	10	12	16	2	1,000 or infinite
Element	Earth	Water	Fire	Air	Ether	*Mahat*, i.e. mind, ego and intellect	Beyond all elements
Bīja mantra	*Laṁ*	*Vaṁ*	*Rāṁ*	*Yaṁ*	*Haṁ*	*Kṣam* or *Oṁ*	*Visarga* or *Oṁ*
Colour of petals	Deep red	Orange-red	Yellow	Blue	Purple	White	Colourless
Physiological relationship	Sacro-coccygeal plexus	Pelvic plexus	Solar plexus	Cardiac plexus	Pharyngeal and laryngeal plexus	Cavernous plexus	Hypothalamic pituitary axis
Endocrine relationship	Perineal body	Testes, ovaries	Adrenal glands	Thymus gland	Thyroid gland	Pituitary gland	Pineal gland

	Mūlādhāra	*Svādhiṣṭhāna*	*Maṇipūra*	*Anāhata*	*Viśuddha*	*Ājnā*	*Sahasrāra*
Vedic astrological sign and ruling planet	Aquarius, Capricorn, Saturn	Sagittarius, Pisces, Jupiter	Aries, Scorpio, Mars	Libra, Taurus, Venus	Gemini, Virgo	Leo – Sun, Cancer – Moon	
Inner sounds	Bumble bee, rumbling motor	Flute, crickets, trickling water	Stringed instrument, sitar, harp	Deep bell or gong	Wind in the trees, rushing water	*Oṁ*, like the roar of the sea	
Positive qualities	Courage, loyalty, steadfastness, perseverance	Openness, willingness, intuition, creativity	Enthusiasm, self-control, loving leadership	Devotion, unconditional love, compassion	Expansiveness, deeply calm, silence	Selfless service, attunement, strong will-power, divine surrender	Beyond all duality, omnipresent, omniscient, *samādhi* bliss
Negative qualities	Stubbornness, prejudice, intolerant	Indecisiveness, vague	Misuse of power and ruthlessness	Attachment, harmful emotions: anger, rage, hatred	Restlessness, boredom, worldly desires	Egotistic, proud, too intellectual, strong sense of 'I, me, mine'	
Prāṇa vāyu (vital force)	*apāṇa*	*vyāṇa*	*samāna*	*prāṇa*	*udāṇa*	all five *prāṇa vāyus*	beyond
Kośa (sheath)	*annamāyā* (physical body)	*prāṇamāyā* (subtle vital body)	*prāṇamāyā* (subtle vital body)	*manomāyā* (mental body)	*vijñānamāyā* (intellectual body)	*vijñānamāyā* (intellectual body)	*ānandamāyā* (blissful causal)

	Mūlādhāra	*Svādhiṣṭhāna*	*Maṇipūra*	*Anāhata*	*Viśuddha*	*Ājnā*	*Sahasrāra*
Tattva (Elements)	*pṛithvī* (earth)	*apās* (water)	*agni* (fire)	*vāyu* (air)	*akaśa* (ether)	*manas* (mind)	Beyond
Yantra (symbolic form)	Yellow square	Silver or white crescent moon	Red inverted triangle	Smoky six-pointed star	White circle	Clear or grey circle	Beyond
Tanmātrā	Smell	Taste	Sight	Touch	Hearing	Mind	Beyond
Jñānedriya	Nose	Tongue	Eyes	Skin	Ears	Mind	Beyond
Kārmendriya	Anus	Sex organs, kidneys, urinary system	Feet	Hands	Vocal cords	Mind	Beyond
Loka (spiritual world)	*Bhūr*	*Bhuvaḥ*	*Svaḥ*	*Manaḥ*	*Janaḥ*	*Tapaḥ*	*Satyam*
Devi (goddess)	Savitri or Ḍākinī	Saraswati or Rākinī	Lakshmi or Lakini	Kali or Kākinī	Sākinī	Hākinī	Śakti
Deva (god)	Gaṇeśa	Viṣṇu	Rudra	Isha	Sadaśiva	Paramśiva	Śiva
Animal	elephant (*airavata*)	crocodile (*makara*)	ram	antelope	white elephant		
Yoni	*tripura*			triangle		triangle	
Lingam	*Svayambhū*	*dhumra*		*bana*		*itarakhya*	
Granthi	Brahma			Viṣṇu		Rudra	Jyotirmāyā

	Mūlādhāra	*Svādhiṣṭhāna*	*Maṇipūra*	*Anāhata*	*Viśuddha*	*Ājnā*	*Sahasrāra*
Alphabet sounds related to the petals	*Vaṁ*	*Baṁ*	*Daṁ*	*Kaṁ*	*Aṁ*	*Ham*	All the alphabet sounds
	Śaṁ	*Bhaṁ*	*Dhaṁ*	*Khaṁ*	*Āṁ*	*Kṣam*	
	Ṣaṁ	*Maṁ*	*Ṇaṁ*	*Gaṁ*	*Īṁ*		
	Saṁ	*Yaṁ*	*Taṁ*	*Ghaṁ*	*Īṁ*		
		Raṁ	*Thaṁ*	*Ṇaṁ*	*Uṁ*		
		Laṁ	*Daṁ*	*Caṁ*	*Ūṁ*		
			Dhaṁ	*Chaṁ*	*Ṛṁ*		
			Naṁ	*Jaṁ*	*Ṛṁ*		
			Paṁ	*Jhaṁ*	*Lṛṁ*		
			Phaṁ	*Ñaṁ*	*Lṛṁ*		
				Ṭaṁ	*Aiṁ*		
				Ṭhaṁ	*Āiṁ*		
					Oṁ		
					Auṁ		
					Aṅ		
					Aḥ		

Appendix 3

The Five Great Elements

	Ether (ākāśa)	*Air (vāyu)*	*Fire (tejas)*	*Water (apās)*	*Earth (pṛithvī)*
Principle	All-pervasive	Motion	Illumination	Cohesion	Stability
Qualities	Expansive, light, clear, subtle, cold, infinite, all-pervasive	Light, like the wind, mobile, clear, rough, dry, erratic	Hot, sharp, penetrating, fluid, luminous, light, ascending, dispersing	Wet, fluid, heavy, cool, lubricating, cohesive, soft, stable	Dense, solid, thick, heavy, stable
Sense	Sound	Touch	Sight	Taste	Smell
Organ	Ears	Skin	Eyes	Tongue	Nose
Action	Speech	Holding	Walking	Procreation	Excretion
Organ of Action	Mouth	Hand	Feet	Genitals	Anus

Glossary

Abhyāsa: Persistent repeated practice.

Adīśvara: The first Lord, Śiva.

Āgāmi karmas: The actions that are being done in this present life and which will bear fruits in a future life. It is this *karma* which preserves our free will, with certain limitations, and ensures our future success.

Ahaṁkāra: Ego.

Ajapā japā: Repetition of a *mantra* is called *japā*. The *japā* becomes *ajapā,* when the *mantra* is repeated in the mind on its own. *Ajapā japā* is continuous repetition of a *mantra* on the subconscious level of the mind.

Ājñā: The sixth *chakra,* located at the eyebrow centre. It has two poles: the negative pole is at the medulla oblongata; the positive pole is at the midpoint between the eyebrows, the Spiritual Eye. The seat of concentration.

Ākāśha: space, ether element, infinite void.

Anāhata: Heart *chakra*, the fourth centre in the *suṣumnā,* the subtle spine.

Ānanda: bliss, infinite joy.

Antaḥkāraṇa: internal instrument of cognition, consisting of consciousness, intellect, ego, and mind.

Antar: Inner, internal.

***Anusvāra*:** Nasalized vowel 'marked with a dot' (ṁ), used in Sanskrit pronunciation (giving a nasal sound pronounced like mm, but influenced according to whatever consonant follows).

Apāna: Downward-moving aspect of *prāṇa;* one of the five major *vāyus;* functions in the region of the navel to the feet.

Āsana: Seat, posture; pose for meditation; the third of eight limbs of Aṣṭāṅga Yoga.

Astādhyāyī: Pānini's 'Eight-Chapter Sanskrit Grammar'.
Aṣṭāṅga: Eight limbs (Aṣṭāṅga Yoga – eight limbs of yoga).
Ātma: The innermost Self, or soul.
Aśvinī: Horse (***aśvinī mudrā*** – horse gesture). The practice is so called because the anal contraction resembles the movement a horse makes with its sphincter immediately after evacuation of its bowels.

Bahir: External (***bahir kumbhaka*** – external breath retention).
Bandha: Literally translates as 'lock'. *Bandhas* are inner actions that direct the subtle power of the breath or *prāṇa*, locking it into a particular part of the body.
Bhūr: Represents earth.
Bhuvaḥ: Represents the subtle worlds with their demigods.
Bhrāmarī: Humming bee (as in *bhrāmarī prāṇāyāma*).
Bhūta Śuddhi: *Bhūta* means 'elements', *śuddhi* means 'purification'; *bhūta śuddhi* is purification of the five subtle elements: earth, water, fire, air, and space (ether).
Bīja: Seed, source (*bīja mantra* – seed-syllable *mantra*).
Brahma muhūrta: Time of God.
Brahman: From the Sanskrit root *brha*, meaning 'expansion', 'knowledge', 'all-pervasiveness'. It indicates the Absolute Supreme Consciousness, the Absolute Reality.
Brahmarandhra: Door of God.

Chakra: Wheel, vortex of energy, energy centre within the body. The *chakras* are transformers for the *prānic* life-energy and consciousness flowing through them. They store energy and distribute it throughout the body.
Cin: Consciousness (*cin mudrā* – gesture of consciousness).
Cit: Consciousness.
Citriṇī: Pale like the moon. *Citriṇī* is one of the *nāḍīs* within the *suṣumnā*.
Citta: Mind-field; mind, field of consciousness.

Damaru: A tiny two-ended drum played by Lord Śiva.
Dandāsana: Stick. This is the basic sitting position with the spine straight and the legs straight out in front of the body. It is from

this position that the forward bending positions are performed.
Devanāgari: Sanskrit script.
Dhyāna: Meditation.

Gāndhāra: One of the seven primary notes (*Ga*) of Hindu music.
Gāyatrī: The most sacred prayer of the *Ṛg Veda*, that is known to all Hindus and concerns Sāvitre. It is the great *Gāyatrī mantra*.
Gheraṇḍa Saṁhitā: The tantric Sanskrit text on Hāṭha Yoga, which is in the form of a dialogue between the sage Gheraṇḍa and an inquirer, Chaṇḍa Kāpāli.

Haṁsa: A *mantra* meaning, 'I am He.' When repeated continuously it becomes *so-ham*, which means 'He (the Absolute) am I.' Either way it has the same meaning.
Hāṭha Yoga: A system of purifying techniques and yoga postures to control the body and mind, through control of *prāṇa*. Hāṭha Yoga is a preparation for Rāja Yoga, the path of meditation.
Hāṭha Yoga Pradīpikā: A classic guide to the practice of Hāṭha Yoga from the 17th century by Yogi Swatmarama.
Hiranyagarbha: Golden Womb; Universal mind.
Hong-sau: Kriyā meditation *mantra*, that means 'I am He.' It deepens the concentration and brings inner calmness.

Icchā: Desire (pronounced *ic-chā*).
Iḍā: One of the three major *nāḍīs* (subtle channels) that runs on the left side of the spine, from the *mūlādhāra chakra* to the *ājñā chakra*. It is associated with lunar energy.

Jāgrat: Waking state – conscious mind.
Jālandhara bandha: Chin lock.
Jīvātma: Individual self; *puruṣa*.
Jña: 'To know' as in Jñanā Yoga (the path of wisdom or higher knowledge) is widely pronounced 'gya'. More accurate is 'gnya', and best is to combine a correct *ja* with a correct *ña*.
Jñanā mudrā: Gesture of intuitive knowledge.

Kanda: Is located between the anus and the root of the reproductive organs, just above *mūlādhāra chakra*. From this source 72,000 *nāḍīs* flow out to the entire subtle circuitry of the astral body.

Kapālabhāti: *Kapāla* means 'skull' and *bhāti* means 'shine'. A Hāṭha Yoga frontal brain purification technique using invigorating breathing.

Karma: Actions that have a binding effect; the law of cause and effect.

Kokanada rakta-kāmāla: Reddish lotus.

Kośas: The five sheaths: *annamāyā* (food), *prāṇamāyā* (vital), *manomāyā* (mind), *vijñānamāyā* (intellect), and *ānandamāyā* (bliss).

Kriyā Yoga: *Kri* from the Sanskrit root *kriyā* means 'to do, to act'. Kriyā Yoga is 'union with the Infinite through the action of *Kriyā*'. An ancient sacred yoga science, that includes advanced techniques of meditation that lead to Self- and God-realization. Kriyā Yoga was revived in this age by Mahavatar Babaji and passed down through a succession of masters to Paramhansa Yogananda.

Kuṇḍalinī Śākti: *Kuṇḍala* means 'coiled'; *Śākti* means 'primordial cosmic energy'. The coiled-up energy that gives power to all the *chakras* and lies dormant at the *mūlādhāra chakra*, at the base of the spine.

Kūtastha: *Kūtastha* means 'that which remains unchanged'. *Kūtastha Caitanya* means 'Christ Consciousness' (the cosmic intelligence of Spirit that is omnipresent in creation). The *Kūtastha* is also used as another name for the Spiritual Eye, located midpoint between the eyebrows.

Laṁ: *Bīja mantra* representing the energy of the earth element at the *mūlādhāra chakra*.

Mahāmudrā: Great Gesture.

Mahat: Cosmic consciousness; cosmic mind.

Mahesvārasutrani: Sounds that are known as the *Mahesvārasutrani* came from the *damaru* played by Lord Śiva.

Mālā beads: Set of 108 beads strung together like a rosary. Used for *mantra japā*, counting repetitions of *mantras* in meditation.

Manas: Recording mind, seat of thinking, mind as receiver of sensation.

Maṇipūra chakra: *Maṇipūra* means 'jewelled city'. The third *chakra* located at the navel centre in the astral spine.

Mantra: From *manas* meaning 'mind', and *tri* meaning 'to cross over'. A subtle transcendental sound that liberates the consciousness.

Mitrāya: Friend.

Mudrā: *Mudrā* means 'gesture'. A *mudrā* is an energy seal that helps in controlling the prānic energy in the body.

Mukti: Liberation.

Mūla bandha: Anal lock. *Mūla* means 'root,' and refers to the region between the anus and the perineum. *Bandha* means 'lock'.

Mūlādhāra chakra: The first *chakra,* at the base of the spine.

Nāda: Inner sound, subtle sound vibration. Eternal pure cosmic sound reverberating throughout endless space.

Nāḍī: *Nāḍī* means 'flow'. Subtle channel in the astral body, through which prānic energy flows.

Nāḍī śodhana: Purifying subtle channel breath. A *prāṇāyāma* breath that uses alternate nostril breathing to purify the *nāḍīs*.

Niralambapuri: Dwelling place without support.

Oṁ: The *Praṇava,* the primordial sound vibration, a *mantra* that symbolizes God. It is the supreme verbal symbol of Brahman both as the Absolute and as the personal God (Īśvara). It is written as *Oṁ,* and repeated or chanted as *Aum.*

Pādma: Lotus.

Pañchamahābhūta: Five Great Elements: ether, air, fire, water and earth.

Pañchikāraṇa: A process of quintuplication that takes place between the five elements (*mahābhūtas*).

Paramātma: Supreme Self.

Parāmhaṇsa: 'Supreme Swan.' A title bestowed on Self-realized gurus or yogis, signifying a spiritual master. 'Swan' (*haṇsa*) symbolizes spiritual discrimination.

Piṅgalā: One of the three major *nāḍīs,* which runs on the right side of the spine, emerging opposite *iḍā,* from the right side of the *mūlādhāra chakra* and intersecting each *chakra* until it reaches the right side of the *ājñā chakra.* It is associated with solar energy.

Prajñā: Knower, undivided consciousness.

Prakṛti: The eternal principle of matter.

Prāṇa: The cosmic vibratory life force that is omnipresent and sustains the universe. *Prāṇa* is also the specific vital energy, the vital air within our bodies. There are five main *prāṇa* currents in the body (*prāṇa, vyāna, samāna, udāṇa, apāṇa*).

Praṇava: *Praṇava* means 'sounding' or 'reverberating' and refers to the vibration of consciousness itself. *Oṁ,* the primordial sound vibration.

Prāṇāyāma: The practice of breath-control, expansion of vital energy.

Prārabdha karmas: Results of past actions which are producing fruit in the present. This is also called *ripe karma,* because it is a debt which is overdue and it is time that it should be paid in the form of sorrow and suffering, gain and loss, whether we like it or not.

Pundarika: White lotus.

Pūraka: Inhalation.

Puruṣa: The Supreme Self, the eternal principle of consciousness.

Rāja Yoga: Rāja means 'royal' or 'king'. The royal path of yoga. The highest path of meditation for realizing God.

Rāṁ: Seed-syllable (*bīja*) *mantra* representing the energy of the fire element at the *maṇipūra chakra.*

Ravaya: Shining One.

Recaka: Exhalation.

Sādhanā: Spiritual practice that is performed regularly for attainment of realization of the Self, and cosmic consciousness.

Sahasrāra: Crown *chakra* at the top of the head, which contains all six main *chakras;* thousand-petalled rayed lotus.

Śākti: The vital power and energy of consciousness. The active creative female principle of the universe.

Samādhi: From the Sanskrit *sam* 'with', *ādhi* 'Lord': 'union with the Lord'. Or *sam-ā-dhā* 'to hold together, to concentrate upon'. The state of superconscious absorption, that is attained when the meditator, the process of meditation, and the object of meditation (God) become One.

Samāna vāyu: One of the five major *vāyus*; the prānic air current functions between the heart and navel in the body; facilitates assimilation.

Śambavī mudrā: A Hāṭha Yoga practice of concentration by gazing at the point between the eyebrows. The practice activates the third eye or *ājñā chakra.*

Saṁskāras: Latent impressions stored in the subtle body and subconscious mind; deep mental impressions produced by past experiences; dormant impressions of our past lives.

Saṁskṛta: Sanskrit. Sanskrit is a refined and literary language, and it is also capable of communicating in a direct, practical manner the important facts of the spiritual life. Sanskrit possesses many precise terms for spiritual concepts and disciplines.

Sañcita karmas: Those actions that have accumulated in several previous lifetimes.

Saptarsi: Seven great Seers who appeared in a mythological story.

Sarasvatī: The goddess of the creative arts, science and knowledge, and speech; bestower of wisdom. Consort of Brahma. She is the creative power and the knowledge behind the power of Brahma.

Śiva: 'In whom all things lie'; 'The Auspicious One'; 'Great Lord'. Pure Consciousness. Name of the deity representing the cosmic state of consciousness.

Śivalingam: A symbol of *Ātma,* the soul or inner spirit; consciousness. *Linga* or *lingam* is a natural oval-shaped stone representing the subtle bodies.

Śivasvarodāya: A scripture in the form of a dialogue between Śiva and Śākti which begins with the nature of the universe and the essential knowledge on living a happy, healthy and inspired life.

Śiva-Śākti: In Tantra, Śiva is *Param Puruṣa,* the Male Principle and Śākti is the Female Principle, and the cosmos has evolved from their union. Śiva and Śākti are inseparable. God is inseparable from His energy or power. There are images and statue deities known as Ardhanarisvāra or Hara Gauri, the half of which is Śiva and the other half is Śākti or Gauri; in other words the one is inseparable from the other.

Śiva Saṁhitā: A Sanskrit text on yoga. In the five chapters are discussed and elaborated the essentials necessary for the practice of yoga, the importance of yoga, principles of *prāṇāyāma, āsanas,* *kuṇḍalinī* and its awakening, the various forms of yoga, etc.

Savikalpa samādhi: In the state of *savikalpa samādhi* the mind is conscious only of the blissful Spirit within, it is not conscious of the exterior world.

Sāvitre: Means 'vivifier' or 'one who brings forth or inspires', and it connotes Sūrya's power. Sāvitre is the guiding principle in the heart that leads one to higher states of consciousness. Sāvitre is known to us through the *Gāyatrī mantra* Prayer.

Śodhana: Purification.

Sparśa: Touch.

Sūkshma Prāṇa: Subtle vital air.

Sūrya Namaskāra: Salutations to the Sun. A sequence of 12 yoga poses.

Suṣumnā: The main subtle channel running through the spine, along which six *chakras* are located. When awakened, the *kuṇḍalinī śākti* rises upward through the *suṣumnā.*

Suṣhupti: Deep sleep state – unconscious mind.

Svapna: Dream state – subconscious mind.

Svāra: Vowels of Sanskrit, of which there are thirteen.

Svāra yoga: A precise science, it has an emphasis on the analysis of the breath and the significance of prāṇic rhythms

Svādhiṣṭhāna chakra: 'One's own abode'. The second *chakra* located in the sacral region.

Svaḥ: Represents the third dimension or celestial region, known as *Svarga Loka* and all the luminous *lokas* (spheres) above.

Tāḍāsana: Mountain pose, a standing yoga posture. In this pose you stand straight like a mountain, firm and strong at the base and ascending upwards. The standing *āsanas* all start from this position.

Taijasa 'Luminous one'. The manifestation of the individual in the subtle body, that develops a false identification of the self with ego.

Turīya: Transcendent; the fourth state of consciousness in Vedanta philosophy. *Turīya* is distinguished from the three physical states (waking, dreaming, dreamless sleep).

Upaniṣads: The *Upaniṣads* form part of the tradition of the Vedic literature. They were composed from about 700 BCE.

Vairāgya: Detachment; dispassion; freedom from worldly desires.
Vajrāsana: Thunderbolt pose. A kneeling posture.
Vajriṇī: Sunlike. One of the inner *nāḍīs* within the *suṣumnā*.
Vaṁ: *Bīja mantra* of *svādhiṣṭhāna chakra*.
Varnamāla: Sanskrit alphabet.
Virat: Cosmic manifestation.
Viṣṇu: The all-pervading one, name of one of the gods of the Hindu Trinity. He is the Preserver and descends to earth in the form of a divine incarnation when the world especially needs His grace. Viṣṇu is mainly worshipped in the form of his incarnations Kṛṣṇa (Krishna) and Rāma.
Viṣṇu mudrā: A hand position that becomes a *mudrā* or 'seal' for directing and regulating the breath in each nostril, as in alternate nostril breathing.
Viśuddha chakra: The fifth *chakra,* which corresponds to the cervical plexus, at the level of the throat.

Viśva: The individual self, the experiencer of the waking state, bound and conditioned by matter, and associated with the phenomenal world and the gross body.
Vṛttis: Subtle vortices of energy created by *saṁskāras,* karmic actions, and the waves of like and dislike that create our mental tendencies, desires and habits, enter the subconscious mind and then get submerged in these lower *chakras.*
Vyāhṛtis: Rhythms.
Vyanjana: Consonants of Sanskrit, of which there are 34.

Yantra: Diagrammatic symbol used as a focal point for concentration and meditation.

Bibliography

Avalon, Arthur [Sir John Woodroffe], *The Serpent Power*, New York: Dover Publications, 1974

Bryant, E F, *The Yoga Sutras of Patañjali*, New York: North Point Press, 2009

Chopra, D, *Power, Freedom and Grace*, San Rafael, CA: Amber-Allen Publishing, 2006

Dasgupta, S, *A History of Indian Philosophy*, Volume 1, Cambridge, 1922

Feuerstein, G, with Brenda Feuerstein, *The Bhagavad Gītā – A New Translation*, Boston & London: Shambhala Publications, 2011

_____, *The Yoga Tradition*, Arizona: Hohm Press, 2008

Feuerstein, G, Subhash Kak & David Frawley, *In Search of the Cradle of Civilisation*, Delhi: Motilal Banarsidass Publishers, 2008

Kriyānanda, Swami [J Donald Walters], *The Essence of the Bhagavad Gītā*, Nevada City, CA: Hansa Press, 2006

Lipski, A, *The Teaching of Śrī Ānandamāyī Mā*, Delhi: Motilal Banarsidass Publishers, 1988

Sturgess, S R, *The Yoga Book*, London, UK: Watkins Publishing, 2002

_____, *Yoga Meditation*, London, UK: Watkins Publishing, 2013

Vasu, Rai Bahadur Srisa Chandra, *The Siva Samhita*, New Delhi: Munshiram Manoharlal Publishers, 1996

_____, *The Gheranda Samhita*, New Delhi: Munshiram Manoharlal Publishers, 1996

Venkatesananda, Swami, *The Yoga Sutras of Patañjali*, India: Divine Life Society, 1998

Viṣṇudevananda, Swami, *Hāṭha Yoga Pradīpikā*, New York: Oṁ Lotus Publishing Company, 1987

Yogananda, Paramhansa, *Autobiography of a Yogi*, Nevada City, CA:

Crystal Clarity Publishers, 1994 (reprint of the 1946 edition)

_____, *Karma and Reincarnation – The Wisdom of Yogananda Vol. 2*, Nevada City, CA: Crystal Clarity Publishers, 2007

_____, *Spiritual Relationships – The Wisdom of Yogananda Vol. 3*, Nevada City, CA: Crystal Clarity Publishers, 2007

_____, *How to Have Courage, Calmness, and Confidence – The Wisdom of Yogananda Vol. 5*, Nevada City, CA: Crystal Clarity Publishers, 2010

_____, *How to Achieve Glowing Health and Vitality – The Wisdom of Yogananda Vol. 6*, Nevada City, CA: Crystal Clarity Publishers, 2011

_____, *Where There is Light*, Los Angeles: Self-Realization Fellowship, 1989

_____, *Super Advanced Course 1, Lessons 1–12*, USA: Kessinger Publishing's Rare Reprints

Kriyā Yoga Resources

Kriyā Yoga Meditation Teachers and Centres

England, UK

Stephen Sturgess

email: stephensturgess@hotmail.com
web: www.yogananda-kriyayoga.org.uk

Richard Fish

email: richardfish108@gmail.com
web: www.kriyayogacentre.org.uk

Ireland

David McGrath

email: maliactica4001@hotmail.com
web: www.kriyaireland.com

USA

Roy Eugene Davis [a direct disciple of Paramhansa Yogananda], Center for Spiritual Awareness, PO Box 7, Lakemont, Georgia, GA 30552-0001

email: info@csa-davis.org
web: www.csa-davis.org

Ananda Communities

Ananda Sangha (a worldwide organization founded by Swami Kriyananda, a direct disciple of Paramhansa Yogananda, offers spiritual support and resources based on the teachings of

Paramhansa Yogananda. There are Ananda spiritual communities in Nevada City, Sacramento, Palo Alto, and Los Angeles, California; Seattle, Washington; Portland and Laurelwood, Oregon.

web: www.ananda.org
www.expandinglight.org

Italy

Ananda Assisi (spiritual community and Kriyā Yoga retreat)

web: www.ananda.it

India

Ananda India (spiritual communities near New Delhi and Pune)

web: anandaindia.org

Index